C-2071

CAREER EXAMINATION SERIES

THIS IS YOUR **PASSBOOK**® FOR ...

HUMAN RESOURCES TECHNICIAN

NATIONAL LEARNING CORPORATION®

passbooks.com

PASSBOOK® SERIES

THE *PASSBOOK® SERIES* has been created to prepare applicants and candidates for the ultimate academic battlefield – the examination room.

At some time in our lives, each and every one of us may be required to take an examination – for validation, matriculation, admission, qualification, registration, certification, or licensure.

Based on the assumption that every applicant or candidate has met the basic formal educational standards, has taken the required number of courses, and read the necessary texts, the *PASSBOOK® SERIES* furnishes the one special preparation which may assure passing with confidence, instead of failing with insecurity. Examination questions – together with answers – are furnished as the basic vehicle for study so that the mysteries of the examination and its compounding difficulties may be eliminated or diminished by a sure method.

This book is meant to help you pass your examination provided that you qualify and are serious in your objective.

The entire field is reviewed through the huge store of content information which is succinctly presented through a provocative and challenging approach – the question-and-answer method.

A climate of success is established by furnishing the correct answers at the end of each test.

You soon learn to recognize types of questions, forms of questions, and patterns of questioning. You may even begin to anticipate expected outcomes.

You perceive that many questions are repeated or adapted so that you can gain acute insights, which may enable you to score many sure points.

You learn how to confront new questions, or types of questions, and to attack them confidently and work out the correct answers.

You note objectives and emphases, and recognize pitfalls and dangers, so that you may make positive educational adjustments.

Moreover, you are kept fully informed in relation to new concepts, methods, practices, and directions in the field.

You discover that you arre actually taking the examination all the time: you are preparing for the examination by "taking" an examination, not by reading extraneous and/or supererogatory textbooks.

In short, this PASSBOOK®, used directedly, should be an important factor in helping you to pass your test.

HUMAN RESOURCES TECHNICIAN

DUTIES
Under direct supervision to do selected technical personnel work and to perform othe
related duties as required. Human Resources Technician is a paraprofessional in th
human resources department. Incumbents are trained in technical human resource
activities, and will perform these functions in support of professional staff. Their
assignments typically differ from the journey level analyst or personnel officer by the
assignment of selected duties or only part of a function, as opposed to having
responsibility for a complete function. Supervision will come from professional perso
staff and will diminish as incumbents gain proficiency.

SCOPE OF THE EXAMINATION
The written test will cover knowledge, skills and/or abilities in such areas as:

1. Recruitment, selection and placement;
2. Classification system administration;
3. Interviewing;
4. Interpreting graphs, charts and tables;
5. Understanding and interpreting written material; and
6. Preparing written material.

HOW TO TAKE A TEST

I. YOU MUST PASS AN EXAMINATION

A. WHAT EVERY CANDIDATE SHOULD KNOW

Examination applicants often ask us for help in preparing for the written test. What can I study in advance? What kinds of questions will be asked? How will the test be given? How will the papers be graded?

As an applicant for a civil service examination, you may be wondering about some of these things. Our purpose here is to suggest effective methods of advance study and to describe civil service examinations.

Your chances for success on this examination can be increased if you know how to prepare. Those "pre-examination jitters" can be reduced if you know what to expect. You can even experience an adventure in good citizenship if you know why civil service exams are given.

B. WHY ARE CIVIL SERVICE EXAMINATIONS GIVEN?

Civil service examinations are important to you in two ways. As a citizen, you want public jobs filled by employees who know how to do their work. As a job seeker, you want a fair chance to compete for that job on an equal footing with other candidates. The best-known means of accomplishing this two-fold goal is the competitive examination.

Exams are widely publicized throughout the nation. They may be administered for jobs in federal, state, city, municipal, town or village governments or agencies.

Any citizen may apply, with some limitations, such as the age or residence of applicants. Your experience and education may be reviewed to see whether you meet the requirements for the particular examination. When these requirements exist, they are reasonable and applied consistently to all applicants. Thus, a competitive examination may cause you some uneasiness now, but it is your privilege and safeguard.

C. HOW ARE CIVIL SERVICE EXAMS DEVELOPED?

Examinations are carefully written by trained technicians who are specialists in the field known as "psychological measurement," in consultation with recognized authorities in the field of work that the test will cover. These experts recommend the subject matter areas or skills to be tested; only those knowledges or skills important to your success on the job are included. The most reliable books and source materials available are used as references. Together, the experts and technicians judge the difficulty level of the questions.

Test technicians know how to phrase questions so that the problem is clearly stated. Their ethics do not permit "trick" or "catch" questions. Questions may have been tried out on sample groups, or subjected to statistical analysis, to determine their usefulness.

Written tests are often used in combination with performance tests, ratings of training and experience, and oral interviews. All of these measures combine to form the best-known means of finding the right person for the right job.

II. HOW TO PASS THE WRITTEN TEST

A. NATURE OF THE EXAMINATION

To prepare intelligently for civil service examinations, you should know how they differ from school examinations you have taken. In school you were assigned certain definite pages to read or subjects to cover. The examination questions were quite detailed and usually emphasized memory. Civil service exams, on the other hand, try to discover your present ability to perform the duties of a position, plus your potentiality to learn these duties. In other words, a civil service exam attempts to predict how successful you will be. Questions cover such a broad area that they cannot be as minute and detailed as school exam questions.

In the public service similar kinds of work, or positions, are grouped together in one "class." This process is known as *position-classification*. All the positions in a class are paid according to the salary range for that class. One class title covers all of these positions, and they are all tested by the same examination.

B. FOUR BASIC STEPS

1) Study the announcement

How, then, can you know what subjects to study? Our best answer is: "Learn as much as possible about the class of positions for which you've applied." The exam will test the knowledge, skills and abilities needed to do the work.

Your most valuable source of information about the position you want is the official exam announcement. This announcement lists the training and experience qualifications. Check these standards and apply only if you come reasonably close to meeting them.

The brief description of the position in the examination announcement offers some clues to the subjects which will be tested. Think about the job itself. Review the duties in your mind. Can you perform them, or are there some in which you are rusty? Fill in the blank spots in your preparation.

Many jurisdictions preview the written test in the exam announcement by including a section called "Knowledge and Abilities Required," "Scope of the Examination," or some similar heading. Here you will find out specifically what fields will be tested.

2) Review your own background

Once you learn in general what the position is all about, and what you need to know to do the work, ask yourself which subjects you already know fairly well and which need improvement. You may wonder whether to concentrate on improving your strong areas or on building some background in your fields of weakness. When the announcement has specified "some knowledge" or "considerable knowledge," or has used adjectives like "beginning principles of..." or "advanced ... methods," you can get a clue as to the number and difficulty of questions to be asked in any given field. More questions, and hence broader coverage, would be included for those subjects which are more important in the work. Now weigh your strengths and weaknesses against the job requirements and prepare accordingly.

3) Determine the level of the position

Another way to tell how intensively you should prepare is to understand the level of the job for which you are applying. Is it the entering level? In other words, is this the position in which beginners in a field of work are hired? Or is it an intermediate or advanced level? Sometimes this is indicated by such words as "Junior" or "Senior" in the class title. Other jurisdictions use Roman numerals to designate the level – Clerk I, Clerk II, for example. The word "Supervisor" sometimes appears in the title. If the level is not indicated by the title, check the description of duties. Will you be working under very close supervision, or will you have responsibility for independent decisions in this work?

4) Choose appropriate study materials

Now that you know the subjects to be examined and the relative amount of each subject to be covered, you can choose suitable study materials. For beginning level jobs, or even advanced ones, if you have a pronounced weakness in some aspect of your training, read a modern, standard textbook in that field. Be sure it is up to date and has general coverage. Such books are normally available at your library, and the librarian will be glad to help you locate one. For entry-level positions, questions of appropriate difficulty are chosen – neither highly advanced questions, nor those too simple. Such questions require careful thought but not advanced training.

If the position for which you are applying is technical or advanced, you will read more advanced, specialized material. If you are already familiar with the basic principles of your field, elementary textbooks would waste your time. Concentrate on advanced textbooks and technical periodicals. Think through the concepts and review difficult problems in your field.

These are all general sources. You can get more ideas on your own initiative, following these leads. For example, training manuals and publications of the government agency which employs workers in your field can be useful, particularly for technical and professional positions. A letter or visit to the government department involved may result in more specific study suggestions, and certainly will provide you with a more definite idea of the exact nature of the position you are seeking.

III. KINDS OF TESTS

Tests are used for purposes other than measuring knowledge and ability to perform specified duties. For some positions, it is equally important to test ability to make adjustments to new situations or to profit from training. In others, basic mental abilities not dependent on information are essential. Questions which test these things may not appear as pertinent to the duties of the position as those which test for knowledge and information. Yet they are often highly important parts of a fair examination. For very general questions, it is almost impossible to help you direct your study efforts. What we can do is to point out some of the more common of these general abilities needed in public service positions and describe some typical questions.

1) General information

Broad, general information has been found useful for predicting job success in some kinds of work. This is tested in a variety of ways, from vocabulary lists to questions about current events. Basic background in some field of work, such as sociology or economics, may be sampled in a group of questions. Often these are principles which have become familiar to most persons through exposure rather than through formal training. It is difficult to advise you how to study for these questions; being alert to the world around you is our best suggestion.

2) Verbal ability

An example of an ability needed in many positions is verbal or language ability. Verbal ability is, in brief, the ability to use and understand words. Vocabulary and grammar tests are typical measures of this ability. Reading comprehension or paragraph interpretation questions are common in many kinds of civil service tests. You are given a paragraph of written material and asked to find its central meaning.

3) Numerical ability

Number skills can be tested by the familiar arithmetic problem, by checking paired lists of numbers to see which are alike and which are different, or by interpreting charts and graphs. In the latter test, a graph may be printed in the test booklet which you are asked to use as the basis for answering questions.

4) Observation

A popular test for law-enforcement positions is the observation test. A picture is shown to you for several minutes, then taken away. Questions about the picture test your ability to observe both details and larger elements.

5) Following directions

In many positions in the public service, the employee must be able to carry out written instructions dependably and accurately. You may be given a chart with several columns, each column listing a variety of information. The questions require you to carry out directions involving the information given in the chart.

6) Skills and aptitudes

Performance tests effectively measure some manual skills and aptitudes. When the skill is one in which you are trained, such as typing or shorthand, you can practice. These tests are often very much like those given in business school or high school courses. For many of the other skills and aptitudes, however, no short-time preparation can be made. Skills and abilities natural to you or that you have developed throughout your lifetime are being tested.

Many of the general questions just described provide all the data needed to answer the questions and ask you to use your reasoning ability to find the answers. Your best preparation for these tests, as well as for tests of facts and ideas, is to be at your physical and mental best. You, no doubt, have your own methods of getting into an exam-taking mood and keeping "in shape." The next section lists some ideas on this subject.

IV. KINDS OF QUESTIONS

Only rarely is the "essay" question, which you answer in narrative form, used in civil service tests. Civil service tests are usually of the short-answer type. Full instructions for answering these questions will be given to you at the examination. But in case this is your first experience with short-answer questions and separate answer sheets, here is what you need to know:

1) Multiple-choice Questions

Most popular of the short-answer questions is the "multiple choice" or "best answer" question. It can be used, for example, to test for factual knowledge, ability to solve problems or judgment in meeting situations found at work.

A multiple-choice question is normally one of three types—

- It can begin with an incomplete statement followed by several possible endings. You are to find the one ending which *best* completes the statement, although some of the others may not be entirely wrong.
- It can also be a complete statement in the form of a question which is answered by choosing one of the statements listed.
- It can be in the form of a problem – again you select the best answer.

Here is an example of a multiple-choice question with a discussion which should give you some clues as to the method for choosing the right answer:

When an employee has a complaint about his assignment, the action which will *best* help him overcome his difficulty is to
- A. discuss his difficulty with his coworkers
- B. take the problem to the head of the organization
- C. take the problem to the person who gave him the assignment
- D. say nothing to anyone about his complaint

In answering this question, you should study each of the choices to find which is best. Consider choice "A" – Certainly an employee may discuss his complaint with fellow employees, but no change or improvement can result, and the complaint remains unresolved. Choice "B" is a poor choice since the head of the organization probably does not know what assignment you have been given, and taking your problem to him is known as "going over the head" of the supervisor. The supervisor, or person who made the assignment, is the person who can clarify it or correct any injustice. Choice "C" is, therefore, correct. To say nothing, as in choice "D," is unwise. Supervisors have and interest in knowing the problems employees are facing, and the employee is seeking a solution to his problem.

2) True/False Questions

The "true/false" or "right/wrong" form of question is sometimes used. Here a complete statement is given. Your job is to decide whether the statement is right or wrong.

SAMPLE: A roaming cell-phone call to a nearby city costs less than a non-roaming call to a distant city.

This statement is wrong, or false, since roaming calls are more expensive.

This is not a complete list of all possible question forms, although most of the others are variations of these common types. You will always get complete directions for answering questions. Be sure you understand *how* to mark your answers – ask questions until you do.

V. RECORDING YOUR ANSWERS

Computer terminals are used more and more today for many different kinds of exams.

For an examination with very few applicants, you may be told to record your answers in the test booklet itself. Separate answer sheets are much more common. If this separate answer sheet is to be scored by machine – and this is often the case – it is highly important that you mark your answers correctly in order to get credit.

An electronic scoring machine is often used in civil service offices because of the speed with which papers can be scored. Machine-scored answer sheets must be marked with a pencil, which will be given to you. This pencil has a high graphite content which responds to the electronic scoring machine. As a matter of fact, stray dots may register as answers, so do not let your pencil rest on the answer sheet while you are pondering the correct answer. Also, if your pencil lead breaks or is otherwise defective, ask for another.

Since the answer sheet will be dropped in a slot in the scoring machine, be careful not to bend the corners or get the paper crumpled.

The answer sheet normally has five vertical columns of numbers, with 30 numbers to a column. These numbers correspond to the question numbers in your test booklet. After each number, going across the page are four or five pairs of dotted lines. These short dotted lines have small letters or numbers above them. The first two pairs may also have a "T" or "F" above the letters. This indicates that the first two pairs only are to be used if the questions are of the true-false type. If the questions are multiple choice, disregard the "T" and "F" and pay attention only to the small letters or numbers.

Answer your questions in the manner of the sample that follows:

32. The largest city in the United States is
    A. Washington, D.C.
    B. New York City
    C. Chicago
    D. Detroit
    E. San Francisco

1) Choose the answer you think is best. (New York City is the largest, so "B" is correct.)
2) Find the row of dotted lines numbered the same as the question you are answering. (Find row number 32)
3) Find the pair of dotted lines corresponding to the answer. (Find the pair of lines under the mark "B.")
4) Make a solid black mark between the dotted lines.

VI. BEFORE THE TEST

Common sense will help you find procedures to follow to get ready for an examination. Too many of us, however, overlook these sensible measures. Indeed, nervousness and fatigue have been found to be the most serious reasons why applicants fail to do their best on civil service tests. Here is a list of reminders:

- Begin your preparation early – Don't wait until the last minute to go scurrying around for books and materials or to find out what the position is all about.
- Prepare continuously – An hour a night for a week is better than an all-night cram session. This has been definitely established. What is more, a night a week for a month will return better dividends than crowding your study into a shorter period of time.
- Locate the place of the exam – You have been sent a notice telling you when and where to report for the examination. If the location is in a different town or otherwise unfamiliar to you, it would be well to inquire the best route and learn something about the building.
- Relax the night before the test – Allow your mind to rest. Do not study at all that night. Plan some mild recreation or diversion; then go to bed early and get a good night's sleep.
- Get up early enough to make a leisurely trip to the place for the test – This way unforeseen events, traffic snarls, unfamiliar buildings, etc. will not upset you.
- Dress comfortably – A written test is not a fashion show. You will be known by number and not by name, so wear something comfortable.
- Leave excess paraphernalia at home – Shopping bags and odd bundles will get in your way. You need bring only the items mentioned in the official notice you received; usually everything you need is provided. Do not bring reference books to the exam. They will only confuse those last minutes and be taken away from you when in the test room.
- Arrive somewhat ahead of time – If because of transportation schedules you must get there very early, bring a newspaper or magazine to take your mind off yourself while waiting.
- Locate the examination room – When you have found the proper room, you will be directed to the seat or part of the room where you will sit. Sometimes you are given a sheet of instructions to read while you are waiting. Do not fill out any forms until you are told to do so; just read them and be prepared.
- Relax and prepare to listen to the instructions
- If you have any physical problem that may keep you from doing your best, be sure to tell the test administrator. If you are sick or in poor health, you really cannot do your best on the exam. You can come back and take the test some other time.

VII. AT THE TEST

The day of the test is here and you have the test booklet in your hand. The temptation to get going is very strong. Caution! There is more to success than knowing the right answers. You must know how to identify your papers and understand variations in the type of short-answer question used in this particular examination. Follow these suggestions for maximum results from your efforts:

1) Cooperate with the monitor

The test administrator has a duty to create a situation in which you can be as much at ease as possible. He will give instructions, tell you when to begin, check to see that you are marking your answer sheet correctly, and so on. He is not there to guard you, although he will see that your competitors do not take unfair advantage. He wants to help you do your best.

2) Listen to all instructions

Don't jump the gun! Wait until you understand all directions. In most civil service tests you get more time than you need to answer the questions. So don't be in a hurry. Read each word of instructions until you clearly understand the meaning. Study the examples, listen to all announcements and follow directions. Ask questions if you do not understand what to do.

3) Identify your papers

Civil service exams are usually identified by number only. You will be assigned a number; you must not put your name on your test papers. Be sure to copy your number correctly. Since more than one exam may be given, copy your exact examination title.

4) Plan your time

Unless you are told that a test is a "speed" or "rate of work" test, speed itself is usually not important. Time enough to answer all the questions will be provided, but this does not mean that you have all day. An overall time limit has been set. Divide the total time (in minutes) by the number of questions to determine the approximate time you have for each question.

5) Do not linger over difficult questions

If you come across a difficult question, mark it with a paper clip (useful to have along) and come back to it when you have been through the booklet. One caution if you do this – be sure to skip a number on your answer sheet as well. Check often to be sure that you have not lost your place and that you are marking in the row numbered the same as the question you are answering.

6) Read the questions

Be sure you know what the question asks! Many capable people are unsuccessful because they failed to *read* the questions correctly.

7) Answer all questions

Unless you have been instructed that a penalty will be deducted for incorrect answers, it is better to guess than to omit a question.

8) Speed tests

It is often better NOT to guess on speed tests. It has been found that on timed tests people are tempted to spend the last few seconds before time is called in marking answers at random – without even reading them – in the hope of picking up a few extra points. To discourage this practice, the instructions may warn you that your score will be "corrected" for guessing. That is, a penalty will be applied. The incorrect answers will be deducted from the correct ones, or some other penalty formula will be used.

9) Review your answers

     If you finish before time is called, go back to the questions you guessed or omitted to give them further thought. Review other answers if you have time.

10) Return your test materials

     If you are ready to leave before others have finished or time is called, take ALL your materials to the monitor and leave quietly. Never take any test material with you. The monitor can discover whose papers are not complete, and taking a test booklet may be grounds for disqualification.

VIII. EXAMINATION TECHNIQUES

    1) Read the general instructions carefully. These are usually printed on the first page of the exam booklet. As a rule, these instructions refer to the timing of the examination; the fact that you should not start work until the signal and must stop work at a signal, etc. If there are any *special* instructions, such as a choice of questions to be answered, make sure that you note this instruction carefully.

    2) When you are ready to start work on the examination, that is as soon as the signal has been given, read the instructions to each question booklet, underline any key words or phrases, such as *least, best, outline, describe* and the like. In this way you will tend to answer as requested rather than discover on reviewing your paper that you *listed without describing*, that you selected the *worst* choice rather than the *best* choice, etc.

    3) If the examination is of the objective or multiple-choice type – that is, each question will also give a series of possible answers: A, B, C or D, and you are called upon to select the best answer and write the letter next to that answer on your answer paper – it is advisable to start answering each question in turn. There may be anywhere from 50 to 100 such questions in the three or four hours allotted and you can see how much time would be taken if you read through all the questions before beginning to answer any. Furthermore, if you come across a question or group of questions which you know would be difficult to answer, it would undoubtedly affect your handling of all the other questions.

    4) If the examination is of the essay type and contains but a few questions, it is a moot point as to whether you should read all the questions before starting to answer any one. Of course, if you are given a choice – say five out of seven and the like – then it is essential to read all the questions so you can eliminate the two that are most difficult. If, however, you are asked to answer all the questions, there may be danger in trying to answer the easiest one first because you may find that you will spend too much time on it. The best technique is to answer the first question, then proceed to the second, etc.

    5) Time your answers. Before the exam begins, write down the time it started, then add the time allowed for the examination and write down the time it must be completed, then divide the time available somewhat as follows:

- If 3-1/2 hours are allowed, that would be 210 minutes. If you have 80 objective-type questions, that would be an average of 2-1/2 minutes per question. Allow yourself no more than 2 minutes per question, or a total of 160 minutes, which will permit about 50 minutes to review.
- If for the time allotment of 210 minutes there are 7 essay questions to answer, that would average about 30 minutes a question. Give yourself only 25 minutes per question so that you have about 35 minutes to review.

6) The most important instruction is to *read each question* and make sure you know what is wanted. The second most important instruction is to *time yourself properly* so that you answer every question. The third most important instruction is to *answer every question.* Guess if you have to but include something for each question. Remember that you will receive no credit for a blank and will probably receive some credit if you write something in answer to an essay question. If you guess a letter – say "B" for a multiple-choice question – you may have guessed right. If you leave a blank as an answer to a multiple-choice question, the examiners may respect your feelings but it will not add a point to your score. Some exams may penalize you for wrong answers, so in such cases *only*, you may not want to guess unless you have some basis for your answer.

7) Suggestions
   a. Objective-type questions
      1. Examine the question booklet for proper sequence of pages and questions
      2. Read all instructions carefully
      3. Skip any question which seems too difficult; return to it after all other questions have been answered
      4. Apportion your time properly; do not spend too much time on any single question or group of questions
      5. Note and underline key words – *all, most, fewest, least, best, worst, same, opposite,* etc.
      6. Pay particular attention to negatives
      7. Note unusual option, e.g., unduly long, short, complex, different or similar in content to the body of the question
      8. Observe the use of "hedging" words – *probably, may, most likely,* etc.
      9. Make sure that your answer is put next to the same number as the question
      10. Do not second-guess unless you have good reason to believe the second answer is definitely more correct
      11. Cross out original answer if you decide another answer is more accurate; do not erase until you are ready to hand your paper in
      12. Answer all questions; guess unless instructed otherwise
      13. Leave time for review

   b. Essay questions
      1. Read each question carefully
      2. Determine exactly what is wanted. Underline key words or phrases.
      3. Decide on outline or paragraph answer

4. Include many different points and elements unless asked to develop any one or two points or elements
5. Show impartiality by giving pros and cons unless directed to select one side only
6. Make and write down any assumptions you find necessary to answer the questions
7. Watch your English, grammar, punctuation and choice of words
8. Time your answers; don't crowd material

8) Answering the essay question

Most essay questions can be answered by framing the specific response around several key words or ideas. Here are a few such key words or ideas:

M's: manpower, materials, methods, money, management
P's: purpose, program, policy, plan, procedure, practice, problems, pitfalls, personnel, public relations
   a. Six basic steps in handling problems:
      1. Preliminary plan and background development
      2. Collect information, data and facts
      3. Analyze and interpret information, data and facts
      4. Analyze and develop solutions as well as make recommendations
      5. Prepare report and sell recommendations
      6. Install recommendations and follow up effectiveness

   b. Pitfalls to avoid
      1. *Taking things for granted* – A statement of the situation does not necessarily imply that each of the elements is necessarily true; for example, a complaint may be invalid and biased so that all that can be taken for granted is that a complaint has been registered
      2. *Considering only one side of a situation* – Wherever possible, indicate several alternatives and then point out the reasons you selected the best one
      3. *Failing to indicate follow up* – Whenever your answer indicates action on your part, make certain that you will take proper follow-up action to see how successful your recommendations, procedures or actions turn out to be
      4. *Taking too long in answering any single question* – Remember to time your answers properly

IX. AFTER THE TEST

Scoring procedures differ in detail among civil service jurisdictions although the general principles are the same. Whether the papers are hand-scored or graded by machine we have described, they are nearly always graded by number. That is, the person who marks the paper knows only the number – never the name – of the applicant. Not until all the papers have been graded will they be matched with names. If other tests, such as training and experience or oral interview ratings have been given, scores will be combined. Different parts of the examination usually have different weights. For example, the written test might count 60 percent of the final grade, and a rating of training and experience 40 percent. In many jurisdictions, veterans will have a certain number of points added to their grades.

After the final grade has been determined, the names are placed in grade order and an eligible list is established. There are various methods for resolving ties between those who get the same final grade – probably the most common is to place first the name of the person whose application was received first. Job offers are made from the eligible list in the order the names appear on it. You will be notified of your grade and your rank as soon as all these computations have been made. This will be done as rapidly as possible.

People who are found to meet the requirements in the announcement are called "eligibles." Their names are put on a list of eligible candidates. An eligible's chances of getting a job depend on how high he stands on this list and how fast agencies are filling jobs from the list.

When a job is to be filled from a list of eligibles, the agency asks for the names of people on the list of eligibles for that job. When the civil service commission receives this request, it sends to the agency the names of the three people highest on this list. Or, if the job to be filled has specialized requirements, the office sends the agency the names of the top three persons who meet these requirements from the general list.

The appointing officer makes a choice from among the three people whose names were sent to him. If the selected person accepts the appointment, the names of the others are put back on the list to be considered for future openings.

That is the rule in hiring from all kinds of eligible lists, whether they are for typist, carpenter, chemist, or something else. For every vacancy, the appointing officer has his choice of any one of the top three eligibles on the list. This explains why the person whose name is on top of the list sometimes does not get an appointment when some of the persons lower on the list do. If the appointing officer chooses the second or third eligible, the No. 1 eligible does not get a job at once, but stays on the list until he is appointed or the list is terminated.

X. HOW TO PASS THE INTERVIEW TEST

The examination for which you applied requires an oral interview test. You have already taken the written test and you are now being called for the interview test – the final part of the formal examination.

You may think that it is not possible to prepare for an interview test and that there are no procedures to follow during an interview. Our purpose is to point out some things you can do in advance that will help you and some good rules to follow and pitfalls to avoid while you are being interviewed.

What is an interview supposed to test?

The written examination is designed to test the technical knowledge and competence of the candidate; the oral is designed to evaluate intangible qualities, not readily measured otherwise, and to establish a list showing the relative fitness of each candidate – as measured against his competitors – for the position sought. Scoring is not on the basis of "right" and "wrong," but on a sliding scale of values ranging from "not passable" to "outstanding." As a matter of fact, it is possible to achieve a relatively low score without a single "incorrect" answer because of evident weakness in the qualities being measured.

Occasionally, an examination may consist entirely of an oral test – either an individual or a group oral. In such cases, information is sought concerning the technical knowledges and abilities of the candidate, since there has been no written examination for this purpose. More commonly, however, an oral test is used to supplement a written examination.

Who conducts interviews?

The composition of oral boards varies among different jurisdictions. In nearly all, a representative of the personnel department serves as chairman. One of the members of the board may be a representative of the department in which the candidate would work. In some cases, "outside experts" are used, and, frequently, a businessman or some other representative of the general public is asked to serve. Labor and management or other special groups may be represented. The aim is to secure the services of experts in the appropriate field.

However the board is composed, it is a good idea (and not at all improper or unethical) to ascertain in advance of the interview who the members are and what groups they represent. When you are introduced to them, you will have some idea of their backgrounds and interests, and at least you will not stutter and stammer over their names.

What should be done before the interview?

While knowledge about the board members is useful and takes some of the surprise element out of the interview, there is other preparation which is more substantive. It *is* possible to prepare for an oral interview – in several ways:

1) Keep a copy of your application and review it carefully before the interview

This may be the only document before the oral board, and the starting point of the interview. Know what education and experience you have listed there, and the sequence and dates of all of it. Sometimes the board will ask you to review the highlights of your experience for them; you should not have to hem and haw doing it.

2) Study the class specification and the examination announcement

Usually, the oral board has one or both of these to guide them. The qualities, characteristics or knowledges required by the position sought are stated in these documents. They offer valuable clues as to the nature of the oral interview. For example, if the job involves supervisory responsibilities, the announcement will usually indicate that knowledge of modern supervisory methods and the qualifications of the candidate as a supervisor will be tested. If so, you can expect such questions, frequently in the form of a hypothetical situation which you are expected to solve. NEVER go into an oral without knowledge of the duties and responsibilities of the job you seek.

3) Think through each qualification required

Try to visualize the kind of questions you would ask if you were a board member. How well could you answer them? Try especially to appraise your own knowledge and background in each area, *measured against the job sought*, and identify any areas in which you are weak. Be critical and realistic – do not flatter yourself.

4) Do some general reading in areas in which you feel you may be weak

For example, if the job involves supervision and your past experience has NOT, some general reading in supervisory methods and practices, particularly in the field of human relations, might be useful. Do NOT study agency procedures or detailed manuals. The oral board will be testing your understanding and capacity, not your memory.

5) Get a good night's sleep and watch your general health and mental attitude

You will want a clear head at the interview. Take care of a cold or any other minor ailment, and of course, no hangovers.

What should be done on the day of the interview?

Now comes the day of the interview itself. Give yourself plenty of time to get there. Plan to arrive somewhat ahead of the scheduled time, particularly if your appointment is in the fore part of the day. If a previous candidate fails to appear, the board might be ready for you a bit early. By early afternoon an oral board is almost invariably behind schedule if there are many candidates, and you may have to wait. Take along a book or magazine to read, or your application to review, but leave any extraneous material in the waiting room when you go in for your interview. In any event, relax and compose yourself.

The matter of dress is important. The board is forming impressions about you – from your experience, your manners, your attitude, and your appearance. Give your personal appearance careful attention. Dress your best, but not your flashiest. Choose conservative, appropriate clothing, and be sure it is immaculate. This is a business interview, and your appearance should indicate that you regard it as such. Besides, being well groomed and properly dressed will help boost your confidence.

Sooner or later, someone will call your name and escort you into the interview room. *This is it.* From here on you are on your own. It is too late for any more preparation. But remember, you asked for this opportunity to prove your fitness, and you are here because your request was granted.

What happens when you go in?

The usual sequence of events will be as follows: The clerk (who is often the board stenographer) will introduce you to the chairman of the oral board, who will introduce you to the other members of the board. Acknowledge the introductions before you sit down. Do not be surprised if you find a microphone facing you or a stenotypist sitting by. Oral interviews are usually recorded in the event of an appeal or other review.

Usually the chairman of the board will open the interview by reviewing the highlights of your education and work experience from your application – primarily for the benefit of the other members of the board, as well as to get the material into the record. Do not interrupt or comment unless there is an error or significant misinterpretation; if that is the case, do not hesitate. But do not quibble about insignificant matters. Also, he will usually ask you some question about your education, experience or your present job – partly to get you to start talking and to establish the interviewing "rapport." He may start the actual questioning, or turn it over to one of the other members. Frequently, each member undertakes the questioning on a particular area, one in which he is perhaps most competent, so you can expect each member to participate in the examination. Because time is limited, you may also expect some rather abrupt switches in the direction the questioning takes, so do not be upset by it. Normally, a board member will not pursue a single line of questioning unless he discovers a particular strength or weakness.

After each member has participated, the chairman will usually ask whether any member has any further questions, then will ask you if you have anything you wish to add. Unless you are expecting this question, it may floor you. Worse, it may start you off on an extended, extemporaneous speech. The board is not usually seeking more information. The question is principally to offer you a last opportunity to present further qualifications or to indicate that you have nothing to add. So, if you feel that a significant qualification or characteristic has been overlooked, it is proper to point it out in a sentence or so. Do not compliment the board on the thoroughness of their examination – they have been sketchy, and you know it. If you wish, merely say, "No thank you, I have nothing further to add." This is a point where you can "talk yourself out" of a good impression or fail to present an important bit of information. Remember, *you close the interview yourself.*

The chairman will then say, "That is all, Mr. _____, thank you." Do not be startled; the interview is over, and quicker than you think. Thank him, gather your belongings and take your leave. Save your sigh of relief for the other side of the door.

How to put your best foot forward

Throughout this entire process, you may feel that the board individually and collectively is trying to pierce your defenses, seek out your hidden weaknesses and embarrass and confuse you. Actually, this is not true. They are obliged to make an appraisal of your qualifications for the job you are seeking, and they want to see you in your best light. Remember, they must interview all candidates and a non-cooperative candidate may become a failure in spite of their best efforts to bring out his qualifications. Here are 15 suggestions that will help you:

1) Be natural – Keep your attitude confident, not cocky

If you are not confident that you can do the job, do not expect the board to be. Do not apologize for your weaknesses, try to bring out your strong points. The board is interested in a positive, not negative, presentation. Cockiness will antagonize any board member and make him wonder if you are covering up a weakness by a false show of strength.

2) Get comfortable, but don't lounge or sprawl

Sit erectly but not stiffly. A careless posture may lead the board to conclude that you are careless in other things, or at least that you are not impressed by the importance of the occasion. Either conclusion is natural, even if incorrect. Do not fuss with your clothing, a pencil or an ashtray. Your hands may occasionally be useful to emphasize a point; do not let them become a point of distraction.

3) Do not wisecrack or make small talk

This is a serious situation, and your attitude should show that you consider it as such. Further, the time of the board is limited – they do not want to waste it, and neither should you.

4) Do not exaggerate your experience or abilities

In the first place, from information in the application or other interviews and sources, the board may know more about you than you think. Secondly, you probably will not get away with it. An experienced board is rather adept at spotting such a situation, so do not take the chance.

5) If you know a board member, do not make a point of it, yet do not hide it

Certainly you are not fooling him, and probably not the other members of the board. Do not try to take advantage of your acquaintanceship – it will probably do you little good.

6) Do not dominate the interview

Let the board do that. They will give you the clues – do not assume that you have to do all the talking. Realize that the board has a number of questions to ask you, and do not try to take up all the interview time by showing off your extensive knowledge of the answer to the first one.

7) Be attentive

You only have 20 minutes or so, and you should keep your attention at its sharpest throughout. When a member is addressing a problem or question to you, give him your undivided attention. Address your reply principally to him, but do not exclude the other board members.

8) Do not interrupt

A board member may be stating a problem for you to analyze. He will ask you a question when the time comes. Let him state the problem, and wait for the question.

9) Make sure you understand the question

Do not try to answer until you are sure what the question is. If it is not clear, restate it in your own words or ask the board member to clarify it for you. However, do not haggle about minor elements.

10) Reply promptly but not hastily

A common entry on oral board rating sheets is "candidate responded readily," or "candidate hesitated in replies." Respond as promptly and quickly as you can, but do not jump to a hasty, ill-considered answer.

11) Do not be peremptory in your answers

A brief answer is proper – but do not fire your answer back. That is a losing game from your point of view. The board member can probably ask questions much faster than you can answer them.

12) Do not try to create the answer you think the board member wants

He is interested in what kind of mind you have and how it works – not in playing games. Furthermore, he can usually spot this practice and will actually grade you down on it.

13) Do not switch sides in your reply merely to agree with a board member

Frequently, a member will take a contrary position merely to draw you out and to see if you are willing and able to defend your point of view. Do not start a debate, yet do not surrender a good position. If a position is worth taking, it is worth defending.

14) Do not be afraid to admit an error in judgment if you are shown to be wrong

The board knows that you are forced to reply without any opportunity for careful consideration. Your answer may be demonstrably wrong. If so, admit it and get on with the interview.

15) Do not dwell at length on your present job

The opening question may relate to your present assignment. Answer the question but do not go into an extended discussion. You are being examined for a *new* job, not your present one. As a matter of fact, try to phrase ALL your answers in terms of the job for which you are being examined.

Basis of Rating

Probably you will forget most of these "do's" and "don'ts" when you walk into the oral interview room. Even remembering them all will not ensure you a passing grade. Perhaps you did not have the qualifications in the first place. But remembering them will help you to put your best foot forward, without treading on the toes of the board members.

Rumor and popular opinion to the contrary notwithstanding, an oral board wants you to make the best appearance possible. They know you are under pressure – but they also want to see how you respond to it as a guide to what your reaction would be under the pressures of the job you seek. They will be influenced by the degree of poise you display, the personal traits you show and the manner in which you respond.

ABOUT THIS BOOK

This book contains tests divided into Examination Sections. Go through each test, answering every question in the margin. At the end of each test look at the answer key and check your answers. On the ones you got wrong, look at the right answer choice and learn. Do not fill in the answers first. Do not memorize the questions and answers, but understand the answer and principles involved. On your test, the questions will likely be different from the samples. Questions are changed and new ones added. If you understand these past questions you should have success with any changes that arise. Tests may consist of several types of questions. We have additional books on each subject should more study be advisable or necessary for you. Finally, the more you study, the better prepared you will be. This book is intended to be the last thing you study before you walk into the examination room. Prior study of relevant texts is also recommended. NLC publishes some of these in our Fundamental Series. Knowledge and good sense are important factors in passing your exam. Good luck also helps. So now study this Passbook, absorb the material contained within and take that knowledge into the examination. Then do your best to pass that exam.

———

EXAMINATION SECTION

EXAMINATION SECTION
TEST 1

DIRECTIONS: Each question or incomplete statement is followed by several suggested answers or completions. Select the one that BEST answers the question or completes the statement. *PRINT THE LETTER OF THE CORRECT ANSWER IN THE SPACE AT THE RIGHT.*

1. Competent civil service personnel cannot come just from initial employment on a competitive basis and equal pay for equal work.
   The one of the following additional factors which is of GREATEST importance in building up a body of competent civil service employees is

   A. analysis of work methods and introduction of streamlined procedures
   B. training for skill improvement and creating a sense of belonging
   C. rotation of employees from organization to organization in order to prevent stagnation
   D. treating personnel problems on a more impersonal basis in order to maintain an objective viewpoint
   E. recruiting for all higher positions from among the body of present employees

   1.____

2. A comment made by an employee about a training course was: *Half of the group seem to know what the course is about, the rest of us can't keep up with them.*
   The FUNDAMENTAL error in training methods to which this criticism points is

   A. insufficient student participation
   B. failure to develop a feeling of need or active want for the material being presented
   C. that the training session may be too long
   D. that no attempt may have been made to connect the new material with what was already known by any member of the group
   E. that insufficient provision has been made by the instructor for individual differences

   2.____

3. The one of the following which is NOT a major purpose of an employee suggestion plan is to

   A. provide an additional method by means of which an employee's work performance can be evaluated
   B. increase employee interest in the work of the organization
   C. provide an additional channel of communication between the employee and top management
   D. utilize to the greatest extent possible the ideas and proposals of employees
   E. provide a formal method for rewarding the occasional valuable idea

   3.____

4. The pay plan is a vital aspect of a duties classification. In fact, in most areas of personnel administration, pay plan and classification are synonymous.
   This statement is

   A. *correct* in general; while the two are not, in general, synonymous, the pay plan is such a vital aspect that without it the classification plan is meaningless and useless
   B. *not correct;* while the pay plan is a vital aspect of a classification plan, it is not the only one

   4.____

C. *correct* in general; pay plan and duties classification are simply two different aspects of the same problem - *equal pay for equal work*
D. *not correct;* although classification is usually a vital element of a pay plan, a pay plan is not essential to the preparation of a duties classification
E. *meaningless* unless the specific nature of the classification plan and the pay plan are set forth

5. The one of the following objectives which is MOST characteristic of intelligent personnel management is the desire to   5.____

   A. obtain competent employees, and having them to provide the climate which will be most conducive to superior performance, proper attitudes, and harmonious adjustments
   B. coordinate the activities of the workers in an organization so that the output will be maximized and cost minimized
   C. reduce the dependence of an organization on the sentiments, ambitions, and idiosyncracies of individual employees and thus advance the overall aims of the organization
   D. recruit employees who can be trained to subordinate their interests to the interests of the organization and to train them to do so
   E. mechanize the procedures involved so that problems of replacement and training are reduced to a minimum

6. An organizational structure which brings together, in a single work unit, work divisions which are non-homogeneous in work, in technology, or in purpose will tend to decrease the danger of friction.
   This opinion is, in general,   6.____

   A. *correct;* individious comparisons tend to be made when everyone is doing the same thing
   B. *not correct;* a homogeneous organization tends to develop a strong competitive spirit among its employees
   C. *correct;* work which is non-homogeneous tends to be of greater interest to the employee, resulting in less friction
   D. *not correct;* persons performing the same type of work tend to work together more efficiently
   E. *correct;* the presence of different kinds of work permits better placement of employees, resulting in better morale

7. Of the following, the MOST accurate statement of current theory concerning the ultimate responsibility for employee training is that   7.____

   A. ultimate responsibility for training is best separated from responsibility for production and administration
   B. ultimate responsibility for training should be in the hands of a training specialist in the central personnel agency
   C. a committee of employees selected from the trainees should be given ultimate responsibility for the training program
   D. a departmental training specialist should be assigned ultimate responsibility for employee training
   E. each official should be ultimately responsible for the training of all employees under his direction

8. The BEST of the following ways to reduce the errors in supervisors' ratings of employee performance caused by variations in the application of the rating standards is to

    A. construct a method for translating each rating into a standard score
    B. inform each supervisor of the distribution of ratings expected in his unit
    C. review and change any rating which does not seem justified by the data presented by the rating supervisor
    D. arrange for practice sessions for supervisors at which rating standards will be applied and discussed
    E. confer with the supervisor when a case of disagreement is discovered between supervisor and review board

8.____

9. Which capsule description, among the following, constitutes an optimum arrangement of the hierarchical organization of a large-city central personnel agency?

    A. Three commissioners who appoint a Director of Personnel to carry out the administrative functions but who handle the quasi-judicial and quasi-legislative duties themselves
    B. A Director of Personnel and two Commissioners all three of whom participate in all aspects of the agency's functions
    C. A Director of Personnel who is responsible for making the final decision in all matters pertaining to personnel administration in a city
    D. A Director of Personnel who is the chief administrator and two Commissioners who, together with the Director, handle the quasi-judicial and quasi-legislative duties
    E. Three Commissioners who have review powers over the acts of the Director of Personnel who is appointed on the basis of a competitive examination

9.____

10. The one of the following which is a major objective expected to be gained by setting up a personnel council composed of representatives of the central personnel agency and departmental personnel officers is to

    A. provide an appeal board to which employees who feel grieved can appeal
    B. allow the departments to participate in making the day-to-day decisions faced by the central personnel agency
    C. prevent the departments from participating in making the day-to-day decisions faced by the central personnel agency
    D. establish good communications between the central personnel agency and the departments
    E. develop a broad base of responsibility for the actions of the central personnel agency

10.____

11. The one of the following which should be the starting point in the development of an accident reduction or prevention program is the

    A. institution of an interorganizational safety contest
    B. improvement of the conditions of work so that accidents are prevented
    C. inauguration of a safety education program to reduce accidents due to carelessness
    D. organization of unit safety committees to bring home the importance of safety to the individual worker
    E. determination of the number, character, and causes of accidents

11.____

12. An orientation program for a group of new employees would NOT usually include   12.____

    A. a description of the physical layout of the organization
    B. a statement of the rules pertaining to leave, lateness, overtime, and so forth
    C. detailed instruction on the job each employee is to perform
    D. an explanation of the lines of promotion
    E. a talk on the significance of the role the department plays in the governmental structure

13. The device of temporary assignment of an employee to the duties of the higher position   13.____
is sometimes used to determine promotability.
The use of this procedure, especially for top positions, is

    A. *desirable;* no test or series of tests can measure fitness to the same extent as actual trial on the job
    B. *undesirable;* the organization will not have a responsible head during the trial period
    C. *desirable;* employees who are on trial tend to operate with greater efficiency
    D. *undesirable;* the organization would tend to deteriorate if no one of the candidates for the position was satisfactory
    E. *desirable;* the procedure outlined is simpler and less expensive than any series of tests

14. Frequently, when accumulating data for a salary standardization study, the salaries for   14.____
certain basic positions are compared with the salaries paid in other agencies, public and private.
The one of the following which would MOST usually be considered one of these basic positions is

    A. Office Manager   B. Administrative Assistant
    C. Chief Engineer   D. Junior Typist
    E. Chemist

15. The emphasis in public personnel administration during recent years has been less on   15.____
the

    A. need for the elimination of the spoils system and more on the development of policy and techniques of administration that contribute to employee selection and productivity
    B. development of policy and techniques of administration that contribute to employee selection and productivity and more on the need for the elimination of the spoils system
    C. human relation aspects of personnel administration and more on the technical problems of classification and placement
    D. problems of personnel administration of governmental units in the United States and more on those of international organizations
    E. problems of personnel administration in international organizations and more on those of governmental units in the United States

16. The recommendation has been made that explicit information be made available to all   16.____
city employees concerning the procedure to be followed when appealing from a performance rating.
To put this recommendation into effect would be

A. *desirable,* primarily because employees would tend to have greater confidence in the performance rating system
B. *undesirable,* primarily because a greater number of employees would submit appeals with no merit
C. *desirable,* primarily because the additional publicity would spotlight the performance rating system
D. *undesirable,* primarily because all appeals should be treated as confidential matters and all efforts to make them public should be defeated
E. *desirable,* primarily because committing the appeal procedure to paper would tend to standardize it

17. The one of the following which in most cases is the BEST practical measure of the merits of the overall personnel policies of one organization as compared to the policies of similar organizations in the same area is the

17.____

A. extent to which higher positions in the hierarchy are filled by career employees
B. degree of loyalty and enthusiasm manifested by the work force
C. rate at which replacements must be made in order to maintain the work force
D. percentage of employees who have joined labor unions and the militancy of these unions
E. scale of salaries

18. Classification may most properly be viewed as the building of a structure. The fundamental unit in the classification structure is the

18.____

A. assignment   B. position   C. service
D. rank   E. grade

19. The one of the following which is NOT usually included in a class specification is

19.____

A. a definition of the duties and responsibilities covered
B. the class title
C. a description of the recruitment method to be used
D. a statement of typical tasks performed
E. the statement of minimum qualifications necessary to perform the work

20. The one of the following which is usually NOT considered part of a classification survey is

20.____

A. grouping positions on the basis of similarities
B. preparing job specifications
C. analyzing and recording specific job duties
D. adjusting job duties to employee qualifications
E. allocating individual positions to classes

21. The one of the following which is MOST generally accepted as a prerequisite to the development of a sound career service is

21.____

A. agreement to accept for all higher positions the senior eligible employee
B. the recruitment of an adequate proportion of beginning employees who will eventually be capable of performing progressively more difficult duties
C. strict adherence to the principle of competitive promotion from within for all positions above the entrance level

D. the development of a program of periodically changing an employee's duties in order to prevent stagnation

E. the existence of administrators who can stimulate employees and keep their production high

22. The determination of the fitness of a person to fill a position solely on the basis of his experience is

22.____

A. *desirable;* experience is the best test of aptitude for a position when it is rated properly

B. *undesirable;* the applicant may not be giving correct factual information in regard to his experience

C. *desirable;* a uniform rating key can be applied to evaluate experience

D. *undesirable;* it is difficult to evaluate from experience records how much the applicant has gained from his experience

E. *desirable;* there will be more applicants for a position if no written or oral tests are required

23. The performance rating standards in a city department have been criticized by its employees as unfair.
The one of the following procedures which would probably be HOST effective in reducing this criticism is to

23.____

A. publish a detailed statement showing how the standards were arrived at

B. provide for participation by employee representatives in revising the standards

C. allow individual employees to submit written statements about the standards employed

D. arrange for periodic meetings of the entire staff at which the standards are discussed

E. appoint a review board consisting of senior supervisory employees to reconsider the standards

24. The statement has been made that personnel administration is the MOST fundamental and important task of the head of any organization.
This statement is based, for the most part, on the fact that

24.____

A. success or failure of an organization to reach its objectives depends on the attitudes and abilities of the people in the organization

B. the influence of personnel administration on organization success varies in proportion to the number, the complexity, and the rarity of the virtues and qualities that are requisite to superior performance of the tasks involved

C. a sound philosophy of personnel administration emphasizes the basic objective of superior service over any other consideration

D. relative autonomy is permitted each department, particularly with respect to the handling of personnel

E. diversity of personnel practices as to salaries, hours, etc., leads to poor morale

25. The requirement imposed by most civil service laws in the United States that tests shall be *practical in character and deal in so far as possible with the actual duties of the position,* has led to a wide use of

25.____

A. tests of social outlook   B. aptitude tests
C. achievement tests   D. objective tests
E. oral tests

26. In general, the one of the following which is the first step in the construction of a test for the selection of personnel is to

     26.____

    A. determine what the duties of the position to be filled are
    B. investigate the relationships among abilities and capacities required for success in the position to be filled
    C. study examinations which have been given in the' past for similar positions
    D. evaluate existing examining instruments to determine their adequacy for making the desired selection
    E. set up the outline and start preliminary preparation of the examining instruments

27. The one of the following situations which is MOST likely to result from a too highly specified assignment or definition of responsibility is that

     27.____

    A. there will be no standard against which to measure the efficiency of the organization
    B. duplication and overlapping of functions will be encouraged
    C. sufficient channels to collect, synthesize, and coordinate all performances may not be provided
    D. essential tasks which have not been explicitly mentioned in the assignment may not get done
    E. there will be a tendency to overlook the need for training

28. Assume that you are interviewing a new entrance level clerical employee for the purpose of determining where he would be best placed.
In making your determination, the characteristic to which you should give GREATEST weight is the employee's

     28.____

    A. interest in the jobs you describe to him
    B. mechanical aptitude
    C. poise and self-assurance
    D. fluency of verbal expression
    E. educational background and his hobbies

29. The use of the probationary period in the public service has become an approved practice especially where state tenure laws guarantee long-term continuous employment. Of the following, the MOST important use of the probationary period is that it

     29.____

    A. provides supervisory contact which will help the new employee regardless of retention at the end of the probationary period
    B. supplies confirming evidence of academic and cultural fitness not measurable in formal test procedures
    C. introduces the new employee to the office and the work situation which conditions future performance
    D. provides the new employee with a sound basis for self-improvement
    E. reveals aspects of performance and attitude toward the job not adequately measured by formal examination

30. The first prerequisite to the formulation of any compensation plan for a public agency is the collection and analysis of certain basic data.
Data are NOT usually collected for this purpose in regard to

   A. working conditions in the agency
   B. the wage paid in the agency at present
   C. labor turnover in the agency
   D. the cost of living in the area
   E. the age and sex distribution of the employees

30.____

31. The one of the following personnel administration techniques which when properly utilized will yield information concerning current training needs of an organization is the

   A. classification plan   B. performance rating
   C. personnel register   D. compensation plan
   E. employee handbook

31.____

32. In administering the activities of a personnel office with a staff of fifteen employees, including seven personnel technicians, the personnel officer should

   A. delegate full authority and responsibility to each staff member and discharge those who do not meet his standards
   B. endeavor to keep tab on the work of each individual on his staff
   C. make sure each job is being done properly or do it himself
   D. plan work programs, make assignments, and check on performance
   E. concern himself only with major policies and expect subordinates to carry out actual functions

32.____

33. The one of the following factors which is MOST influential in determining the proportion of qualified applicants who refuse public employment when offered is the

   A. interim between application and offer of a position
   B. specific nature of the duties of the position
   C. general nature of economic conditions at the time when the position is offered
   D. salary paid
   E. general undesirable nature of public employment

33.____

34. A placement officer in a department follows the procedure of consulting the supervisor of the unit in which a vacancy exists concerning the kind of worker he wants before attempting to fill the vacancy.
This procedure is, in general,

   A. *undesirable;* it makes the selection process dependent on the whim of the supervisor
   B. *desirable;* it will make for a more effectively working organization
   C. *undesirable;* if the kind of worker the supervisor wants is not available, he will be dissatisfied
   D. *desirable;* the more people who are consulted about a matter of this kind, the more chance there is that no mistake will be made
   E. *undesirable;* the wishes of the worker as well as those of the supervisor should be taken into consideration

34.____

35. In a large organization, proper recruitment is not possible without the existence of an effective position classification system.
    The one of the following which BEST explains why this is the case is that otherwise effective means of determining the capabilities and characteristics of prospective employees are of little value

    A. unless these are related to the salary scale and current economic conditions
    B. without a knowledge of the essential character of the work to be performed in each position
    C. where no attempt to classify the different recruitment approaches has been made in advance
    D. if there has been no attempt made to obtain the cooperation of the employees involved
    E. to personnel officers who tend to place new employees in positions without reference to capabilities

35.____

36. The recommendation has been made that a departmental grievance board be set up, which would handle all employee grievances from their inception to conclusion.
    Of the following comments for and against the acceptance of this recommendation, the one which is NOT valid is that it is

    A. *desirable,* primarily because it will remove a constant source of friction between supervisor and employee and place the problem in the hands of an objective board
    B. *undesirable,* primarily because handling grievances is an integral part of the supervisory process and the immediate supervisor must be afforded the opportunity to deal with the situation
    C. *desirable,* primarily because no supervisor will have to determine whether he has been unfair to one of his subordinates and no subordinate will have a grievance
    D. *desirable,* primarily because the handling of grievances will tend to be expedited as the board will have only one function
    E. *undesirable,* primarily because the handling of grievances will tend to be delayed as the board will not have all the necessary information available

36.____

37. The one of the following which is frequently given as a major argument against a tightly knit promotion-from-within policy is that

    A. it takes too long for an employee in the lower grades to reach the top
    B. all persons both in and out of the government are equally entitled to civil service jobs
    C. persons are placed in executive jobs who are too well acquainted with the existing organization
    D. it leads to the presence in executive jobs of clerks who still operate as clerks
    E. it is not desirable to guarantee to all employees promotion to new responsibilities from time to time

37.____

38. Of the following factors which are influential in determining which employment a young man or woman will choose, government employ is generally considered superior in

    A. incentives to improve efficiency
    B. opportunities to move into other similar organizations
    C. prestige and recognition
    D. leave and retirement benefits
    E. salaries

38.____

39. Training programs, to be fully effective, should be concerned not only with the acquisition   39.____
or improvement of skills but also with

    A. employee attitude and will to work
    B. the personality problems of the individual employees
    C. time and motion studies for the development of new procedures
    D. the recruitment of the best persons available to fill a given position
    E. such theoretical background material as is deemed necessary

Questions 40-45.

DIRECTIONS: Questions 40 through 45 are to be answered on the basis of the following
             paragraphs.

Plan 1   Hire broadly qualified people, work out their assignments from time to time to suit
the needs of the enterprise and aptitudes of individuals. Let their progress and
recognition be based on the length and overall quality of the service, regardless of
the significance of individual assignments which they periodically assume.

Plan 2   Hire experts and assign them well-defined duties. Their compensation, for the
most part, should be dependent on the duties performed.

40. For Plan 1 to be successful, there must be assured, to a much greater extent than for   40.____
Plan 2, the existence of

    A. a well-developed training program
    B. a widely publicized recruitment program
    C. in general, better working conditions
    D. more skilled administrators
    E. a greater willingness to work together toward a common goal

41. Plan 1 would tend to develop employees who were   41.____

    A. dissatisfied because of the impossibility of advancing rapidly to positions of impor-
tance
    B. conversant only with problems in the particular field in which they were employed
    C. in general, not satisfied with the work they perform
    D. intensely competitive
    E. able to perform a variety of functions

42. Large governmental organizations in the United States tend, in general, to use Plan   42.____

    A. 1
    B. 2
    C. 1 for technical positions and Plan 2 for clerical positions
    D. 2 for administrative positions and Plan 1 for clerical and technical positions
    E. 1 for office machine operators and Plan 2 for technical positions

43. In organizations which operate on the basis of Plan 1, placement of a man in the proper job after selection is much more difficult than in those which operate on the basis of Plan 2.
This statement is, in general,

    A. *correct;* the organization would have only specific positions open and generalists would be forced into technical positions
    B. *not correct;* specific aptitudes and abilities would tend to be determined in advance as would be the case with Plan 2
    C. *correct;* it is much more difficult to determine specific aptitudes and abilities than general qualifications
    D. *not correct;* placement would be based on the needs of the organization, consequently only a limited number of positions would be available
    E. *correct;* the selection is not on the basis of specific aptitudes and abilities

43.____

44. Administration in an organization operating on the basis of Plan 1 would tend to be less flexible than one operating on the basis of Plan 2.
This statement is, in general,

    A. *correct;* recruitment of experts permits rapid expansion
    B. *not correct;* the absence of well-defined positions permits wide and rapid recruitment without an extensive selection period
    C. *correct;* well-defined positions allow for replacement on an assembly-line basis without an extensive breaking-in period and thus permits greater flexibility
    D. *not correct;* Plan 1 presents greater freedom in movement of individuals from one position to another and in re-defining positions according to capabilities of employees and the needs of the moment
    E. *correct;* Plan 1 presents greater freedom in adjusting an organizational structure to unexpected stresses since the clear definition of duties shows where the danger points are

44.____

45. To a greater extent than Plan 2, Plan 1 leads to conflict and overlapping in administrative operations.
In general, this is the case because

    A. employees paid on the basis of duties performed tend to be more conscious of overlapping operations and tend to limit their activities
    B. experts refuse to accept responsibilities in fields other than their own
    C. the lack of carefully defined positions may conceal many points at which coordination and reconciliation are necessary
    D. there tends to be more pressure for *empire building* where prestige is measured solely in terms of assignment
    E. there is less need, under Plan 1, to define lines of responsibility and authority and consequently conflict will arise

45.____

46. Some organizations interview employees who resign or are discharged.
This procedure is USUALLY

    A. of great value in reducing labor turnover and creating good will toward the organization
    B. of little or no value as the views of incompetent or disgruntled employees are of questionable validity

46.____

C. dangerous; it gives employees who are leaving an organization the opportunity to pay off old scores
D. of great value in showing the way to more efficient methods of production and the establishment of higher work norms
E. dangerous; it may lead to internal friction as operating departments believe that it is not the function of the personnel office to check on operations

47. The one of the following which is the MOST common flaw in the administration of an employee performance rating system is the   47._____

A. failure to explain the objectives of the system to employees
B. lack of safeguards to prevent supervisors from rating employees down for personal reasons
C. tendency for rating supervisors to rate their employees much too leniently
D. fact that employees are aware of the existence of the system
E. increasing number of committees and boards required

48. As a result of its study of the operations of the Federal government, the Hoover Commission recommended that, for purposes of reduction in force, employees be ranked from the standpoint of their overall usefulness to the agency in question.   48._____
The one of the following which is a major disadvantage of this proposal is that it would probably result in

A. efficient employees becoming indifferent to the social problems posed
B. a sense of insecurity on the part of employees which might tend to lower efficiency
C. the retention of employees who are at or just past their peak performance
D. the retention of generalists rather than specialists
E. the loss of experience in the agency, as ability rather than knowledge will be the criterion

49. A personnel officer checking the turnover rate in his department found that, over a period of five years, the rate at which engineers left the organization was exactly the same as the rate at which junior clerks left the department.   49._____
This information tends to indicate

A. that something may be amiss with the organization; the rate for engineers under ordinary circumstances should be higher than for clerks
B. that the organization is in good shape; neither the technical nor clerical aspects are being overemphasized
C. nothing which would be of value in determining the state of the organization
D. that the organization is in good shape; working conditions, in general, are equivalent for all employees
E. that something may be amiss with the organization; the turnover rate for engineers under ordinary circumstances should be lower than for clerks

50. Of the following, the MOST essential feature of a grievance procedure is that   50._____

A. those who appeal be assured of expert counsel
B. the administration have opportunity to review cases early in the procedure
C. it afford assurance that those who use it will not be discriminated against
D. general grievances be publicized
E. it be simple to administer

KEY (CORRECT ANSWERS)

1.	B	11.	E	21.	B	31.	B	41.	E
2.	E	12.	C	22.	D	32.	D	42.	B
3.	A	13.	A	23.	B	33.	A	43.	E
4.	D	14.	D	24.	A	34.	B	44.	D
5.	A	15.	A	25.	C	35.	B	45.	C
6.	D	16.	A	26.	A	36.	B	46.	A
7.	E	17.	C	27.	D	37.	D	47.	C
8.	D	18.	B	28.	A	38.	D	48.	B
9.	D	19.	C	29.	E	39.	A	49.	E
10.	D	20.	D	30.	E	40.	A	50.	C

TEST 2

DIRECTIONS: Each question or incomplete statement is followed by several suggested answers or completions. Select the one that BEST answers the question or completes the statement. *PRINT THE LETTER OF THE CORRECT ANSWER IN THE SPACE AT THE RIGHT.*

1. In which of the following fields could two or more groups duplicating each other's work USUALLY be best justified?   1._____

    A. Accounting   B. Personnel
    C. Public relations   D. Research and development
    E. Systems and procedures

2. Which of the following statements is MOST nearly accurate? A span of control   2._____

    A. of 5 people is better than that of 10 people
    B. of 5 people may be better or worse than that of 10 people
    C. of 5 people is worse than that of 10 people
    D. is rarely over 20 minutes at any one time
    E. means the same as the scalar system

3. A linear responsibility chart is   3._____

    A. a graphical method of showing each sub-project making up a total project with the time it takes to complete each
    B. a graphical method of showing jobs, functions, and, by the use of appropriate symbols, the relationship of each job to each function
    C. a graphical method of solving linear equations used in doing Operations Research
    D. a new method of procedures analysis which makes it possible to focus on both the employees and the equipment they use
    E. another name for a special organization chart

4. An administrator of a public agency is faced with the problem of deciding which of two divisions should be responsible for the statistical reporting of the agency. This work is now located in one of them but each of the two division chiefs believes that the work should be located within his division because of its relationship to other activities under his supervision. The Organization Planning Section is located in one of the two divisions. Assuming that in this situation the administrator can select any one of the following courses of action, the BEST for him to take would be to   4._____

    A. assign a staff member from the Organization Planning Section to study the problem, who for the duration of the assignment would report directly to the administrator
    B. assign staff from the Organization Planning Section to study the problem
    C. assign the statistical work to the other division for a trial period because of the problems which exist under the present arrangement
    D. call in an outside consultant or refer it to a competent staff employee not assigned to the divisions involved
    E. leave the organization as it is because the advantages of a change are not entirely clear to all concerned

5. The problem of whether office services such as filing, duplicating, and stenography
should be centralized or decentralized arises in every business organization.
One advantage of decentralizing these services is that

    A. greater facility exists in such matters as finding correspondence
    B. greater flexibility exists in rotating workers during vacations
    C. higher production is attained at a lower cost per unit
    D. knowledge of the purpose and use of work acts as an incentive for production
    E. reduction in investment results from the use of less machinery

5.____

6. Research to date on the relationship between productivity and morale shows that

    A. high productivity and high morale nearly always go together
    B. high productivity and low morale nearly always go together
    C. low productivity and high morale nearly always go together
    D. low productivity and low morale nearly always go together
    E. there is no clear relationship between productivity and morale

6.____

7. Which one of the following statements BEST describes *work measurement* as commonly
used in government?
It is

    A. a method of establishing an equitable relationship between volume of work per-
formed and manpower utilized
    B. a new technique which may be substituted for traditional accounting methods
    C. the amount of work turned out by an organization in a given time period
    D. the same as the work count, as used in Work Simplification
    E. the same as time-motion study

7.____

8. Critics of work measurement have contended that any increase in production is more
than offset by deterioration in standards of quality or service.
The BEST answer to this charge is to

    A. argue that increases in production have not been offset by decreased quality
    B. define work units in terms of both quality and quantity
    C. ignore it
    D. point out that statistical quality control can be used to control quality
    E. point out that work measurement is not concerned with quality, and hence that the
argument is irrelevant

8.____

9. When it is determined that a given activity or process is so intangible that it cannot be
reflected adequately by
a work unit, it is BEST for a work measurement system to

    A. combine that activity with others that are measurable
    B. discuss the activity only in narrative reports
    C. exclude it from the work measurement system
    D. include only the time devoted to that activity or process
    E. select the best available work unit, as better than none

9.____

10. Which one of the following is frequently referred to as the father of Statistical Quality   10._____
    Control?

    A. Ralph M. Barnes   B. John M. Pfiffner
    C. Benjamin Selekman   D. Walter A. Shewhart
    E. Donald C. Stone

11. Which one of the following BEST explains the use and value of the *upper control limit*   11._____
    (and *lower control limit* where applicable) in Statistical Quality Control?
    It

    A. automatically keeps production under control
    B. indicates that unit costs are too high or too low
    C. is useful as a training device for new workers
    D. tells what pieces to discard or errors to correct
    E. tells when assignable causes as distinguished from chance causes are at work

12. A manager skilled in human relations can BEST be defined as one who   12._____

    A. can identify interpersonal problems and work out solutions to them
    B. can persuade people to do things his way
    C. gets along well with people and has many friends
    D. plays one role with his boss, another with his subordinates, and a third with his
       peers
    E. treats everyone fairly

13. The BEST way to secure efficient management is to   13._____

    A. allow staff agencies to solve administrative problems
    B. equip line management to solve its own problems
    C. get employees properly classified and trained
    D. prescribe standard operating procedures
    E. set up a board of control

14. The composition of the work force in American government and industry is changing.   14._____
    There has been an increase in the proportion of white collar to blue collar employees and
    an increase in the proportion of higher educated to lower educated employees.
    This change will MOST likely result in

    A. a more simplified forms control system
    B. closer supervision of employees
    C. further decentralization of decision-making
    D. more employee grievances
    E. organization by process instead of purpose

15. In which of the following professional journals would you be MOST apt to find articles on   15._____
    organization theory?

    A. Administrative Science Quarterly
    B. Factory Management and Maintenance
    C. Harvard Business Review
    D. O and M
    E. Public Administration Review

16. Which of the following organizations is MOST noted for its training courses in various management subjects? 16.____

    A. American Management Association
    B. American Political Science Association
    C. American Society for Public Administration
    D. Society for the Advancement of Management
    E. Systems and Procedures Association

17. A *performance budget* puts emphasis on 17.____

    A. achieving greatest economy
    B. expenditures for salaries, travel, rent, supplies, etc.
    C. revenues rather than on expenditures
    D. tables of organization or staffing patterns
    E. what is accomplished, e.g., number of applications processed, trees planted, buildings inspected, etc.

18. Which of the following statements MOST accurately defines *Operations Research?* 18.____

    A. A highly sophisticated reporting system used in the analysis of management problems
    B. A specialized application of electronic data processing in the analysis of management problems
    C. Research on operating problems
    D. Research on technological problems
    E. The application of sophisticated mathematical tools to the analysis of management problems

19. Which of the following characteristics of a system would MOST likely lead to the conclusion that manual methods should be used rather than punch card equipment? 19.____

    A. High volume
    B. Low volume but complex computations
    C. Operations of a fixed sequence
    D. Relatively simple work
    E. Repetitive work

20. Assume that a computer with typing software costs $1100 and an electric typewriter costs $300. Except for speed of production, assume that in all other pertinent respects they are the same, including a life expectancy of 10 years each. 20.____
    What is the approximate amount of time $7.40 per hour typist must save and re-invest in work to have her computer recoup the difference in purchase price?

    A. 11 hours annually   B. 110 hours annually
    C. 550 hours annually   D. 1100 hours annually
    E. One hour a day

21. The principal justification for using office machines to replace hand labor is to   21.____

    A. achieve automation   B. eliminate errors
    C. increase productivity   D. make work easier
    E. reduce labor problems

22. An analog computer is one which   22.____

    A. is classified as *medium* size
    B. is used primarily for solving scientific and engineering problems rather than for data processing
    C. operates on the principle of creating a physical, often electrical, analogy of the mathematical problem to be solved
    D. uses transistors rather than vacuum tubes
    E. works on the basis of logarithms

23. The binary numbering system used in computers is one which   23.____

    A. is much more complicated than the usual decimal numbering system
    B. uses a radix or base of 8
    C. uses letters of the alphabet rather than numerical digits
    D. uses only two digits, 0 and 1
    E. uses the customary ten digits, 0 through 9

24. An electronic computer performs various arithmetic operations by   24.____

    A. adding and subtracting
    B. adding, subtracting, dividing, and multiplying
    C. Boolean algebra
    D. multiplying and dividing
    E. all operations listed in B and C

25. The MOST effective basis for an analysis of the flow of work in a large governmental agency is the   25.____

    A. analysis of descriptions written by employees
    B. discussion of routines with selected employees
    C. discussion of operations with supervisors
    D. initiation of a series of general staff meetings to discuss operational procedures
    E. observation of actual operations

26. The BEST reason for prescribing definite procedures for certain work in an organization is to   26.____

    A. enable supervisor to keep *on top of* details of work
    B. enable work to be processed speedily and consistently
    C. facilitate incorporation of new policies
    D. prevent individual discretion
    E. reduce training periods

27. Which one of the following is the MOST important difference between clerks in small offices and those in large offices?
Clerks in

    27.____

    A. large offices are less closely supervised
    B. large offices have more freedom to exercise originality in their work
    C. small offices are more restricted by standardized procedures
    D. small offices are more specialized in their duties
    E. small offices need a greater variety of clerical skills

28. After taking the necessary steps to analyze a situation, an employee reaches a decision which is reviewed by his supervisor and found to be incorrect.
Of the following possible methods of dealing with this incident, the MOST constructive for the employee would be for the supervisor to

    28.____

    A. correct the decision and give the employee an explanation
    B. correct the decision and suggest more detailed analysis in the future
    C. help the employee discover what is wrong with the basis for decision
    D. set up a temporary control on this type of decision until the employee demonstrates he can handle it
    E. suggest that the employee review future cases of this type with him before reaching a decision

29. Which one of the following is NOT a purpose ordinarily served by charts?

    29.____

    A. Aid in training employees
    B. Assist in presenting and selling recommendations
    C. Detect gaps or discrepancies in data collected
    D. Put facts in proper relationships to each other
    E. Show up problems of human relationships

30. Which of the following descriptive statements does NOT constitute a desirable standard in evaluating an administrative sequence or series of tasks having a definite objective?

    30.____

    A. All material should be routed as directly as possible to reduce the cost of time and motion.
    B. Each form must clear the section chief before going to another section.
    C. Each task should be assigned to the lowest-ranking employee who can perform it adequately.
    D. Each task should contribute positively to the basic purpose of the sequence.
    E. Similar tasks should be combined.

31. Which one of the following is NOT a principle of motion economy?

    31.____

    A. Continuous curved motions are preferable to straight-line motions involving sudden and sharp changes in direction.
    B. Motions of the arms should be made in the same direction and should be made simultaneously.
    C. The hands should be relieved of all work that can be performed more advantageously by the feet.
    D. The two hands should begin and complete their motions at the same time.
    E. Two or more tools should be combined whenever possible.

32. Generally, the first step in the measurement of relative efficiency of office employees engaged in machine operation is the

    A. analysis of the class of positions involved to determine the duties and responsibilities and minimum qualifications necessary for successful job performance
    B. analysis of those skills which make for difference in the production of various employees
    C. development of a service rating scale which can be scored accurately
    D. development of a standard unit of production that can be widely applied and that will give comparable data
    E. selection of an appropriate sampling of employees whose duties involve the specific factors to be measured

33. In the course of a survey, a disgruntled employee of Unit A comes to your office with an offer to *tell all* about Unit B, where he used to work.
    You should

    A. listen to him but ignore any statements he makes
    B. listen to him carefully, but verify his assertions before acting on them
    C. make him speak to you in the presence of the persons he is criticizing
    D. reprimand him for not minding his own business
    E. report him to the security officer

34. Combining several different procedures into a single flow of work would MOST likely achieve which of the following advantages?

    A. Better teamwork
    B. Higher quality decisions
    C. Improved morale
    D. Reduced fluctuations in workload
    E. Reduced problems of control

35. After conducting a systems survey in the Personnel Division you find that there is not sufficient work in the Division to keep a recently hired employee gainfully employed.
    The BEST solution to this problem is usually to

    A. lay off the employee with a full month's salary
    B. leave the employee in the Division because the workload may increase
    C. leave the employee in the Personnel Division, but assign him overflow work from other divisions
    D. reassign the employee when an appropriate opening occurs elsewhere in the organization
    E. request the employee to resign so that no unfavorable references will appear on his personnel record

36. You are making a study of a central headquarters office which processes claims received 36.____
    from a number of regional offices. You notice the following problems: some employees
    are usually busy while others assigned to the same kind of work in the same grade have
    little to do; high-level professional people frequently spend considerable time searching
    for files in the file room.
    Which of the following charts would be MOST useful to record and analyze the data
    needed to help solve these problems?
    _____ chart.

    A. forms distribution   B. layout
    C. operation   D. process
    E. work distribution

37. A *therblig* is BEST defined as a   37.____

    A. follower of Frederick W. Taylor
    B. small element or task of an operation used in time-motion study
    C. special type of accounting machine
    D. type of curve used in charting certain mathematical relationships
    E. unit for measuring the effectiveness of air conditioning

38. One of the following advantages which is LEAST likely to accrue to a large organization 38.____
    as a result of establishing a centralized typing and stenographic unit is that

    A. less time is wasted
    B. morale of the stenographers increases
    C. the stenographers receive better training
    D. wages are more consistent
    E. work is more equally distributed

39. In the communications process, the work *noise* is used to refer to   39.____

    A. anything that interferes with the message between transmitter and receiver
    B. meaningless communications
    C. the amplitude of verbal communication
    D. the level of general office and environmental sounds other than specific verbal
       communications
    E. the product of the grapevine

40. Which of the following is NOT an advantage of oral instructions as compared with written 40.____
    instructions when dealing with a small group?

    A. Oral instructions are more adaptable to complex orders
    B. Oral instructions can be changed more easily and quickly.
    C. Oral instructions facilitate exchange of information between the order giver and
       order receiver.
    D. Oral instructions make it easier for order giver and order receiver.
    E. The oral medium is suitable for instructions that will be temporary.

41. The employee opinion or attitude survey has for some time been accepted as a valuable communications device.
Of the following, the benefit which is LEAST likely to occur from the use of such a survey is:

    A. A clearer view of employee understanding of management policies is obtained
    B. Improved morale may result
    C. Information useful for supervisory and executive development is obtained
    D. The reasons why management policies were adopted are clarified
    E. Useful comparisons can be made between organization units

41.____

42. Which of the following is the MOST important principle to remember in preparing written reports that are to be submitted to a superior?

    A. Avoid mentioning in writing errors or mistakes
    B. Include human interest anecdotes
    C. Put all information into graphical or tabular form
    D. Report everything that has happened
    E. Report results in relation to plan

42.____

43. In conducting an electronic data processing study, with which one of the following should you be LEAST concerned?

    A. Computer characteristics; i.e., word length requirements, type storage characteristics, etc.
    B. Data collection requirements
    C. Methods used by other governmental jurisdictions
    D. System input/output requirements and volume
    E. System integration and flow of work

43.____

44. The MOST significant difference between a random access and a sequential type data processing computer system is

    A. Generally, a random access system has lower *locating* or access times
    B. Random access provides the potential for processing data on a *first come-first served* basis without the necessity of batching or pre-arranging the data in some sequence
    C. Random access systems are more often disk type storage systems
    D. Random access systems can operate more easily in conjunction with sequential tape or card oriented computer systems
    E. Random access systems have larger storage capacities

44.____

45. The most effective leader would MOST likely be one who

    A. is able to use a variety of leadership styles depending on the circumstances
    B. issues clear, forceful directives
    C. knows the substance of the work better than any of his subordinates
    D. supervises his subordinates closely
    E. uses democratic methods

45.____

46. One large office is a more efficient operating unit than the same number of square feet split into smaller offices.
    Of the following, the one that does NOT support this statement is:

    A. Better light and ventilation are possible
    B. Changes in layout are less apt to be made thus avoiding disruption of work flow
    C. Communication between individual employees is more direct
    D. Space is more fully utilized
    E. Supervision and control are more easily maintained

46._____

47. The major purpose for adopting specific space standards is to

    A. allocate equal space to employees doing the same kind of work
    B. cut costs
    C. keep space from becoming a status symbol
    D. prevent empire-building
    E. provide an accurate basis for charging for space allocated to each organization unit

47._____

48. The modular concept in office space planning is

    A. a method of pre-planning office space for economical use
    B. expensive because it complicates the air conditioning and electrical systems
    C. outdated because it lacks flexibility
    D. used as a basis for planning future space requirements
    E. used primarily for executive offices

48._____

49. Which one of the following statements is NOT correct?

    A. A general conference or committee room may eliminate the need for a number of private offices.
    B. In designing office space the general trend is toward the use of a standard color scheme.
    C. Private offices should be constructed in such a way as to avoid cutting off natural light and ventilation.
    D. Private offices result in a larger investment in equipment and furnishings.
    E. Transparent or translucent glass can be used in the upper portion of the partition for private offices.

49._____

50. Which one of the following is NOT a good general rule of communications in an organization?

    A. All supervisors should know the importance of communications.
    B. Oral communications are better than written where persuasion is needed.
    C. People should be told facts that make them feel they *belong*.
    D. The grapevine should be eliminated.
    E. The supervisor should hear information before his subordinates.

50._____

KEY (CORRECT ANSWERS)

1. D	11. E	21. C	31. B	41. D
2. B	12. A	22. C	32. D	42. E
3. B	13. B	23. D	33. B	43. C
4. D	14. C	24. A	34. D	44. B
5. D	15. A	25. E	35. D	45. A
6. E	16. A	26. B	36. E	46. B
7. A	17. E	27. E	37. B	47. A
8. B	18. E	28. C	38. B	48. A
9. D	19. B	29. E	39. A	49. B
10. D	20. A	30. B	40. A	50. D

EXAMINATION SECTION
TEST 1

DIRECTIONS: Each question or incomplete statement is followed by several suggested answers or completions. Select the one that BEST answers the question or completes the statement. *PRINT THE LETTER OF THE CORRECT ANSWER IN THE SPACE AT THE RIGHT.*

1. In management terms, when one sees the word "appraisal," what does that mean?
   A. A system used to improve the performance of personnel
   B. The core method for determining employee wages
   C. A rewards system that retailers use to attract more customers
   D. A way to evaluate an individual employee's performance over a given amount of time

1.____

2. Dave's management style tends to be very tight in his control of employees working underneath him. He makes nearly all of the decisions for his group and any information is usually run through him before making it to the rest of his team. What type of management style is Dave displaying?
   A. Authoritarian   B. Democratic
   C. Egalitarian   D. Draconian

2.____

3. If you are working for a company that is extremely ineffective in the way it planned its workforce, which of the following scenarios would MOST likely be true of your company?
   A. Constantly offering retraining to current employees
   B. Problems with recruiting and selecting employees
   C. Outsourcing production to other companies
   D. None of the above

3.____

4. You are brought in as a consultant to a firm that is trying to figure out the best managerial style for their employees. As you learn more about the company, you would be influenced to recommend leadership styles based on which of the following factors?
   A. The acceptance that "Yes men/women" are favored more than those who disagree
   B. Workers should be left to be in more control of their own working environment
   C. Expected skills of each employee
   D. Offering profit sharing as part of the employee remuneration package

4.____

5. You are speaking to a group of employees and you keep mentioning the word *empowerment* as an important concept to understand. After your presentation is over, one of the employees approaches you and tells you he was confused when you mentioned that word. Which of the following would BEST help him understand what you meant by the word *empowerment*?
    A. It is a method of ensuring employees gain more autonomy and decision-making powers.
    B. It is a system that inspires employees to move within the workforce with less restrictions
    C. It is essentially a synonym for profit sharing.
    D. It is a type of leadership that depends on having control.

6. Your company is about to begin a huge recruitment project to infuse your workforce with new employees. As you start your search, which of the following factors would MOST influence how you recruit and select employees for your company?
    A. The state of the economy
    B. The training program the company currently has in place
    C. Your company's size
    D. None of the above

7. Recruitment is BEST defined as
    A. attempting to fill gaps that exist in the skills of your current labor force
    B. paying attention to someone's work habits and noting how they perform their duties
    C. a system of beliefs that holds the fundamental objectives of your company
    D. the way a company fills the need to find new employees

8. You schedule a meeting with the higher-ups in your company because you are greatly concerned with low morale at your company. Which of the following would NOT be a reason to tell them for why you believe morale is low?
    A. High turnover rate
    B. High levels of personal productivity
    C. High levels of absenteeism
    D. Bad external image

9. Sarah describes herself as someone who *manages by objectives*. What does that mean?
    A. She doles out authority to carry out certain jobs by those beneath her
    B. A style that brings experts together onto one team
    C. A style that focuses on setting benchmarks to achieve corporate goals
    D. She prefers the organization control rest with those in the *headquarters*

10. As a young manager at your firm, you prefer to delegate as a way to empower your employees. One of the veteran managers offers you some advice when she tells you that delegation works great, but there is one thing you should never delegate. Which one of these would she MOST likely tell you to never delegate?
    A. Responsibility
    B. Authority
    C. Workload
    D. Department representation at meetings

10._____

11. What type of interview will MOST likely see a set of standardized questions?
    A. Phone   B. Structured   C. Group   D. Multi-tiered

11._____

12. Which of the following would be considered an organizational incentive plan?
    A. Employee stock ownership   B. Profit-sharing
    C. Scanlon plans   D. All of the above

12._____

13. Shawna works as a local union representative for her full-time employment. By what term is she generally known?
    A. Union organizer   B. Business agent
    C. Steward   D. None of the above

13._____

14. Which of the following programs uses simulation training for their employees?
    A. Apprenticeships   B. On-the-job
    C. Job instruction   D. Near-the-job

14._____

15. You currently have John, an exempt employee, working for you. Which of the following is NOT true about John as it relates to your company?
    A. He is allowed to collectively bargain because of the Tart-Hartley Act.
    B. He is subjected to the overtime provisions of the Fair Labor Standards Act just like non-exempt employees.
    C. He is allowed to have a modified work schedule.
    D. He is paid an hourly wage rate.

15._____

16. The management process consists of planning, organizing, _____, leading, and controlling.
    A. staffing   B. motivating
    C. preparing   D. consolidating

16._____

17. Jon is a new manager at the company and he is nervous about his first managerial job. As his *guide*, you offer advice and tell him the bottom line in managing is simple; you have to
    A. motivate subordinates   B. get results
    C. exercise authority   D. micromanage

17._____

18. Your role as an employee advocate extends to all of the following EXCEPT   18._____
    A. creating a learning environment
    B. inferred power, functional control, line authority
    C. defining how management should treat employees
    D. coordinating function, service function, functional control

19. As the globalization of a business increases, it results in   19._____
    A. non-traditional jobs   B. advancements in technology
    C. less competition   D. more competition

20. How can Human Resources create value for a company?   20._____
    A. By measuring employee behaviors
    B. Measuring outcomes of employee behaviors
    C. By engaging in activities that produce needed employee behaviors
    D. None of the above

21. The combined knowledge, education, skills, and expertise of an organization's   21._____
    workers is known as
    A. demographics   B. human diversity
    C. human resources   D. human capital

22. A firm's vision is BEST defined as   22._____
    A. identifying and executing the company's mission by matching its
       capabilities with demands of its environment
    B. a formal summary of the aims and values of the organization
    C. the continuous planning, monitoring, analysis, and assessment of the
       organization in order to meet its goals and objectives
    D. a study undertaken to identify internal strengths and weaknesses

23. Which of the following is the FIRST step in the recruiting and selection process?   23._____
    A. Succession planning   B. Personnel planning
    C. Applications   D. Trend analysis

24. Tina works in HR and wants to start planning for employment requirements.   24._____
    You tell her that will require forecasting which of the following?
    A. The amount of inside candidates   B. The amount of outside candidates
    C. Personnel needs   D. All of the above

25. Which of the following would NOT be a good way to determine which   25._____
    employees are available for promotion or transfer?
    A. Trend analysis   B. Personnel inventory
    C. Qualifications inventories   D. Both A and B

KEY (CORRECT ANSWERS)

1.	D		11.	B
2.	A		12.	D
3.	B		13.	C
4.	C		14.	D
5.	A		15.	B
6.	C		16.	A
7.	D		17.	B
8.	B		18.	A
9.	C		19.	D
10.	A		20.	C

21.	D
22.	A
23.	B
24.	C
25.	D

TEST 2

DIRECTIONS: Each question or incomplete statement is followed by several suggested answers or completions. Select the one that BEST answers the question or completes the statement. *PRINT THE LETTER OF THE CORRECT ANSWER IN THE SPACE AT THE RIGHT.*

1. What is the MOST important tool that you can use when selecting employees for hire?
   A. Pre-employment test   B. Background check
   C. Calling references   D. Personal interview

   1.____

2. Of the following types of interviews, which one is likely to be MOST reliable and valid because it focuses on asking the same questions to each potential employee?
   A. Directive   B. Job-related
   C. Unstructured   D. Stress

   2.____

3. Which of the following questions would be MOST appropriate if you were trying to ask an applicant a situational interview question?
   A. "So, tell me about yourself."
   B. "What do you do if you discover an employee stealing company property?"
   C. "What three words best describe you?"
   D. "Do you have any questions for me?"

   3.____

4. Why should you always take notes during an interview?
   A. It helps you stay busy during the interview.
   B. It helps you stay focused on what the interviewee is saying.
   C. It helps you jog your memory after the interview.
   D. None of the above

   4.____

5. Of the following, which is NOT a part of a successful implementation of employee orientation?
   A. Making the new hire feel at ease
   B. Give the applicant an understanding of the organization
   C. Start the new hire contract
   D. Be clear on employee expectations with regards to work and behavior

   5.____

6. Your boss comes to you and asks you to figure out how to increase motivation in trainees. Which of the following should you tell him to do?
   A. Allow the trainees to make errors
   B. Allow the trainees time to practice
   C. Provide positive feedback to the trainees
   D. All of the above

   6.____

7. Which of the following is NOT an actual advantage of on-the-job training?
   A. The overall cost of the program   B. Lack of need for off-site facilities
   C. How quick trainees get feedback   D. Trainees learn by doing

   7.____

8. What type of training focuses on helping new hires learn off the job with equipment they will use when they are on the job?

    A. Computer-based   B. Simulated

    C. EPSS   D. On-the-job training

8.____

9. In order to bring about a change in organizational philosophy, what must a manager understand?

    A. How to break through resistance to change

    B. How to lead organizational change

    C. How to use organizational development

    D. All of the above

9.____

10. What is the goal whenever you are managing someone's performance?

    A. Make certain workers' performances are supporting the company's strategic goals.

    B. Evaluate the employee's performance against expectations.

    C. Make sure the employee has the prerequisite training to perform his or her job.

    D. None of the above

10.____

11. If you are someone who likes simple, popular, and productive appraisal methods, which of the following would be the BEST one for you to use?

    A. 360-degree feedback   B. Critical incident method

    C. Alternation ranking   D. Weighted checklist method

11.____

12. After meeting with an employee during a performance appraisal, you realize you made a mistake and should not have followed which of the following steps during the meeting?

    A. Define the job

    B. Prepare detailed forms and procedures to be used

    C. Appraise performance

    D. Give feedback

12.____

13. Increasingly, companies are using performance management more and more each year. Which of the following statements cannot be inferred from this rise in popularity concerning performance management?

    A. That total quality management concepts are well received

    B. Traditional models of performance appraisal were not accurately measuring performance

    C. Every employee's efforts must focus on helping their company achieve its strategic objectives

    D. None of the above

13.____

14. Someone who is critical of the "management by objectives" appraisal method would cite which of the following reasons for why they are against it?
    A. It is time consuming
    B. It encourages face-to-face communication
    C. It is flexible
    D. None of the above

14.____

15. You notice that one manager tends to give certain employees high marks in several trait areas when really they are only doing one thing well. When you talk to this manager about fixing this, you mention that he is exhibiting the _____ effect(s).
    A. bias
    B. halo
    C. unclear standards
    D. both A and C

15.____

16. While you like the idea of adding "self-evaluations" for performance reviews, what is one of the problems you may encounter if you decide to include them?
    A. It forces the employee to look at past performance and set future objectives.
    B. Employees must focus on their inconsistencies and try to find appropriate solutions for them.
    C. Many employees overvalue the quality of their own performance relative to others.
    D. Both A and B

16.____

17. Why do many critics feel that pay for performance plans are largely ineffective?
    A. It increases motivation and competition among employees.
    B. It connects employee productivity to how much they get paid.
    C. Not all rewards are suited to all situations.
    D. Each employee must expect to receive a reward.

17.____

18. Merit raises are BEST defined as which of the following?
    A. A raise that is awarded to an individual based on the person's performance.
    B. A type of compensation where part of the pay is guaranteed and the rest is incentive to pay
    C. A one-time pay raise made a particular time of the year, usually based on company performance, not individual
    D. Incentive where pay plan establishes a fixed unit of time for completion of a task. The sooner the task is completed, the higher the bonus.

18.____

19. You are asked to join a new company at the ground floor. During the initial meeting of executives, one states that the company should use the _____ method because it is easy to administer. You point out that while that it is true, it could also be the most discriminatory.
    A. classification
    B. ranking
    C. point factor
    D. guide chart

19.____

20. Which of the following BEST describes a skills inventory?   20.____
    A. It details the requisite skills for a specific position.
    B. It is an article most commonly used to validate reducing employees in a non-union setting.
    C. It is a cumulative compilation of skills required in a business.
    D. It catalogues the experiences and abilities of an organization's workforce.

21. Jay Noto, your boss, was made aware of another employee's test score at   21.____'
    the time they were hired, and you know that his awareness of the score
    affected the employee's job performance rating. If this in fact is true, which of
    the following human resources issues has your supervisor fallen prey to?
    A. Correlation   B. Criterion contamination
    C. Criterion relevance   D. Contextual performance

22. When putting together a training program with the sole purpose of helping   22.____
    supervisors cultivate skills in training employees, an instructor should include
    which of the following?
    A. Case analysis   B. Workshop lectures
    C. Programmed instruction   D. Role playing

23. John O'Toole is preparing to become a Human Resources manager and   23.____
    one of his training sessions focuses on making ethically responsible choices.
    The following scenarios are given to him. Which one should he choose as the
    MOST ethical?
    A. Eliminating low-paying businesses from salary survey results of HR positions
    B. Choosing not to stand up against a discriminatory decision made by superiors
    C. Endorsing a qualified friend for an opening in a department different from his own
    D. None of the above

24. You are asked to improve employee retention in your company. Since the   24.____
    business is flat in structure, what is the MOST effective way to increase the
    ability to hold onto your employees?
    A. Offer dual career ladders
    B. Create an effective employee assistance program
    C. Allow employees to telecommute for part of the work week
    D. Create a mentorship program in succession planning

25. What does the "forced ranking" appraisal method rate employees against?   25.____
    A. Standards of performance
    B. Employees are rated against one another
    C. They are rated against their own past performance
    D. Employees are rated against a bell curve

KEY (CORRECT ANSWERS)

1.	D		11.	C
2.	A		12.	B
3.	B		13.	D
4.	C		14.	A
5.	C		15.	B
6.	D		16.	C
7.	A		17.	C
8.	B		18.	A
9.	D		19.	B
10.	A		20.	D

21.	B
22.	D
23.	C
24.	A
25.	B

TEST 3

DIRECTIONS: Each question or incomplete statement is followed by several suggested answers or completions. Select the one that BEST answers the question or completes the statement. *PRINT THE LETTER OF THE CORRECT ANSWER IN THE SPACE AT THE RIGHT.*

1. What criteria are used when determining an employee's pay equation?
   A. Years of experience, tenure, and grade level
   B. Market pricing, merit, and demonstrated performance
   C. Hourly pay, performance bonus, and cash awards
   D. All of the above

   1.____

2. The matrix organization is suited to managing a group of activities that is
   A. narrow and interrelated
   B. broad in focus and unrelated
   C. diverse and unrelated
   D. diverse and interrelated

   2.____

3. When desirous of building employer brand equity, what is the MOST important aspect to consider?
   A. A clear profile of target candidates
   B. Calculated recruitment marketing and an advertising plan
   C. A single, unified, reliable message
   D. Thorough testing of marketing writings

   3.____

4. You are judging the objectivity of an employee's performance appraisal. It is MOST important to consider which of the following?
   A. Looking at and rating the biases of the employee's boss
   B. The candidate's potential for promotion
   C. The amount of employees in the department
   D. The training and knowledge of the employee's boss

   4.____

5. Which of the following does a flow diagram serve as?
   A. A way to improve utilization of an operator and a machine
   B. A chart depicting right and left-hand motions
   C. To analyze people and/or materials on the move
   D. Used to look at the ergonomics of a job

   5.____

6. During a meeting, the idea of job expansion is brought up. One coworker states that it would be good for the company because employees could learn new skills and reduce boredom. Playing devil's advocate, you want to bring up a few disadvantages. Which of the following should you NOT include when talking about disadvantages of job expansion?
   A. Lower wage rates
   B. Higher capital costs
   C. Individual differences
   D. Smaller labor pool

   6.____

7. If demand for the product varies, but the company manages to keep its current level of employment, wher4e might those cost savings come from?
   A. Decrease in hiring costs
   B. Decrease in firing costs
   C. Unemployment insurance
   D. All of the above

   7.____

8. You attend a meeting in which the topic of external stakeholders is discussed. A coworker asks you what is meant by the phrase "external stakeholders". You explain the basics and then give her an example. Which of the following would be the BEST example of an external stakeholder?

    A. Suppliers   B. Shareholders
    C. Customers   D. Municipal employees

8._____

9. Of the following, the only one that does NOT relate to work scheduling is

    A. flexible workweek   B. telecommuting schedule
    C. part-time status   D. ergonomics

9._____

10. Why are labor standards necessary?

    A. They determine the steps that are required to perform a task.
    B. They define cost and time estimates prior to production.
    C. They help regulate the machines required by the process.
    D. They mandate the raw materials to be consumed in the process.

10._____

11. Which of the following BEST defines a knowledge-based system of payment?

    A. One that rewards employees for developing understanding or talent
    B. Type of payment in which a worker is paid a fixed rate for each unit produced
    C. A system of payment whereby the wage is fixed on the understanding that a specific level of work performance will be maintained
    D. An incentive plan that depends on the company's profitability in addition to employees' regular salary and bonuses

11._____

12. What is the difference between job enrichment and job enlargement?

    A. Enriched jobs have a greater amount of tasks similar to one another, while enlarged jobs include some of the planning and control necessary for job accomplishment.
    B. Enriched jobs allow employees to do a number of tedious tasks instead of only one.
    C. Enlarged jobs allow for a larger number of similar tasks, whereas enriched ones include some of the planning and control necessary for accomplishing tasks.
    D. All of the above are differences.

12._____

13. A behavior-centered rating scale combines the features of a traditional rating scale with which of the following methods?

    A. Ranking   B. Critical incidences
    C. Paired comparison   D. None of the above

13._____

14. Which of the following Human Resources measures helps to identify employee performance and operation on a period more than a year after hiring?

    A. Quality of hire   B. Accomplishment index
    C. Cost per hire   D. Coworker commitment index

14._____

15. Which level of the company is responsible for preparing a staffing plan?   15._____
    A. Strategic   B. Managerial
    C. Operational   D. None of the above

16. You are tasked with creating a "Best HR Practices" presentation. Which   16._____
    of the following foundations should your presentation, and all HR practices, be
    built upon?
    A. One that relies on people as a source of competitive advantage
    B. HR organizations should focus on continuous improvement, not radical
       transformations
    C. HR should develop an enduring and relevant HR philosophy and mission
    D. All of the above

17. Which of the following challenges do most HR departments face across   17._____
    the industry?
    A. Competition and diversity   B. Deregulation and diversity
    C. Globalization and deregulation   D. Both A and C

18. As diversity increases, heavier and heavier demands are made of which   18._____
    of the following management teams?
    A. Production   B. Human Resources
    C. Finance   D. All of the above

19. The following choices are a list of different companies, each with a brief   19._____
    description. Which of the following would be unlikely to offer fringe benefits?
    A. Ma & Pa's Cupcakes, a small business
    B. Toys4Chap, a Forbes Fortune 500 company
    C. All Natural Foods, a regional, organic-based grocery chain
    D. P&G Inc., an international crop company

20. POSD CORB, an H acronym, stands for: planning, organizing, _____,   20._____
    directing, coordinating, _____, and budgeting.
    A. placating; rating   B. pursuing; regulating
    C. preparing; reparation   D. planning; reporting

21. When one talks of task specialization, what are they referring to?   21._____
    A. The division of the total assignment into individual jobs
    B. The recruitment, selection, development, training, and compensation of
       personnel
    C. The process of identifying and determining particular job duties and
       requirements and the relative importance of these duties for a given job
    D. The specification of contents, methods, and relationships of jobs in order
       to satisfy technological and organizational requirements

22. You are running a workshop on the importance of avoiding workplace accidents. You want your listeners to remember three basic reasons for accidents, so you tell them the three are
    A. unsanitary conditions, hazardous conditions, and unsafe acts
    B. chance occurrences, hazardous conditions, and unsafe acts
    C. chance occurrences, unsafe conditions, and unsafe acts
    D. unsanitary conditions, unsafe acts, and chance occurrences

22.____

23. Which of the following would NOT be considered a "statutory benefit"?
    A. Social Security
    B. Medical insurance
    C. Workman's Compensation
    D. Unemployment Benefits

23.____

24. If a business is unable to _____ a solid group of employees, it could cause a bottleneck for production.
    A. motivate and compensate
    B. compensate and recruit
    C. motivate the recruit
    D. recruit and maintain

24.____

25. Which of the following are three main reasons for safety programs?
    A. Ergonomic, morale, and social
    B. Social, legal, and ethical
    C. Legal, executive, and judicial
    D. Moral, legal, and economic

25.____

KEY (CORRECT ANSWERS)

1.	B		11.	A
2.	D		12.	C
3.	C		13.	B
4.	A		14.	A
5.	C		15.	C
6.	A		16.	D
7.	D		17.	C
8.	B		18.	B
9.	D		19.	A
10.	B		20.	D

21.	A
22.	C
23.	B
24.	D
25.	D

TEST 4

DIRECTIONS: Each question or incomplete statement is followed by several suggested answers or completions. Select the one that BEST answers the question or completes the statement. *PRINT THE LETTER OF THE CORRECT ANSWER IN THE SPACE AT THE RIGHT.*

1.   You are part of a human resource management group, and you are trying to   1.____
     formulate a strategy. Which of the following should be decided FIRST?
     A. The mission and goals of the company
     B. Outside openings and competition
     C. The internal strengths and weaknesses
     D. The abilities and skills of employees

2.   As HR manager, you are well aware of the four-fifths rule. When hiring, if you   2.____
     decide to employ 7 Caucasians out of 72 (which is your highest rate), then you
     must hire how many Asian people out of 63 (which is your smallest)?
     A. 8   B. 5   C. 11   D. 9

3.   Which of the following is considered a phase of career development?   3.____
     A. Performance   B. Loyalty
     C. Recruitment   D. Development

4.   A main Human Resources function is the performance appraisal that   4.____
     connects workers and businesses and provides input for other processes
     through what three means?
     A. Testing, Direction, Improvement
     B. Enrollment, Selection, Responsibility
     C. Identification, Measurement, Management
     D. Management, Talent, Development

5.   There are two types of compensation that HR managers generally refer to: 5.____
     direct and indirect compensation. Which of the following would be considered
     an indirect form of compensation?
     A. Base Pay   B. Variable Pay
     C. Statutory Benefits   D. Stock Benefits

6.   Which of the following group rewards do NOT allow for a "Pay for Performance"   6.____
     aspect to them?
     A. Merit   B. Bonus
     C. Awards   D. All of the above

7.   What does EEO stand for?   7.____
     A. Employee's Equal Opportunity   B. Equal Employment Opportunity
     C. Equitable Excellence in Occupation D. Employee Excellence Optimum

8.   Protections and privileges that are negotiated for and provided by a legal   8.____
     and binding accord for employees are called _____ rights.
     A. guaranteed   B. liability   C. privileged   D. contractual

9. Warren is in the process of fixing a telephone pole when part of his harness breaks, sending him tumbling to the ground. While the accident was not fatal, it did leave Warren in a wheelchair for the next five months. Atlantic Gas and Electric, the company Warren works for, refuses to pay for the expenses from Warren's injury. This is a violation of which of the following benefits that Warren receives as part of his contractual agreement?
   A. Workers Compensation Insurance
   B. Medical Insurance
   C. Employer's Compensation Insurance
   D. Unemployment Benefits

9.____

10. The Assessment Phase of Career Development is focused on which of the following?
   A. Shaping the type of career that employees desire and the actions they should take to realize their career goals
   B. Measuring performance of employee goals over a given period of time
   C. Helping employees identify their strengths and weaknesses that may affect future performance
   D. None of the above

10.____

11. Which of the following acts are responsible for things like retirement income, disability income, health benefits, and survivor benefits?
   A. COBRA
   B. Social Security Act of 1935
   C. The Federal Employment Compensation Act
   D. American Disability Act of 1973

11.____

12. Many states use "at will" employment for their businesses, which means an employer or employee can terminate a working relationship at any time for any reason. With that said, which of the following are exceptions to the "at will" employment?
   A. Public policy exceptions
   B. Implied contracts
   C. Lack of good faith and fair dealing
   D. All of the above

12.____

13. You overhear your father complain that his employers and the union are in a contract negotiation that has become embittered and negative. He feels that the employers are not really interested in bargaining with the union, but rather are stalling in an effort to make the union workers desperate. You tell your dad that he should seek legal action because the employer is violating which of the following acts?
   A. Employee Free Choice Act   B. Wagner Act
   C. The Clayton Act   D. Davis-Bacon Act

13.____

14. Cultural dimension that affects the success of HR management in many countries where relative emphasis is on a status of hierarchy is called
   A. masculinity/femininity   B. collectivism
   C. power distance   D. all of the above

14.____

15. There are many potential problems with measuring the quality of employee performance in an appraisal such as
    - A. rater bias
    - B. business politics
    - C. successful sales
    - D. both A and B

15.____

16. Which of the following is NOT an example of a gainsharing plan?
    - A. Stock options
    - B. Scanlon plan
    - C. Rucker plan
    - D. Improshare

16.____

17. Which of the following measures should be taken in order to maintain the integrity and security of Human Resources data?
    - A. Back up the data at pre-arranged intervals
    - B. Download the data to hard copies
    - C. Allow properly trained IT staff to access the data
    - D. Delete the data on a yearly basis to reduce the likelihood of theft

17.____

18. HR departments have started to develop systems known as _____ that help show potential issues ahead of time giving HR representatives time to develop plans and strategies to avoid the problem or minimize its impact.
    - A. fire detectors
    - B. lie detectors
    - C. smoke detectors
    - D. burglar alarms

18.____

19. One way for HR departments to keep employees from feeling bored or lacking investment in the company is to convince managers to create individual "Challenge Plans" for each employee. This will help HR dramatically increase which of the following?
    - A. Payroll effectiveness
    - B. Recidivism
    - C. Power distance
    - D. Retention rates

19.____

20. The owner of the company you work for has decided to consolidate many of the management positions, which means there are fewer opportunities for promotion. He asks you how he should stimulate workers to ensure they continue to develop their skills. You recommend _____ transfer and job rotation plans.
    - A. supervised
    - B. horizontal
    - C. vertical
    - D. both A and C

20.____

21. At your company, the "Higher Education" committee, which you are on, focuses on providing employees with a way to continue their certifications and education in different areas the company is interested in. One day, a newly hired employee approaches you, confused about what it means when the company says it will pay for employees to partake in formal education, and she is looking for an example of what "formal education" means. Which of the following would be an APPROPRIATE example of "formal education"?
    - A. Courses by consultants
    - B. Internships
    - C. Assessment centers
    - D. 360-degree feedback

21.____

22. _____ are considered a tool of measurement that gathers the effectiveness of a manager's use of skills associated with success in management.   22._____
    A. 360-degree feedback
    B. Management assessment
    C. Employee standards
    D. Benchmarks

23. Job _____ is when a company moves employees through various job assignments in one or more areas.   23._____
    A. enlargement   B. rotation   C. sharing   D. transfer

24. While internships are defined as temporary positions with an emphasis on on-the-job training rather than merely employment, externships tend to focus on development through which of the following?   24._____
    A. A part-time temporary position at another company
    B. A full-time temporary position at another company
    C. A part-time permanent position at another company
    D. A full-time permanent position at another company

25. When a more experienced, senior employee actively aids a less experienced colleague, it is commonly referred to as which of the following?   25._____
    A. Trainer-trainee
    B. Mentorship
    C. Tutoring
    D. Leading

KEY (CORRECT ANSWERS)

1.	A		11.	B
2.	B		12.	D
3.	D		13.	B
4.	C		14.	C
5.	C		15.	D
6.	A		16.	A
7.	B		17.	A
8.	D		18.	C
9.	A		19.	D
10.	C		20.	B

21.	A
22.	D
23.	C
24.	B
25.	B

EXAMINATION SECTION
TEST 1

DIRECTIONS: Each question or incomplete statement is followed by several suggested answers or completions. Select the one that BEST answers the question or completes the statement. *PRINT THE LETTER OF THE CORRECT ANSWER IN THE SPACE AT THE RIGHT.*

1. A supervisor notices that one of his more competent subordinates has recently been showing less interest in his work. The work performed by this employee has also fallen off and he seems to want to do no more than the minimum acceptable amount of work. When his supervisor questions the subordinate about his decreased interest and his mediocre work performance, the subordinate replies: *Sure, I've lost interest in my work. I don't see any reason why I should do more than I have to. When I do a good job, nobody notices it. But, let me fall down on one minor job and the whole place knows about it! So why should I put myself out on this job?*
   If the subordinate's contentions are true, it would be correct to assume that the

   A. subordinate has not received adequate training
   B. subordinate's workload should be decreased
   C. supervisor must share responsibility for this employee's reaction
   D. supervisor has not been properly enforcing work standards

   1.____

2. *How many subordinates should report directly to each supervisor? While there is agreement that there are limits to the number of subordinates that a manager can supervise well, this limit is determined by a number of important factors.*
   Which of the following factors is most likely to increase the number of subordinates that can be effectively supervised by one supervisor in a particular unit?

   A. The unit has a great variety of activities
   B. A staff assistant handles the supervisor's routine duties
   C. The unit has a relatively inexperienced staff
   D. The office layout is being rearranged to make room for more employees

   2.____

3. Mary Smith, an Administrative Assistant, heads the Inspection Records Unit of Department Y. She is a dedicated supervisor who not only strives to maintain an efficient operation, but she also tries to improve the competence of each individual member of her staff. She keeps these considerations in mind when assigning work to her staff. Her bureau chief asks her to compile some data based on information contained in her records. She feels that any member of her staff should be able to do this job. The one of the following members of her staff who would probably be given LEAST consideration for this assignment is

   A. Jane Abel, a capable Supervising Clerk with considerable experience in the unit
   B. Kenneth Brown, a Senior Clerk recently transferred to the unit who has not had an opportunity to demonstrate his capabilities
   C. Laura Chance, a Clerk who spends full time on a single routine assignment
   D. Michael Dunn, a Clerk who works on several minor jobs but still has the lightest workload

   3.____

4. *There are very few aspects of a supervisor's job that do not involve communication, either in writing or orally.*
   Which of the following statements regarding oral and written orders is NOT correct?

   4.____

A. Oral orders usually permit more immediate feedback than do written orders.
B. Written orders, rather than oral orders, should generally be given when the subordinate will be held strictly accountable.
C. Oral orders are usually preferable when the order contains lengthy detailed instructions.
D. Written orders, rather than oral orders, should usually be given to a subordinate who is slow to understand or is forgetful.

5. Assume that you are the head of a large clerical unit in Department R. Your department's personnel office has appointed a Clerk, Roberta Rowe, to fill a vacancy in your unit. Before bringing this appointee to your office, the personnel office has given Roberta the standard orientation on salary, fringe benefits, working conditions, attendance and the department's personnel rules. In addition, he has supplied her with literature covering these areas. Of the following, the action that you should take FIRST after Roberta has been brought to your office is to   5.____

A. give her an opportunity to read the literature furnished by the personnel office so that she can ask you questions about it
B. escort her to the desk she will use and assign her to work with an experienced employee who will act as her trainer
C. explain the duties and responsibilities of her job and its relationship with the jobs being performed by the other employees of the unit
D. summon the employee who is currently doing the work that will be performed by Roberta and have him explain and demonstrate how to perform the required tasks

6. Your superior informs you that the employee turnover rate in your office is well above the norm and must be reduced. Which one of the following initial steps would be LEAST appropriate in attempting to overcome this problem?   6.____

A. Decide to be more lenient about performance standards and about employee requests for time off, so that your office will gain a reputation as an easy place to work
B. Discuss the problem with a few of your key people whose judgment you trust to see if they can shed some light on the underlying causes of the problem
C. Review the records of employees who have left during the past year to see if there is a pattern that will help you understand the problem
D. Carefully review your training procedures to see whether they can be improved

7. In issuing instructions to a subordinate on a job assignment, the supervisor should ordinarily explain why the assignment is being made. Omission of such an explanation is best justified when the   7.____

A. subordinate is restricted in the amount of discretion he can exercise in carrying out the assignment
B. assignment is one that will be unpopular with the subordinate
C. subordinate understands the reason as a result of previous similar assignments
D. assignment is given to an employee who is in need of further training

8. When a supervisor allows sufficient time for training and makes an appropriate effort in the training of his subordinates, his chief goal is to   8.____

    A.   increase the dependence of one subordinate upon another in their everyday work activities
    B.   spend more time with his subordinates in order to become more involved in their work
    C.   increase the capability and independence of his subordinates in carrying out their work
    D.   increase his frequency of contact with his subordinates in order to better evaluate their performance

9.   In preparing an evaluation of a subordinate's performance, which one of the following items is usually irrelevant?   9._____

    A.   Remarks about tardiness or absenteeism
    B.   Mention of any unusual contributions or accomplishments
    C.   A summary of the employee's previous job experience
    D.   An assessment of the employee's attitude toward the job

10.   The ability to delegate responsibility while maintaining adequate controls is one key to a supervisor's success. Which one of the following methods of control would minimize the amount of responsibility assumed by the subordinate?   10._____

    A.   Asking for a monthly status report in writing
    B.   Asking to receive copies of important correspondence so that you can be aware of potential problems
    C.   Scheduling periodic project status conferences with your subordinate
    D.   Requiring that your subordinate confer with you before making decisions on a project

11.   You wish to assign an important project to a subordinate who you think has good potential. Which one of the following approaches would be most effective in successfully completing the project while developing the subordinate's abilities?   11._____

    A.   Describe the project to the subordinate in general terms and emphasize that it must be completed as quickly as possible
    B.   Outline the project in detail to the subordinate and emphasize that its successful completion could lead to career advancement
    C.   Develop a detailed project outline and timetable, discuss the details and timing with him and assign the subordinate to carry out the plan on his own
    D.   Discuss the project objectives and suggested approaches with the subordinate, and ask the subordinate to develop a detailed project outline and timetable of your approval

12.   Research studies reveal that an important difference between high-production and low-production supervisors lies not in their interest in eliminating mistakes, but in their manner of handling mistakes. High-production supervisors are most likely to look upon mistakes as primarily   12._____

    A.   an opportunity to provide training
    B.   a byproduct of subordinate negligence
    C.   an opportunity to fix blame in a situation
    D.   a result of their own incompetence

13. Supervisors should try to establish what has been called *positive discipline*, an atmo-   13.____
sphere in which subordinates willingly abide by rules which they consider fair. When a
supervisor notices a subordinate violating an important rule, his FIRST course of action
should be to

    A. stop the subordinate and tell him what he is doing wrong
    B. wait a day or two before approaching the employee involved
    C. call a meeting of all subordinates to discuss the rule
    D. forget the matter in the hope that it will not happen again

14. The working climate is the feeling, degree of freedom, the tone and the mood of the   14.____
working environment. Which of the following contributes most to determining the working
climate in a unit or group?

    A. The rules set for rest periods
    B. The example set by the supervisor
    C. The rules set for morning check-in
    D. The wages paid to the employees

15. John Polk is a bright, ingenious clerk with a lot of initiative. He has made many good sug-   15.____
gestions to his supervisor in the Training Division of Department T, where he is
employed. However, last week one of his bright ideas literally *blew up*. In setting up some
electronic equipment in the training classroom, he crossed some wires resulting in a
damaged tape recorder and a classroom so filled with smoke that the training class had
to be held in another room. When Mr. Brown, his supervisor, learned of this occurrence,
he immediately summoned John to his private office. There Mr. Brown spent five minutes
bawling John out, calling him an overzealous, overgrown kid, and sent him back to his job
without letting John speak once. Of the following, the action of Mr. Brown that most
deserves approval is that he

    A. took disciplinary action immediately without regard for past performance
    B. kept the disciplinary interview to a brief period
    C. concentrated his criticism on the root cause of the occurrence
    D. held the disciplinary interview in his private office .

16. Typically, when the technique of *supervision by results* is practiced, higher management   16.____
sets down, either implicitly or explicitly, certain performance standards or goals that the
subordinate is expected to meet. So long as these standards are met, management
interferes very little. The most likely result of the use of this technique is that it will

    A. lead to ambiguity in terms of goals
    B. be successful only to the extent that close direct supervision is practiced
    C. make it possible to evaluate both employee and supervisory effectiveness
    D. allow for complete autonomy on the subordinate's part

17. Assume that you, an Administrative Assistant, are the supervisor of a large clerical unit   17.____
performing routine clerical operations. One of your clerks consistently produces much
less work than other members of your staff performing similar tasks. Of the following, the
action you should take FIRST is to

    A. ask the clerk if he wants to be transferred to another unit

B. reprimand the clerk for his poor performance and warn him that further disciplinary action will be taken if his work does not improve
C. quietly ask the clerk's co-workers whether they know why his performance is poor
D. discuss this matter with the clerk to work out plans for improving his performance

18. When making written evaluations and reviews of the performance of subordinates, it is usually advisable to

18.____

    A. avoid informing the employee of the evaluation if it is critical because it may create hard feelings
    B. avoid informing the employee of the evaluation whether critical or favorable because it is tension-producing
    C. permit the employee to see the evaluation but not to discuss it with him because the supervisor cannot be certain where the discussion might lead
    D. discuss the evaluation openly with the employee because it helps the employee understand what is expected of him

19. There are a number of well-known and respected human relations principles that successful supervisors have been using for years in building good relationships with their employees. Which of the following does NOT illustrate such a principle?

19.____

    A. Give clear and complete instructions
    B. Let each person know how he is getting along
    C. Keep an open-door policy
    D. Make all relationships personal ones

20. Assume that it is your responsibility as an Administrative Assistant to maintain certain personnel records that are continually being updated. You have three senior clerks assigned specifically to this task. Recently you have noticed that the volume of work has increased substantially, and the processing of personnel records by the clerks is backlogged. Your supervisor is now receiving complaints due to the processing delay. Of the following, the best course of action for you to take FIRST is to

20.____

    A. have a meeting with the clerks, advise them of the problem, and ask that they do their work faster; then confirm your meeting in writing for the record
    B. request that an additional position be authorized for your unit
    C. review the procedures being used for processing the work, and try to determine if you can improve the flow of work
    D. get the system moving faster by spending some of your own time processing the backlog

21. Assume that you are in charge of a payroll unit consisting of four clerks. It is Friday, November 14. You have just arrived in the office after a conference. Your staff is preparing a payroll that must be forwarded the following Monday. Which of the following new items on your desk should you attend to FIRST?

21.____

    A. A telephone message regarding very important information needed for the statistical summary of salaries paid for the month of November
    B. A memorandum regarding a new procedure that should be followed in preparing the payroll
    C. A telephone message from an employee who is threatening to endorse his paycheck *Under Protest* because he is dissatisfied with the amount

D. A memorandum from your supervisor reminding you to submit the probationary period report on a new employee

22. You are an Administrative Assistant in charge of a unit that orders and issues supplies. On a particular day you are faced with the following four situations. Which one should you take care of FIRST?

    A. One of your employees who is in the process of taking the quarterly inventory of supplies has telephoned and asked that you return his call as soon as possible

    B. A representative of a company that is noted for producing excellent office supplies will soon arrive with samples for you to distribute to the various offices in your agency

    C. A large order of supplies which was delivered this morning has been checked and counted and a deliveryman is waiting for you to sign the receipt

    D. A clerk from the purchase division asks you to search for a bill you failed to send to them which is urgently needed in order for them to complete a report due this morning

22.____

23. As an Administrative Assistant, assume that it is necessary for you to give an unpleasant assignment to one of your subordinates. You expect this employee to raise some objections to this assignment. The most appropriate of the following actions for you to take FIRST is to issue the assignment

    A. orally, with the further statement that you will not listen to any complaints

    B. in writing, to forestall any complaints by the employee

    C. orally, permitting the employee to express his feelings

    D. in writing, with a note that any comments should be submitted in writing

23.____

24. Assume that you are an Administrative Assistant supervising the Duplicating and Reproduction Unit of Department B. One of your responsibilities is to prepare a daily schedule showing when and on which of your unit's four duplicating machines jobs are to be run off. Of the following, the factor that should be given LEAST consideration in preparing the schedule is the

    A. priority of each of the jobs to be run off

    B. production speed of the different machines that will be used

    C. staff available to operate the machines

    D. date on which the job order was received

24.____

25. *Cycling is an arrangement where papers are processed throughout a period according to an orderly plan rather than as a group all at one time. This technique has been used for a long time by public utilities in their cycle billing.* Of the following practices, the one that best illustrates this technique is that in which

    A. paychecks for per annum employees are issued bi-weekly and those for per diem employees are issued weekly

    B. field inspectors report in person to their offices one day a week, on Fridays, when they do all their paperwork and also pick up their paychecks

    C. the dates for issuing relief checks to clients vary depending on the last digit of the clients' social security numbers

    D. the last day for filing and paying income taxes is the same for Federal, State and City income taxes

25.____

26. The employees in your division have recently been given an excellent up-to-date office manual, but you find that a good number of employees are not following the procedures outlined in it. Which one of the following would be most likely to ensure that employees begin using the manual effectively?

    A. Require each employee to keep a copy of the manual in plain sight on his desk
    B. Issue warnings periodically to those employees who deviate most from procedures prescribed in the manual
    C. Tell an employee to check his manual when he does not follow the proper procedures
    D. Suggest to the employees that the manual be studied thoroughly

26.____

27. The one of the following factors which should be considered FIRST in the design of office forms is the

    A. information to be included in the form
    B. sequence of the information
    C. purpose of the form
    D. persons who will be using the form

27.____

28. *Window envelopes are being used to an increasing extent by government and private industry.* The one of the following that is NOT an advantage of window envelopes is that they

    A. cut down on addressing costs
    B. eliminate the need to attach envelopes to letters being sent forward for signature by a superior
    C. are less costly to buy than regular envelopes
    D. reduce the risk of having letters placed in wrong envelopes

28.____

29. Your bureau head asks you to prepare the office layouts for several of his units being moved to a higher floor in your office building. Of the following possibilities, the one that you should AVOID in preparing the layouts is to

    A. place the desks of the first-line supervisors near those of the staffs they supervise
    B. place the desks of employees whose work is most closely related near one another
    C. arrange the desks so that employees do not face one another
    D. locate desks with many outside visitors farthest from the office entrance

29.____

30. Which one of the following conditions would be LEAST important in considering a change of the layout in a particular office?

    A. Installation of a new office machine
    B. Assignment of five additional employees to your office
    C. Poor flow of work
    D. Employees' personal preferences of desk location

30.____

31. Suppose Mr. Bloom, an Administrative Assistant, is dictating a letter to a stenographer. His dictation begins with the name of the addressee and continues to the body of the letter. However, Mr. Bloom does not dictate the address of the recipient of the letter. He expects the stenographer to locate it. The use of this practice by Mr. Bloom is

    A. acceptable, especially if he gives the stenographer the letter to which he is responding

31.____

B. acceptable, especially if the letter is lengthy and detailed
C. unacceptable, because it is not part of a stenographer's duties to search for information
D. unacceptable, because he should not rely on the accuracy of the stenographer

32. Assume that there are no rules, directives or instructions concerning the filing of materials in your office or the retention of such files. A system is now being followed of placing in *inactive files any materials that are more than one year old. Of the following, the most appropriate thing to do with material that has been in an inactive* file in your office for more than one year is to

A. inspect the contents of the files to decide how to dispose of them
B. transfer the material to a remote location, where it can be obtained if necessary
C. keep the material intact for a minimum of another three years
D. destroy the material which has not been needed for at least a year

32.____

33. Suppose you, an Administrative Assistant, have just returned to your desk after engaging in an all-morning conference. Joe Burns, a Clerk, informs you that Clara McClough, an administrator in another agency, telephoned during the morning and that, although she requested to speak with you, he was able to give her the desired information. Of the following, the most appropriate action for you to take in regard to Mr. Burns' action is to

A. thank him for assisting Ms. McClough in your absence
B. explain to him the proper telephone practice to use in the future
C. reprimand him for not properly channeling Ms. McClough's call
D. issue a memo to all clerical employees regarding proper telephone practices

33.____

34. *When interviewing subordinates with problems, supervisors frequently find that asking direct questions of the employee results only in evasive responses. The supervisor may therefore resort to the non-directive interview technique. In this technique the supervisor avoids pointed questions; he leads the employee to continue talking freely uninfluenced by the supervisor's preconceived notions. This technique often enables the employee to bring his problem into sharp focus and to reach a solution to his problem.*
Suppose that you are a supervisor interviewing a subordinate about his recent poor attendance record. On calling his attention to his excessive lateness record, he replies:
I just don't seem to be able to get up in the morning. Frankly, I've lost interest in this job. I don't care about it. When I get up in the morning, I have to skip breakfast and I'm still late. I don't care about this job.
If you are using the *non-directive* technique in this interview, the most appropriate of the following responses for you to make is

A. *You don't care about this job?*
B. *Don't you think you are letting your department down?*
C. *Are you having trouble at home?*
D. *Don't you realize your actions are childish?*

34.____

35. An employee in a work group made the following comment to a co-worker: *It's great to be a lowly employee instead of an Administrative Assistant because you can work without thinking. The Administrative Assistant is getting paid to plan, schedule and think. Let him see to it that you have a productive day.*
Which one of the following statements about this quotation best reflects an understanding of good personnel management techniques and the role of the supervising Administrative Assistant?

35.____

A. The employee is wrong in attitude and in his perception of the role of the Administrative Assistant
B. The employee is correct in attitude but is wrong in his perception of the role of the Administrative Assistant
C. The employee is correct in attitude and in his perception of the role of the Administrative Assistant
D. The employee is wrong in attitude but is right in his perception of the role of the Administrative Assistant

---

KEY (CORRECT ANSWERS)

1.	C	11.	D	26.	C
2.	B	12.	A	27.	C
3.	A	13.	A	28.	C
4.	C	14.	B	29.	D
5.	C	15.	D	30.	D
6.	A	16.	C/D	31.	A
7.	C	17.	D	32.	A/B
8.	C	18.	D	33.	A
9.	C	19.	D	34.	A
10.	D	20.	C	35.	D
		21.	B		
		22.	C		
		23.	C		
		24.	D		
		25.	C		

TEST 2

DIRECTIONS: Each question or incomplete statement is followed by several suggested answers or completions. Select the one that BEST answers the question or completes the statement. *PRINT THE LETTER OF THE CORRECT ANSWER IN THE SPACE AT THE RIGHT.*

Questions 1 through 5 are to be answered solely on the basis of the following passage:

General supervision, in contrast to close supervision, involves a high degree of delegation of authority and requires some indirect means to ensure that employee behavior conforms to management needs. Not everyone works well under general supervision, however. General supervision works best where subordinates desire responsibility. General supervision also works well where individuals in work groups have strong feelings about the quality of the finished work products. Strong identification with management goals is another trait of persons who work well under general supervision. There are substantial differences in the amount of responsibility people are willing to accept on the job. One person may flourish under supervision that another might find extremely restrictive.

Psychological research provides evidence that the nature of a person's personality affects his attitude toward supervision. There are some employees with a low need for achievement and high fear of failure who shy away from challenges and responsibilities. Many seek self-expression off the job and ask only to be allowed to daydream on it. There are others who have become so accustomed to the authoritarian approach in their culture, family and previous work experience that they regard general supervision as no supervision at all. They abuse the privileges it bestows on them and refuse to accept the responsibilities it demands.

Different groups develop different attitudes toward work. Most college graduates, for example, expect a great deal of responsibility and freedom. People with limited education, on the other hand, often have trouble accepting the concept that people should make decisions for themselves, particularly decisions concerning work. Therefore, the extent to which general supervision will be effective varies greatly with the subordinates involved.

1. According to the above passage, which one of the following is a necessary part of management policy regarding general supervision?   1.____

    A.   Most employees should formulate their own work goals
    B.   Deserving employees should be rewarded periodically
    C.   Some controls on employee work patterns should be established
    D.   Responsibility among employees should generally be equalized

2. It can be inferred from the above passage that an employee who avoids responsibilities and challenges is most likely to   2.____

    A.   gain independence under general supervision
    B.   work better under close supervision than under general supervision
    C.   abuse the liberal guidelines of general supervision
    D.   become more restricted and cautious under general supervision

3. Based on the above passage, employees who succeed under general supervision are most likely to   3.____

    A.   have a strong identification with people and their problems
    B.   accept work obligations without fear
    C.   seek self-expression off the job
    D.   value the intellectual aspects of life

4. Of the following, the best title for the passage is 4.____

    A. Benefits and Disadvantages of General Supervision
    B. Production Levels of Employees Under General Supervision
    C. Employee Attitudes Toward Work and the Work Environment
    D. Employee Background and Personality as a Factor in Utilizing General Supervision

5. It can be inferred from the above passage that the one of the following employees who is 5.____
most likely to work best under general supervision is one who

    A. is a part-time graduate student
    B. was raised by very strict parents
    C. has little self-confidence
    D. has been closely supervised in past jobs

Questions 6 through 10 are to be answered solely on the basis of the information in the following passage:

The concept of *program management* was first developed in order to handle some of the complex projects undertaken by the U.S. Department of Defense in the 1950's. Program management is an administrative system combining planning and control techniques to guide and coordinate all the activities which contribute to one overall program or project. It has been used by the federal government to manage space exploration and other programs involving many contributing organizations. It is also used by state and local governments and by some large firms to provide administrative integration of work from a number of sources, be they individuals, departments or outside companies.

One of the specific administrative techniques for program management is Program Evaluation Review Technique (PERT). PERT begins with the assembling of a list of all the activities needed to accomplish an overall task. The next step consists of arranging these activities in a sequential network showing both how much time each activity will take and which activities must be completed before others can begin. The time required for each activity is estimated by simple statistical techniques by the persons who will be responsible for the work, and the time required to complete the entire string of activities along each sequential path through the network is then calculated. There may be dozens or hundreds of these paths, so the calculation is usually done by computer. The longest path is then labeled the *critical path* because no matter how quickly events not on this path are completed, the events along the longest path must be finished before the project can be terminated. The overall starting and completion dates are then pinpointed, and target dates are established for each task. Actual progress can later be checked by comparison to the network plan.

6. Judging from the information in the above passage, which one of the following projects is 6.____
most suitable for handling by a program management technique?

    A. Review and improvement of the filing system used by a city office
    B. Computerization of accounting data already on file in an office
    C. Planning and construction of an urban renewal project
    D. Announcing a change in city tax regulations to thousands of business firms

7. The passage indicates that program management methods are now in wide use by vari- 7.____
ous kinds of organizations. Which one of the following organizations would you LEAST
expect to make much use of such methods today?

A. An automobile manufacturer
B. A company in the aerospace business
C. The government of a large city
D. A library reference department

8. In making use of the PERT technique, the first step is to determine

8.____

A. every activity that must take place in order to complete the project
B. a target date for completion of the project
C. the estimated time required to complete each activity which is related to the whole
D. which activities will make up the longest path on the chart

9. Who estimates the time required to complete a particular activity in a PERT program?

9.____

A. The people responsible for the particular activity
B. The statistician assigned to the program
C. The organization that has commissioned the project
D. The operator who programs the computer

10. Which one of the following titles best describes the contents of the passage?

10.____

A. *The Need For Computers in Today's Projects*
B. *One Technique For Program Management*
C. *Local Governments Can Now Use Space-Age Techniques*
D. *Why Planning Is Necessary For Complex Projects*

11. An Administrative Assistant has been criticized for the low productivity in the group which he supervises. Which of the following best reflects an understanding of supervisory responsibilities in the area of productivity? An Administrative Assistant should be held responsible for

11.____

A. his own individual productivity and the productivity of the group he supervises, because he is in a position where he maintains or increases production through others
B. his own personal productivity only, because the supervisor is not likely to have any effect on the productivity of subordinates
C. his own individual productivity but only for a drop in the productivity of the group he supervises, since subordinates will receive credit for increased productivity individually
D. his own personal productivity only, because this is how he would be evaluated if he were not a supervisor

12. A supervisor has held a meeting in his office with an employee about the employee's grievance. The grievance concerned the sharp way in which the supervisor reprimanded the employee for an error the employee made in the performance of a task assigned to him. The problem was not resolved. Which one of the following statements about this meeting best reflects an understanding of good supervisory techniques?

12.____

A. It is awkward for a supervisor to handle a grievance involving himself. The supervisor should not have held the meeting.
B. It would have been better if the supervisor had held the meeting at the employee's workplace, even though there would have been frequent distractions, because the employee would have been more relaxed.

C. The resolution of a problem is not the only sign of a successful meeting. The achievement of communication was worthwhile.
D. The supervisor should have been forceful. There is nothing wrong with raising your voice to an employee every once in a while.

13. John Hayden, the owner of a single-family house, complains that he submitted an application for reduction of assessment that obviously was not acted upon before his final assessment notice was sent to him. The timely receipt of the application has been verified in a departmental log book. As the supervisor of the clerical unit through which this application was processed and where this delay occurred, you should be LEAST concerned with

    A. what happened   B. who is responsible
    C. why it happened   D. what can be learned from it

13.____

14. The one of the following that applies most appropriately to the role of the first-line supervisor is that usually he is

    A. called upon to help determine agency policy
    B. involved in long-range agency planning
    C. responsible for determining some aspects of basic organization structure
    D. a participant in developing procedures and methods

14.____

15. Sally Jones, an Administrative Assistant, gives clear and precise instructions to Robert Warren, a Senior Clerk. In these instructions, Ms. Jones clearly delegates authority to Mr. Warren to undertake a well-defined task. In this situation Ms. Jones should expect Mr. Warren to

    A. come to her to check out details as he progresses with the task
    B. come to her only with exceptional problems
    C. ask her permission if he wishes to use his delegated authority
    D. use his authority to redefine the task and its related activities

15.____

16. Planning involves establishing departmental goals and programs and determining ways of reaching them. The main advantage of such planning is that

    A. there will be no need for adjustments once a plan is put into operation
    B. it ensures that everyone is working on schedule
    C. it provides the framework for an effective operation
    D. unexpected work problems are easily overcome

16.____

17. As a result of reorganization, the jobs in a large clerical unit were broken down into highly specialized tasks. Each specialized task was then assigned to a particular employee to perform. This action will probably lead to an increase in

    A. flexibility   B. job satisfaction
    C. need for coordination   D. employee initiative

17.____

18. Your office carries on a large volume of correspondence concerned with the purchase of supplies and equipment for city offices. You use form letters to deal with many common situations. In which one of the following situations would use of a form letter be LEAST appropriate?

18.____

A. Informing suppliers of a change in city regulations concerning purchase contracts
B. Telling a new supplier the standard procedures to be followed in billing
C. Acknowledging receipt of a complaint and saying that the complaint will be investigated
D. Answering a city councilman's request for additional information on a particular regulation affecting suppliers

19. Assume that you are an Administrative Assistant heading a large clerical unit. Because of the great demands being made on your time, you have designated Tom Smith, a Supervising Clerk, to be your assistant and to assume some of your duties. Of the following duties performed by you, the most appropriate one to assign to Tom Smith is to

    19.____

A. conduct the on-the-job training of new employees
B. prepare the performance appraisal reports on your staff members
C. represent your unit in dealings with the heads of other units
D. handle matters that require exception to general policy

20. In establishing rules for his subordinates, a superior should be primarily concerned with

    20.____

A. creating sufficient flexibility to allow for exceptions
B. making employees aware of the reasons for the rules and the penalties for infractions
C. establishing the strength of his own position in relation to his subordinates
D. having his subordinates know that such rules will be imposed in a personal manner

21. The practice of conducting staff training sessions on a periodic basis is generally considered

    21.____

A. poor; it takes employees away from their work assignments
B. poor; all staff training should be done on an individual basis
C. good; it permits the regular introduction of new methods and techniques
D. good; it ensures a high employee productivity rate

22. Suppose, as an Administrative Assistant, you have just announced at a staff meeting with your subordinates that a radical reorganization of work will take place next week. Your subordinates at the meeting appear to be excited, tense and worried. Of the following, the best action for you to take at that time is to

    22.____

A. schedule private conferences with each subordinate to obtain his reaction to the meeting
B. close the meeting and tell your subordinates to return immediately to their work assignments
C. give your subordinates some time to ask questions and discuss your announcement
D. insist that your subordinates do not discuss your announcement among themselves or with other members of the agency

23. Suppose that as an Administrative Assistant you were recently placed in charge of the Duplicating and Stock Unit of Department Y. From your observation of the operations of your unit during your first week as its head, you get the impression that there are inefficiencies in its operations causing low productivity. To obtain an increase in its productivity, the FIRST of the following actions you should take is to

    23.____

A.   seek the advice of your immediate superior on how he would tackle this problem
B.   develop plans to correct any unsatisfactory conditions arising from other than man-power deficiencies
C.   identify the problems causing low productivity
D.   discuss your productivity problem with other unit heads to find out how they handled similar problems

24.   Assume that you are an Administrative Assistant recently placed in charge of a large clerical unit. At a meeting, the head of another unit tells you, *My practice is to give a worker more than he can finish. In that way you can be sure that you are getting the most out of him.* For you to adopt this practice would be

   24.____

A.   advisable, since your actions would be consistent with those practiced in your agency
B.   inadvisable, since such a practice is apt to create frustration and lower staff morals
C.   advisable, since a high goal stimulates people to strive to attain it
D.   inadvisable, since management may, in turn, set too high a productivity goal for the unit

25.   Suppose that you are the supervisor of a unit in which there is an increasing amount of friction among several of your staff members. One of the reasons for this friction is that the work of some of these staff members cannot be completed until other staff members complete related work. Of the following, the most appropriate action for you to take is to

   25.____

A.   summon these employees to a meeting to discuss the responsibilities each has and to devise better methods of coordination
B.   have a private talk with each employee involved and make each understand that there must be more cooperation among the employees
C.   arrange for interviews with each of the employees involved to determine what his problems are
D.   shift the assignments of these employees so that each will be doing a job different from his current one

26.   An office supervisor has a number of responsibilities with regard to his subordinates. Which one of the following functions should NOT be regarded as a basic responsibility of the office supervisor?

   26.____

A.   Telling employees how to solve personal problems that may be interfering with their work
B.   Training new employees to do the work assigned to them
C.   Evaluating employees' performance periodically and discussing the evaluation with each employee
D.   Bringing employee grievances to the attention of higher-level administrators and seeking satisfactory resolutions

27.   One of your most productive subordinates frequently demonstrates a poor attitude toward his job. He seems unsure of himself, and he annoys his co-workers because he is continually belittling himself and the work that he is doing. In trying to help him overcome this problem, which of the following approaches is LEAST likely to be effective?

   27.____

A. Compliment him on his work and assign him some additional responsibilities, telling him that he is being given these responsibilities because of his demonstrated ability
B. Discuss with him the problem of his attitude, and warn him that you will have to report it on his next performance evaluation
C. Assign him a particularly important and difficult project, stressing your confidence in his ability to complete it successfully
D. Discuss with him the problem of his attitude, and ask him for suggestions as to how you can help him overcome it

28. You come to realize that a personality conflict between you and one of your subordinates is adversely affecting his performance. Which one of the following would be the most appropriate FIRST step to take?   28.____

A. Report the problem to your superior and request assistance. His experience may be helpful in resolving this problem.
B. Discuss the situation with several of the subordinate's co-workers to see if they can suggest any remedy.
C. Suggest to the subordinate that he get professional counseling or therapy.
D. Discuss the situation candidly with the subordinate, with the objective of resolving the problem between yourselves.

29. Assume that you are an Administrative Assistant supervising the Payroll Records Section in Department G. Your section has been requested to prepare and submit to the department's budget officer a detailed report giving a breakdown of labor costs under various departmental programs and sub-programs. You have assigned this task to a Supervising Clerk, giving him full authority for seeing that this job is performed satisfactorily. You have given him a written statement of the job to be done and explained the purpose and use of this report. The next step that you should take in connection with this delegated task is to   29.____

A. assist the Supervising Clerk in the step-by-step performance of the job
B. assure the Supervising Clerk that you will be understanding of mistakes if made at the beginning
C. require him to receive your approval for interim reports submitted at key points before he can proceed further with his task
D. give him a target date for the completion of this report

30. Assume that you are an Administrative Assistant heading a unit staffed with six clerical employees. One Clerk, John Snell, is a probationary employee appointed four months ago. During the first three months, John learned his job quickly, performed his work accurately and diligently, and was cooperative and enthusiastic in his attitude. However, during the past few weeks his enthusiasm seems dampened, he is beginning to make mistakes and at times appears bored. Of the following, the most appropriate action for you to take is to   30.____

A. check with John's co-workers to find out whether they can explain John's change in attitude and work habits
B. wait a few more weeks before taking any action, so that John will have an opportunity to make the needed changes on his own initiative
C. talk to John about the change in his work performance and his decreased enthusiasm

D. change John's assignment since this may be the basic cause of John's change in attitude and performance

31. The supervisor of a clerical unit, on returning from a meeting, finds that one of his subor-   31.____
dinates is performing work not assigned by him. The subordinate explains that the group supervisor had come into the office while the unit supervisor was out and directed the employee to work on an urgent assignment. This is the first time the group supervisor had bypassed the unit supervisor. Of the following, the most appropriate action for the unit supervisor to take is to

   A. explain to the group supervisor that bypassing the unit supervisor is an undesirable practice
   B. have the subordinate stop work on the assignment until the entire matter can be clarified with the group supervisor
   C. raise the matter of bypassing a supervisor at the next staff conference held by the group supervisor
   D. forget about the incident

32. Assume that you are an Administrative Assistant in charge of the Mail and Records Unit   32.____
of Department K. On returning from a meeting, you notice that Jane Smith is not at her regular work location. You learn that another employee, Ruth Reed, had become faint, and that Jane took Ruth outdoors for some fresh air. It is a long-standing rule in your unit that no employee is to leave the building during office hours except on official business or with the unit head's approval. Only a few weeks ago, John Duncan was reprimanded by you for going out at 10:00 a.m. for a cup of coffee. With respect to Jane Smith's violation of this rule, the most appropriate of the following actions for you to take is to

   A. issue a reprimand to Jane Smith, with an explanation that all employees must be treated in exactly the same way
   B. tell Jane that you should reprimand her, but you will not do so in this instance
   C. overlook this rule violation in view of the extenuating circumstances
   D. issue the reprimand with no further explanation, treating her in the same manner that you treated John Duncan

33. Assume that you are an Administrative Assistant recently assigned as supervisor of   33.____
Department X's Mail and Special Services Unit. In addition to processing your depart-ment's mail, your clerical employees are often sent on errands in the city. You have learned that, while on such official errands, these clerks sometimes take care of their own personal matters or those of their co-workers. The previous supervisor had tolerated this practice even though it violated a departmental personnel rule. The most appropriate of the following actions for you to take is to

   A. continue to tolerate this practice so long as it does not interfere with the work of your unit
   B. take no action until you have proof that an employee has violated this rule; then give a mild reprimand
   C. wait until an employee has committed a gross violation of this rule; then bring him up on charges
   D. discuss this rule with your staff and caution them that its violation might necessitate disciplinary action

34. *Supervisors who exercise 'close supervision' over their subordinates usually check up on* 34.____
their employees frequently, give them frequent instructions and, in general, limit their
freedom to do their work in their own way. Those who exercise 'general supervision' usu-
ally set forth the objectives of a job, tell their subordinates what they want accomplished,
fix the limits within which the subordinates can work and let the employees (if they are
capable) decide how the job is to be done. Which one of the following conditions would
contribute LEAST to the success of the *general supervision* approach in an organizational unit?

    A. Employees in the unit welcome increased responsibilities
    B. Work assignments in the unit are often challenging
    C. Work procedures must conform with those of other units
    D. Staff members support the objectives of the unit

35. Assume that you are an Administrative Assistant assigned as supervisor of the Clerical 35.____
Services Unit of a large agency's Labor Relations Division. A member of your staff
comes to you with a criticism of a policy followed by the Labor Relations Division. You
also have similar views regarding this policy. Of the following, the most appropriate action
for you to take in response to his criticism is to

    A. agree with him, but tell him that nothing can be done about it at your level
    B. suggest to him that it is not wise for him to express criticism of policy
    C. tell the employee that he should direct his criticism to the head of your agency if he
        wants quick action
    D. ask the employee if he has suggestions for revising the policy

---

KEY (CORRECT ANSWERS)

1. C	11. A	26. A
2. B	12. C	27. B
3. B	13. B	28. D
4. D	14. D	29. D
5. A	15. B	30. C
6. C	16. C	31. D
7. D	17. C	32. C
8. A	18. D	33. D
9. A	19. A	34. C
10. B	20. B	35. D
	21. C	
	22. C	
	23. C	
	24. B	
	25. A	

TEST 3

1. At the request of your bureau head you have designed a simple visitor's referral form. The form will be cut from 8-1/2" x 11" stock.
   Which of the following should be the dimensions of the form if you want to be sure that there is no waste of paper?

   A.   2-3/4" x 4-1/4"   B.   3-1/4" x 4-3/4"
   C.   3-3/4" x 4-3/4"   D.   4-1/2" x 5-1/2"

   1.____

2. An office contains six file cabinets, each containing three drawers. One of your responsibilities as a new Administrative Assistant is to see that there is sufficient filing space. At the present time, 1/4 of the file space contains forms, 2/9 contains personnel records, 1/3 contains reports, and 1/7 of the remaining space contains budget records.
   If each drawer may contain more than one type of record, how much drawer space is now *empty*?

   A.   0 drawers   B.   13/14 of a drawer
   C.   3 drawers   D.   3-1/2 drawers

   2.____

3. Assume that there were 21 working days in March. The five clerks in your unit had the following number of absences in March:
   Clerk H - 2 absences
   Clerk J - 1 absence
   Clerk K - 6 absences
   Clerk L - 0 absences
   Clerk M - 10 absences

   To the nearest day, what was the *average* attendance in March for the five clerks in your unit?

   A.   4   B.   17   C.   18   D.   21

   3.____

Questions 4-12

4. The stenographers who are secretaries to commissioners have more varied duties than the stenographic pool.

   A.   This is an example of effective writing.
   B.   In this sentence there would be a comma after *commissioners* in order to break up the sentence into clauses.
   C.   In this sentence the words *stenographers in* should be inserted after the word *than*.
   D.   In this sentence the word *commissioners* is misspelled.

   4.____

5. A person who becomes an administrative assistant will be called upon to provide leader- 5.____
   ship, to insure proper quantity and quality of production, and many administrative chores
   must be performed.

   A. This sentence is an example of effective writing.
   B. The sentence should be divided into three separate sentences, each describing a
      duty.
   C. The words *many administrative chores must be performed* should be changed to
      to perform many administrative chores.
   D. The words *to provide leadership* should be changed to *to be a leader.*

6. A complete report has been submitted by our branch office, giving details about this 6.____
   transaction.

   A. This sentence is an example of effective writing.
   B. The phrase *giving details about this transaction* should be placed between the
      words *report* and *has.*
   C. A semi-colon should replace the comma after the word *office* to indicate indepen-
      dent clauses.
   D. A colon should replace the comma after the word *office* since the second clause
      provides further explanation.

7. The report was delayed because of the fact that the writer lost his rough draft two days 7.____
   before the deadline.

   A. This sentence is an example of effective writing.
   B. In this sentence the words *of the fact that* are unnecessary and should be deleted.
   C. In this sentence the words *because of the fact that* should be shortened to *due to.*
   D. In this sentence the word *before* should be replaced by *prior to.*

8. Included in this offer are a six months' guarantee, a complete set of instructions, and one 8.____
   free inspection of the equipment.

   A. This sentence is an example of effective writing.
   B. The word *is* should be substituted for the word *are.*
   C. The word *months* should have been spelled *month's.*
   D. The word *months* should be spelled *months.*

9. Certain employees come to the attention of their employers. Especially those with poor 9.____
   work records and excessive absences.

   A. This sentence is an example of effective writing.
   B. The period after the word *employers* should be changed to a comma, and the first
      letter of the word *Especially* should be changed to a small *e.*
   C. The period after the word *employers* should be changed to a semicolon, and the
      first letter of the word *Especially* should be changed to a small *e.*
   D. The period after the word *employers* should be changed to a colon.

10. The applicant had decided to decline the appointment by the time he was called for the 10.____
    interview.

A. This sentence is an example of effective writing.
B. In this sentence the word *had* should be deleted.
C. In this sentence the phrase *was called* should be replaced by *had been called.*
D. In this sentence the phrase *had decided to decline* should be replaced by *declined.*

11. There are two elevaters, each accommodating ten people. 11.____

    A. This sentence is correct.
    B. In this sentence the word *elevaters* should be spelled *elevators.*
    C. In this sentence the word *each* should be replaced by the word *both.*
    D. In this sentence the word *accommodating* should be spelled *accomodating.*

12. With the aid of a special device, it was possible to alter the letterhead on the depart- 12.____
ment's stationary.

    A. This sentence is correct.
    B. The word *aid* should be spelled *aide.*
    C. The word *device* should be spelled *devise.*
    D. The word *stationary* should be spelled *stationery.*

13. Examine the following sentence and then choose from the options below the correct 13.____
word to be inserted in the blank space.
Everybody in both offices _____ involved in the project.

    A. are   B. feel   C. is

Questions 14-18

DIRECTIONS: Answer questions 14 through 18 SOLELY on the basis of the information in the following passage.

A new way of looking at job performance promises to be a major advance in measuring and increasing a person's true effectiveness in business. The fact that individuals differ enormously in their judgment of when a piece of work is actually finished is significant. It is believed that more than half of all people in the business world are defective in the *sense of closure,* that is they do not know the proper time to throw the switch that turns off their effort in one direction and diverts it to a new job. Only a minority of workers at any level have the required judgment and the feeling of responsibility to work on a job to the point of maximum effectiveness. The vast majority let go of each task far short of the completion point.

Very often, a defective sense of closure exists in an entire staff. When that occurs, it usually stems from a long-standing laxness on the part of higher management. A low degree of responsibility has been accepted and it has come to be standard. Combating this requires implementation of a few basic policies. Firstly, it is important to make each responsibility completely clear and to set certain guideposts as to what constitutes complete performance. Secondly, excuses for delays and failures should not be dealt with too sympathetically, but interest should be shown in the encountered obstacles. Lastly, a checklist should be used periodically to determine whether new levels of expectancy and new closure values have been set.

14. According to the above passage, a *majority of* people in the business world 14.____

    A. do not complete their work on time

B. cannot properly determine when a particular job is completed
C. make lame excuses for not completing a job on time
D. can adequately judge their own effectiveness at work

15. It can be *inferred from* the above passage that when a poor sense of closure is observed among all the employees in a unit, the responsibility for raising the performance level belongs to

    15.____

A. non-supervisory employees
B. the staff as a whole
C. management
D. first-line supervisors

16. It is *implied by* the above passage that, by the establishment of work guideposts, employees may develop a

    16.____

A. better understanding of expected performances
B. greater interest in their work relationships
C. defective sense of closure
D. lower level of performance

17. It can be inferred from the above passage that an individual's idea of whether a job is finished is *most closely* associated with his

    17.____

A. loyalty to management
B. desire to overcome obstacles
C. ability to recognize his own defects
D. sense of responsibility

18. Of the following, the BEST heading for the above passage is

    18.____

A. Management's Role in a Large Bureaucracy
B. Knowing When a Job is Finished
C. The Checklist, a Supervisor's Tool for Effectiveness
D. Supervisory Techniques

Questions 19-25

DIRECTIONS: Answer questions 19 through 25 assuming that you are in charge of public information for an office which issues reports and answers questions from other offices and from the public on changes in land use. The charts below represent comparative land use in four neighborhoods. The area of each neighborhood is expressed in city blocks. Assume that all city blocks are the same size.

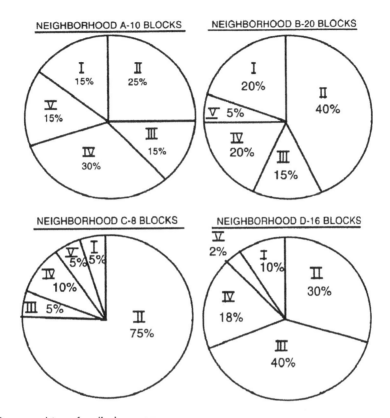

KEY: I   - One- and two-family houses
II - Apartment buildings
III - Office buildings
IV - Retail stores
V - Factories and warehouses

19. In how many of these neighborhoods does residential use (categories I and II together)   19._____
account for *more than 50%* of the land use?

    A. 1   B. 2   C. 3   D. 4

20. How many of the neighborhoods have an area of land occupied by apartment buildings   20._____
which is *greater than* the area of land occupied by apartment buildings in Neighborhood
C?

    A. none   B. 1   C. 2   D. 3

21. Which neighborhood has the LARGEST land area occupied by factories and ware-   21._____
houses?

    A. A   B. B   C. C   D. D

22. In which neighborhood is the LARGEST percentage of the land devoted to *both* office   22._____
buildings and retail stores?

    A. A   B. B   C. C   D. D

23. What is the difference, to the nearest city block, between the amount of land devoted to one- and two-family houses in Neighborhood A and the amount devoted to similar use in Neighborhood C?   23.____

   A.   1 block   B.   2 blocks   C.   5 blocks   D.   10 blocks

24. Which one of the following types of buildings occupies the same amount of land area in Neighborhood B as the amount of land area occupied by retail stores in Neighborhood A?   24.____

   A.   Apartment buildings
   B.   Office buildings
   C.   Retail stores
   D.   Factories and warehouses

25. Based on the information in the charts, which one of the following statements must be TRUE?   25.____

   A.   Factories and warehouses are gradually disappearing from all the neighborhoods except Neighborhood A.
   B.   Neighborhood B has more land area occupied by retail stores than any of the other neighborhoods.
   C.   There are more apartment dwellers living in Neighborhood C than in any of the other neighborhoods.
   D.   All four of these neighborhoods are predominantly residential.

KEY (CORRECT ANSWERS)

1.	A	11.	B
2.	C	12.	D
3.	B	13.	C
4.	C	14.	B
5.	C	15.	C
6.	B	16.	A
7.	B	17.	D
8.	A	18.	B
9.	B	19.	B
10.	A	20.	B

21.	A
22.	D
23.	A
24.	B
25.	B

INTERVIEWING
EXAMINATION SECTION
TEST 1

DIRECTIONS : Each question or incomplete statement is followed by several suggested answers or completions. Select the one that BEST answers the question or completes the statement. *PRINT THE LETTER OF THE CORRECT ANSWER IN THE SPACE AT THE RIGHT.*

1. You are conducting an interview with a client who has been having some difficulties with one of her fellow-workers. The client walks on crutches. You tell the client that she probably finds it difficult to get along with her fellow-workers because of this handicap.
To make such a statement would, *generally,* be

    A. *proper;* people are often prejudiced against persons with physical deformities
    B. *proper;* statements such as this indicate to the client that you are sympathetic toward her
    C. *improper;* this approach would not help the client solve her problem
    D. *improper;* you should have discussed this handicap in relation to the client's continued ability to continue in her job

1.____

2. The information which the interviewer plans to secure from an individual with whom he talks is determined MAINLY by the

    A. purpose of the interview and the functions of the agency
    B. state assistance laws and the desires of the individual
    C. privacy they have while talking and the willingness of the individual to give information
    D. emotional feelings of the individual seeking help and the interviewer's reactions to these feelings

2.____

3. *Generally,* the MOST effective of the following ways of dealing with a person being interviewed who frequently digresses from the subject under discussion or starts to ramble, is for the interviewer to

    A. tell the person that he, the interviewer, will have to terminate the interview unless the former sticks to the point
    B. increase the tempo of the interview
    C. demonstrate that he is a good listener and allow the person to continue in his own way
    D. inject questions which relate to the purpose of the interview

3.____

4. "Being a good listener" is an interviewing technique which, if applied properly, is *desirable* MOSTLY because it

    A. catches the client more easily in misrepresentations and lies
    B. conserves the energies of the interviewer
    C. encourages the client to talk about his personal affairs without restraint
    D. encourages the giving of information which is generally more reliable and complete

4.____

5. When questioning applicants for eligibility, it would be BEST to ask questions that are

5.____

A. *direct,* so that the applicant will realize that the interviewer knows what he is doing
B. *direct,* so that the information received will be as pertinent as possible
C. *indirect,* so that the applicant will not realize the purpose of the interview
D. *indirect,* so that you can trap the applicant into making admissions that he would not otherwise make

6. The CHIEF reason for conducting an interview with a new applicant in complete privacy is that the

      6.____

A. interviewer will be better able to record the facts without any other worker reading his case notes
B. applicant will be impressed by the business-like atmosphere of the agency
C. interviewer will be able to devote more time to questioning the applicant without interruption
D. applicant will be more likely to speak frankly

7. When conducting an interview with a client who is upset because of an increase in rent, it would be BEST for the interviewer to

      7.____

A. agree with the client that the agency was wrong in raising his rent, as a basis for further discussion
B. tell the client that unless he calms down the interview will be ended
C. prevent the client from becoming emotional
D. tell the client the reasons for the increase

8. At an interview to determine whether an applicant is eligible, the applicant gives information different from that which he submitted on his application.
The MOST advisable action to take is to

      8.____

A. cross out the old information, enter the new information, and initial the entry
B. re-enter the old information on the application form and initial the entry
C. give the applicant another application form, have him fill it out correctly, and resume the interview
D. give the applicant another application form to fill out, and set a later date for another interview

9. After you have secured, in an interview, all the necessary information from an applicant, he shows no intention of leaving, but starts to tell you a long personal story.
Of the following, the MOST advisable action for you to take is to

      9.____

A. explain to the applicant why personal stories are out of place in a business office
B. listen carefully to the story for whatever relevant information it may contain
C. interrupt him tactfully, thank him for the information he has already given, and terminate the interview
D. inform your supervisor that the time required for this interview will prevent you from completing the interviews scheduled for the day

10. In interviewing, the practice of anticipating an applicant's answers to questions is, *generally,*

      10.____

A. *desirable* because it is effective and economical when it is necessary to interview large numbers of applicants
B. *desirable* because many applicants have language difficulties

C. *undesirable* because it is the inalienable right of every person to answer as he sees fit

D. *undesirable* because applicants may tend to agree with the answer proposed by the interviewer even when the answer is not entirely correct

11. A follow-up interview was arranged for an applicant in order that he might furnish certain requested evidence. At this follow-up interview, the applicant still fails to furnish the necessary evidence.
It would be MOST advisable for you to

11.____

A. advise the applicant that he is now considered ineligible
B. ask the applicant how soon he can get the necessary evidence and set a date for another interview
C. question the applicant carefully and thoroughly to determine if he has misrepresented or falsified any information
D. set a date for another interview and tell the applicant to get the necessary evidence by that time

12. When an initial interview is being conducted, one way of starting is to explain the purpose of the interview to the applicant.
The practice of starting the interview with such an explanation is, *generally,*

12.____

A. *desirable* because the applicant can then understand why the interview is necessary and what will be accomplished by it
B. *desirable* because it creates the rapport which is necessary to successful interviewing
C. *undesirable* because time will be saved by starting off directly with the questions which must be asked
D. *undesirable* because the interviewer should have the choice of starting an interview in any manner he prefers

13. Empathy can be defined as the ability of one individual to respond sensitively and imaginatively to another's feelings.
For an interviewer to be empathic during an interview is *usually*

13.____

A. *undesirable*, mainly because an interviewer should never be influenced by the feelings of the one being interviewed
B. *desirable*, mainly because an interview will not be productive unless the interviewer takes the side of the person interviewed
C. *undesirable*, mainly because empathy usually leads an interviewer to be biased in favor of the person being interviewed
D. *desirable*, mainly because this ability allows the interviewer to direct his questions more effectively to the person interviewed

14. Assume that you must interview several people who know each other.
To gather them all in one group and question them TOGETHER, is, *generally,*

14.____

A. *good practice,* since any inaccurate information offered by one person would be corrected by others in the group
B. *poor practice,* since people in a group rarely pay adequate attention to questions
C. *good practice,* since the interviewer will save much time and effort in this way
D. *poor practice,* since the presence of several people can inhibit an individual from speaking

15. An effective interviewer should know that the one of the following reasons which LEAST   15.____
describes why there is a wide range of individual behavior in human relations is that

    A. socio-economic status influences human behavior
    B. physical characteristics do not influence human behavior
    C. education influences human behavior
    D. childhood experience influences human behavior

16. An interviewer encounters an uncooperative interviewee. Of the following, the FIRST   16.____
thing the interviewer should do in such a situation is to

    A. try various appeals to win the interviewee over to a cooperative attitude
    B. try to ascertain the reason for non-cooperation
    C. promise the interviewee that all data will be kept confidential
    D. alter his interviewing technique with the uncooperative interviewee

17. You discover that an interviewee who was requested to bring with him specific docu-   17.____
ments for his initial employment interview has forgotten the documents.
Of the following, the BEST course of action to take is to

    A. give the person a reasonable amount of time to furnish the documents
    B. tell the person you will let him know how much additional time he has
    C. mark the person disqualified for employment; he has failed to provide reasonably
       requested data on time
    D. mark the person provisionally qualified for employment; upon receipt of the docu-
       ments he will be permanently qualified

18. In checking interviewees' work experience, you realize that the person whom you are to   18.____
interview is only marginally fluent in English and has, therefore, requested permission to
bring a translator with him.
Of the following, the BEST course of action is to inform the interviewee that

    A. outside translators may not be used
    B. only city translators may be used
    C. state law requires fluency in English of all civil servants
    D. he may be assisted in the interview by his translator

19. Assume that, during the course of an interview, you are verbally attacked by the person   19.____
being interviewed.
Of the following, it would be MOST advisable to

    A. answer back in a matter-of-fact manner
    B. ask the person to apologize and discontinue the interview
    C. ignore the attack but adjourn the interview to another day
    D. use restraint and continue the interview

20. Assume that you find that the person you are interviewing has difficulty finishing his sen-   20.____
tences and seems to be groping for words.
In such a case, the BEST approach for you to take is to

    A. say what you think the person has in mind
    B. proceed patiently without calling attention to the problem
    C. ask the person why he finds it difficult to finish his sentences
    D. interrupt the interview until the person feels more relaxed

21. The one of the following which BEST describes the effect of the *sympathetic approach* in interviewing on the interviewee is that it will

    A. have no discernible effect on the interviewee
    B. calm the interviewee
    C. lead the interviewee to underemphasize his problems
    D. mislead the interviewee

21.____

22. The one of the following characteristics which is a PRIMARY requisite for a successful interview is

    A. total *curiosity*
    B. total *sympathy*
    C. complete *attention*
    D. complete *dedication*

22.____

23. Assume that you have been assigned to conduct a follow-up interview with a primary witness.
The one of the following which is MOST important in arranging such an interview is to

    A. keep the witness cooperative
    B. conduct the matter in secret
    C. allow the witness to determine where and when the interview takes place
    D. conduct the interview as soon as possible to insure a strong case

23.____

24. By examining a candidate's employment record, an interviewer can determine many things about the candidate. Of the following, the one which is LEAST apparent from an employment record is the candidate's

    A. character
    B. willingness to work
    C. capacity to get along with co-workers
    D. potential for advancing in civil service

24.____

25. Assume that you are conducting an interview in which the person being interviewed is using the interview as a forum for venting his anti-civil service feelings.
Of the following, the FIRST thing that you should do is to

    A. agree with the person; perhaps that will shorten the outburst
    B. respectfully disagree with the person; the decorum of the interview has already been disrupted
    C. courteously and objectively direct the interview to the relevant issue
    D. reschedule the interview to another mutually agreeable time

25.____

KEY (CORRECT ANSWERS)

1.	C		11.	B
2.	A		12.	A
3.	D		13.	D
4.	D		14.	D
5.	B		15.	B
6.	D		16.	B
7.	D		17.	A
8.	A		18.	D
9.	C		19.	D
10.	D		20.	B

21.	C
22.	C
23.	A
24.	D
25.	C

TEST 2

DIRECTIONS: Each question or incomplete statement is followed by several suggested answers or completions. Select the one that BEST answers the question or completes the statement. *PRINT THE LETTER OF THE CORRECT ANSWER IN THE SPACE AT THE RIGHT.*

1.   The pattern of an interview is LARGELY set by the   1.____

    A.   person being interviewed
    B.   person conducting the interview
    C.   nature of the interview
    D.   policy of the agency employing the interviewer

2.   Assume that a person being interviewed, who had been talking freely, suddenly tries to   2.____
change the subject.
To a trained interviewer, this behavior would mean that the person *probably*

    A.   knew very little about the subject
    B.   realized that he was telling too much
    C.   decided that his privacy was being violated
    D.   realized that he was becoming confused

3.   Assume that you receive a telephone call from an unknown individual requesting infor-   3.____
mation about a person you are currently interviewing.
In such a situation, the BEST course of action for you to take is to

    A.   give him the information over the telephone
    B.   tell him to write to your department for the information
    C.   send him the information, retaining a copy for your files
    D.   tell him to call back, giving you additional time to check into the matter

4.   In an interview, assuming that the interviewer was using a *non-directive approach* in this   4.____
interview, of the following, the interviewer's most effective response would be:

    A.   "You know, you are building a bad record of tardiness."
    B.   "Can you tell me more about this situation?"
    C.   "What kind of person is your superior?"
    D.   "Do you think you are acting fairly towards the agency by being late so often?"

5.   In an interview, assuming that the interviewer was using a *directed approach* in this inter-   5.____
view, of the following, the interviewer's response should be:

    A.   "That doesn't seem like much of an excuse to me."
    B.   "What do you mean by saying that you've lost interest?"
    C.   "What problems are there with the supervision you are getting?"
    D.   "How do you think your tardiness looks in your personnel record?"

Questions 6-8.

DIRECTIONS: Answer Questions 6 through 8 only on the basis of information given in the passage below.

.A personnel interviewer, selecting job applicants, may find that he reacts badly to some people even on first contact. This reaction cannot usually be explained by things that the interviewee has done or said. Most of us have had the experience of liking or disliking, of feeling comfortable or uncomfortable with people on first acquaintance, long before we have had a chance to make a conscious, rational decision about them. Often, too, our liking or disliking is transmitted to the other person by subtle processes such as gestures, posture, voice intonations, or choice of words. The point to be kept in mind in this: the relations between people are complex and occur at several levels, from the conscious to the unconscious. This is true whether the relationship is brief or long, formal or informal.

Some of the major dynamics of personality which operate on the unconscious level are projection, sublimation, rationalization, and repression. Encountering these for the first time, one is apt to think of them as representing pathological states. In the extreme, they undoubtedly are, but they exist so universally that we must consider them also to be parts of normal personality.

Without necessarily subscribing to any of the numerous theories of personality, it is possible to describe personality in terms of certain important aspects or elements. We are all aware of ourselves as thinking organisms.

This aspect of personality, the conscious part, is important for understanding human behavior, but it is not enough. Many find it hard to accept the notion that each person also has an unconscious. The existence of the unconscious is no longer a matter of debate. It is not possible to estimate at all precisely what proportion of our total psychological life is conscious, what proportion unconscious. Everyone who has studied the problem, however, agrees that consciousness is the smaller part of personality. Most of what we are and do is a result of unconscious processes. To ignore this is to risk mistakes.

6. The passage above suggests that an interviewer can be MOST effective if he   6._____

    A. learns how to determine other peoples' unconscious motivations
    B. learns how to repress his own unconsciously motivated mannerisms and behavior
    C. can keep others from feeling that he either likes or dislikes them
    D. gains an understanding of how the unconscious operates in himself and in others

7. It may be inferred from the passage above that the "subtle processes, such as gestures,   7._____
   posture, voice intonation, or choice of words," referred to in the first paragraph, are, *usually,*

    A. in the complete control of an expert interviewer
    B. the determining factors in the friendships a person establishes
    C. controlled by a person's unconscious
    D. not capable of being consciously controlled

8. The passage above implies that various different personality theories are, *usually,*   8._____

    A. so numerous and different as to be valueless to an interviewer
    B. in basic agreement about the importance of the unconscious
    C. understood by the interviewer who strives to be effective
    D. in agreement that personality factors such as projection and repression are pathological

Questions 9-10.

DIRECTIONS: Answer Questions 9 and 10 ONLY on the basis of information given in the passage below.

Since we generally assure informants that what they say is confidential, we are not free to tell one informant what the other has told us. Even if the informant says, "I don't care who knows it; tell anybody you want to," we find it wise to treat the interview as confidential. An interviewer who relates to some informants what other informants have told him is likely to stir up anxiety and suspicion. Of course, the interviewer may be able to tell an informant what he has heard without revealing the source of his information. This may be perfectly appropriate where a story has wide currency so that an informant cannot infer the source of the information. But if an event is not widely known, the mere mention of it may reveal to one informant what another informant has said about the situation. How can the data be cross-checked in these circumstances?

9. The passage above implies that the anxiety and suspicion an interviewer may arouse by   9.____
    telling what.has been learned in other interviews is due to the

    A. lack of trust the person interviewed may have in the interviewer's honesty
    B. troublesome nature of the material which the interviewer has learned in other inter-
        views
    C. fact that the person interviewed may not believe that permission was given to
        repeat the information
    D. fear of the person interviewed that what he is telling the interviewer will be
        repeated

10. The paragraph above is *most likely* part of a longer passage dealing with   10.____

    A. ways to verify data gathered in interviews
    B. the various anxieties a person being interviewed may feel
    C. the notion that people sometimes say things they do not mean
    D. ways an interviewer can avoid seeming suspicious

Questions 11-12.

DIRECTIONS: Answer Questions 11 and 12 ONLY on the basis of information given below.

The ability to interview rests not only on any single trait, but on a vast complex of them. Habits, skills, techniques, and attitudes are all involved. Competence in interviewing is acquired only after careful and diligent study, prolonged practice (preferably under supervision), and a good bit of trial and error; for interviewing is not an exact science, it is an art. Like many other arts, however, it can and must draw on science in several of its aspects.

There is always a place for individual initiative, for imaginative innovations, and for new combinations of old approaches. The skilled interviewer cannot be bound by a set of rules. Likewise, there is not a set of rules which can guarantee to the novice that his interviewing will be successful. There are, however, some accepted, general guide-posts which may help the beginner to avoid mistakes, learn how to conserve his efforts, and establish effective working relationships with interviewees; to accomplish, in short, what he set out to do.

11. According to the passage above, rules and standard techniques for interviewing are   11.____

A. helpful for the beginner, but useless for the experienced, innovative interviewer
B. destructive of the innovation and initiative needed for a good interviewer
C. useful for even the experienced interviewer, who may, however, sometimes go beyond them
D. the means by which nearly anybody can become an effective interviewer

12. According to the passage above, the one of the following which is a prerequisite to competent interviewing is

12.____

A. avoiding mistakes
C. imaginative innovation

B. study and practice
D. natural aptitude

Questions 13-16.

DIRECTIONS: Answer Questions 13 through 16 SOLELY on the basis of information given in the following paragraph.

The question of what material is relevant is not as simple as it might seem. Frequently material which seems irrelevant to the inexperienced has, because of the common tendency to disguise and distort and misplace one's feelings, considerable significance. It may be necessary to let the client "ramble on" for a while in order to clear the decks, as it were, so that he may get down to things that really are on his mind. On the other hand, with an already disturbed person, it may be important for the interviewer to know when to discourage further elaboration of upsetting material. This is especially the case where the worker would be unable to do anything about it. An inexperienced interviewer might, for instance, be intrigued with the bizarre elaboration of material that the psychotic produces, but further elaboration of this might encourage the client in his instability. A too random discussion may indicate that the interviewee is not certain in what areas the interviewer is prepared to help him, and he may be seeking some direction. Or again, satisfying though it may be for the interviewer to have the interviewee tell him intimate details, such revelations sometimes need to be checked or encouraged only in small doses. An interviewee who has "talked too much" often reveals subsequent anxiety. This is illustrated by the fact that? frequently after a "confessional" interview ,the interviewee surprises the interviewer by being withdrawn, inarticulate, or hostile, or by breaking the next appointment.

13. Sometimes a client may reveal certain personal information to an interviewer and subsequently, may feel anxious about this revelation.
If, during an interview, a client begins to discuss very personal matters, it would be BEST to

13.____

A. tell the client, in no uncertain terms, that you're not interested in personal details
B. ignore the client at this point
C. encourage the client to elaborate further on the details
D. inform the client that the information seems to be very personal

14. Clients with severe psychological disturbances pose an especially difficult problem for the inexperienced interviewer.
The difficulty lies in the possibility of the client's

    A. becoming physically violent and harming the interviewer
    B. "rambling on" for a while
    C. revealing irrelevant details which may be followed by cancelled appointments
    D. reverting to an unstable state as a result of interview material

14.____

15. An interviewer should be constantly alert to the possibility of obtaining clues from the client as to problem areas.
According to the above passage, a client who discusses topics at random may be

    A. unsure of what problems the interviewer can provide help
    B. reluctant to discuss intimate details
    C. trying to impress the interviewer with his knowledge
    D. deciding what relevant material to elaborate on

15.____

16. The evaluation of a client's responses may reveal substantial information that may aid the interviewer in assessing the problem areas that are of concern to the client. Responses that seemed irrelevant at the time of the interview may be of significance because

    A. considerable significance is attached to all irrelevant material
    B. emotional feelings are frequently masked
    C. an initial "rambling on" is often a prelude to what -is actually bothering the client
    D. disturbed clients often reveal subsequent anxiety

16.____

Questions 17-19.

DIRECTIONS: Answer Questions 17 through 19 SOLELY on the basis of the following paragraph.

The physical setting of the interview may determine its entire potentiality. Some degree of privacy and a comfortable relaxed atmosphere are important. The interviewee is not encouraged to give much more than his name and address if the interviewer seems busy with other things, if people are rushing about, if there are distracting noises. He has a right to feel that, whether the interview lasts five minutes or an hour, he has, for that time, the undivided attention of the interviewer. Interruptions, telephone calls, and so on, should be reduced to a minimum. If the interviewee has waited in a crowded room for what seems to him an interminably long period, he is naturally in no mood to sit down and discuss what is on his mind. Indeed, by that time the primary thing on his mind may be his irritation at being kept waiting, and he frequently feels it would be impolite to express this. If a wait or interruptions have been unavoidable, it is always helpful to give the client some recognition that these are disturbing and that he can naturally understand that they make it more difficult for him to proceed. At the same time if he protests that they have not troubled him, the interviewer can best accept his statements at their face value, as further insistence that they must have been disturbing may be interpreted by him as accusing, and he may conclude that the interviewer has been personally hurt by his irritation.

17. Distraction during an interview may tend to limit the client's responses.   17.____
In a case where an interruption has occurred, it would be BEST for the interviewer to

    A. terminate this interview and have it rescheduled for another time period
    B. ignore the interruption since it is not continuous
    C. express his understanding that the distraction can cause the client to feel disturbed
    D. accept the client's protests that he has been troubled by the interruption

18. To maximize the rapport that can be established with the client, an appropriate physical   18.____
setting is necessary. At the very least, some privacy would be necessary.
In addition, the interviewer should

    A. always appear to be busy in order to impress the client
    B. focus his attention only on the client
    C. accept all the client's statements as being valid
    D. stress the importance of the interview to the client

19. Clients who have been waiting quite some time for their interview may, justifiably, become   19.____
upset. However, a client *may initially* attempt to mask these feelings because he may

    A. personally hurt the interviewer
    B. want to be civil
    C. feel that the wait was unavoidable
    D. fear the consequences of his statement

20. You have been assigned to interview W, a witness, concerning a minor automobile acci-   20.____
dent. Although you have made no breach of the basic rules of contact and approach,
you, nevertheless, recognize that you and W have a personality clash and that a natural
animosity has resulted.
Of the following, you MOST appropriately should

    A. discuss the personality problem with W and attempt to resolve the difference
    B. stop the interview on some pretext and leave in a calm and pleasant manner,
       allowing an associate to continue the interview
    C. ignore the personality problem and continue as though nothing had happened
    D. change the subject matter being discussed since the facts sought may be the
       source of the animosity

21. Assume that you desire to interview W, a reluctant witness to an event that took place   21.____
several weeks previously. Assume further that the interview can take place at a location
to be designated by the interviewer.
Of the following, the place of interview should *preferably* be the

    A. office of the interviewer
    B. home of W
    C. office of W
    D. scene where the event took place

22. Assume that you are interviewing W, a witness. During the interview it becomes apparent   22.____
that W's statements are inaccurate and at variance with the facts previously established.
In these circumstances, it would be BEST for you to

    A. tell W that his statements are inaccurate and point out how they conflict with previ-
       ously established facts

B. reword your questions and ask additional questions about the facts being discussed
C. warn W that he may be required to testify under oath at a later date
D. ignore W's statements if you have other information that support the facts

23. Assume that W, a witness being interviewed by you, shows a tendency to ramble. His answers to your questions are lengthy and not responsive.
In this situation, the BEST action for you to take is to

    23.____

A. permit W to continue because at some point he will tell you the information sought
B. tell W that he is rambling and unresponsive and that more will be accomplished if he is brief and to the point
C. control the interview so that complete and accurate information is obtained
D. patiently listen to W since rambling is W's style and it cannot be changed

24. Assume that you are interviewing a client. Of the following, the BEST procedure for you to follow in regard to the use of your notebook is to

    24.____

A. take out your notebook at the start of the interview and immediately begin taking notes
B. memorize the important facts related during the interview and enter them after the interview has been completed
C. advise the client that all his answers are being taken down to insure that he will tell the truth
D. establish rapport with the client and ask permission to jot down various data in your notebook

25. In order to conduct an effective interview, an interviewer's attention must continuously be directed in two ways, toward himself as well as toward the interviewee. Of the following, the PRIMARY danger in this division of attention is that the

    25.____

A. interviewer's behavior may become less natural and thus alienate the interviewee
B. interviewee's span of attention will be shortened
C. interviewer's response may be interpreted by the interviewee as being antagonistic
D. interviewee's more or less concealed prejudices will come to the surface

KEY (CORRECT ANSWERS)

1.	B	11.	C
2.	B	12.	B
3.	B	13.	D
4.	B	14.	D
5.	C	15.	A
6.	D	16.	B
7.	C	17.	C
8.	B	18.	B
9.	D	19.	B
10.	A	20.	B

21.	A
22.	B
23.	C
24.	D
25.	A

EXAMINATION SECTION

DIRECTIONS: Each question or incomplete statement is followed by several suggested answers or completions. Select the one that BEST answers the question or completes the statement. *PRINT THE LETTER OF THE CORRECT ANSWER IN THE SPACE AT THE RIGHT.*

Questions 1-5.

DIRECTIONS: Each of Questions 1 through 5 consists of a passage which contains one word that is incorrectly used because it is not in keeping with the meaning that the quotation is evidently intended to convey. Determine which word is incorrectly used. Select from the choices lettered A, B, C, and D the word which, when substituted for the incorrectly used word, would BEST help to convey the meaning of the quotation.

1. Whatever the method, the necessity to keep up with the dynamics of an organization is the point on which many classification plans go awry. The budgetary approach to "positions," for example, often leads to using for recruitment and pay purposes a position authorized many years earlier for quite a different purpose than currently contemplated – making perhaps the title, the class, and the qualifications required inappropriate to the current need. This happens because executives overlook the stability that takes place in job duties and fail to reread an initial description of the job before saying, as they scan a list of titles, "We should fill this position right away." Once a classification plan is adopted, it is pointless to do anything less than provide for continuous, painstaking maintenance on a current basis, else once different positions that have actually become similar to each other remain in different classes, and some former cognates that have become quite different continue in the same class. Such a program often seems expensive. But to stint too much on this out-of-pocket cost may create still higher hidden costs growing out of lowered morale, poor production, delayed operating programs, excessive pay for simple work, and low pay for responsible work (resulting in poorly qualified executives and professional men) – all normal concomitants of inadequate, hasty, or out-of-date classification.   1.____

   A. evolution   B. personnel
   C. disapproved   D. forward

2. At first sight, it may seem that there is little or no difference between the usableness of a manual and the degree of its use. But there is a difference. A manual may have all the qualities which make up the usable manual and still not be used. Take this instance as an example: Suppose you have a satisfactory manual but issue instructions from day to day through the avenue of bulletins, memorandums, and other informational releases. Which will the employee use, the manual or the bulletin which passes over his desk? He will, of course, use the latter, for some obsolete material will not be contained in this manual. Here we have a theoretically usable manual which is unused because of the other avenues by which procedural information may be issued.   2.____

   A. countermand   B. discard
   C. intentional   D. worthwhile

3. By reconcentrating control over its operations in a central headquarters, a firm is able to extend the influence of automation to many, if not all, of its functions – from inventory and payroll to production, sales, and personnel. In so doing, businesses freeze all the elements of the corporate function in their relationship to one another and to the overall objectives of the firm. From this total systems concept, companies learn that computers can accomplish much more than clerical and accounting jobs. Their capabilities can be tapped to perform the traditional applications (payroll processing, inventory control, accounts payable, and accounts receivable) as well as newer applications such as spotting deviations from planned programs (exception reporting), adjusting planning schedules, forecasting business trends, simulating market conditions, and solving production problems. Since the office manager is a manager of information and each of these applications revolves around the processing of data, he must take an active role in studying and improving the system under his care.

    A. maintaining   B. inclusion
    C. limited   D. visualize

3.____

4. In addition to the formal and acceptance theories of the source of authority, although perhaps more closely related to the latter, is the belief that authority is generated by personal qualifies of technical competence. Under this heading is the individual who has made, in effect, subordinates of others through sheer force of personality, and the engineer or economist who exerts influence by furnishing answers or sound advice. These may have no actual organizational authority, yet their advice may be so eagerly sought and so unerringly followed that it appears to carry the weight of an order.
But, above all, one cannot discount the importance of formal authority with its institutional foundations. Buttressed by the qualities of leadership implicit in the acceptance theory, formal authority is basic to the managerial job. Once abrogated, it may be delegated or withheld, used or misused, and be effective in capable hands or be ineffective in inept hands.

    A. selected   B. delegation
    C. limited   D. possessed

4.____

5. Since managerial operations in organizing, staffing, directing, and controlling are designed to support the accomplishment of enterprise objectives, planning logically precedes the execution of all other managerial functions. Although all the functions intermesh in practice, planning is unique in that it establishes the objectives necessary for all group effort. Besides, plans must be made to accomplish these objectives before the manager knows what kind of organization relationships and personal qualifications are needed, along which course subordinates are to be directed, and what kind of control is to be applied. And, of course, each of the other managerial functions must be planned if they are to be effective.
Planning and control are inseparable – the Siamese twins of management. Unplanned action cannot be controlled, for control involves keeping activities on course by correcting deviations from plans. Any attempt to control without plans would be meaningless, since there is no way anyone can tell whether he is going where he wants to go – the task of control – unless first he knows where he wants to go – the task of planning. Plans thus preclude the standards of control.

    A. coordinating   B. individual
    C. furnish   D. follow

5.____

Questions 6-7.

DIRECTIONS: Answer Questions 6 and 7 SOLELY on the basis of information given in the fol-
               lowing paragraph.

*In-basket tests are often used to assess managerial potential. The exercise consists of a
set of papers that would be likely to be found in the in-basket of an administrator or manager
at any given time, and requires the individuals participating in the examination to indicate how
they would dispose of each item found in the in-basket. In order to handle the in-basket effectively, they must successfully manage their time, refer and assign some work to subordinates,
juggle potentially conflicting appointments and meetings, and arrange for follow-up of problems generated by the items in the in-basket. In other words, the in-basket test is attempting
to evaluate the participants' abilities to organize their work, set priorities, delegate, control,
and make decisions.*

6.   According to the above paragraph, to succeed in an in-basket test, an administrator must   6._____

    A.   be able to read very quickly
    B.   have a great deal of technical knowledge
    C.   know when to delegate work
    D.   arrange a lot of appointments and meetings

7.   According to the above paragraph, all of the following abilities are indications of manage-   7._____
     rial potential EXCEPT the ability to

    A.   organize and control   B.   manage time
    C.   write effective reports   D.   make appropriate decisions

Questions 8-9.

DIRECTIONS: Answer Questions 8 and 9 SOLELY on the basis of information given in the fol-
               lowing paragraph.

*One of the biggest mistakes of government executives with substantial supervisory
responsibility is failing to make careful appraisals of performance during employee probationary periods. Many a later headache could have been avoided by prompt and full appraisal
during the early months of an employee's assignment. There is not much more to say about
this except to emphasize the common prevalence of this oversight, and to underscore that for
its consequences, which are many and sad, the offending managers have no one to blame
but themselves.*

8.   According to the above passage, probationary periods are   8._____

    A.   a mistake, and should not be used by supervisors with large responsibilities
    B.   not used properly by government executives
    C.   used only for those with supervisory responsibility
    D.   the consequence of management mistakes

9. The one of the following conclusions that can MOST appropriately be drawn from the above passage is that

    A. management's failure to appraise employees during their probationary period is a common occurrence
    B. there is not much to say about probationary periods, because they are unimportant
    C. managers should blame employees for failing to use their probationary periods properly
    D. probationary periods are a headache to most managers

9.____

Questions 10-12.

DIRECTIONS: Answer Questions 10 through 12 SOLELY on the basis of information given in the following paragraph.

The common sense character of the merit system seems so natural to most Americans that many people wonder why it should ever have been inoperative. After all, the American economic system, the most phenomenal the world has ever known, is also founded on a rugged selective process which emphasizes the personal qualities of capacity, industriousness, and productivity. The criteria may not have always been appropriate and competition has not always been fair, but competition there was, and the responsibilities and the rewards – with exceptions, of course – have gone to those who could measure up in terms of intelligence, knowledge, or perseverance. This has been true not only in the economic area, in the money-making process, but also in achievement in the professions and other walks of life.

10. According to the above paragraph, economic rewards in the United States have

    A. always been based on appropriate, fair criteria
    B. only recently been based on a competitive system
    C. not gone to people who compete too ruggedly
    D. usually gone to those people with intelligence, knowledge, and perseverance

10.____

11. According to the above passage, a merit system is

    A. an unfair criterion on which to base rewards
    B. unnatural to anyone who is not American
    C. based only on common sense
    D. based on the same principles as the American economic system

11.____

12. According to the above passage, it is MOST accurate to say that

    A. the United States has always had a civil service merit system
    B. civil service employees are very rugged
    C. the American economic system has always been based on a merit objective
    D. competition is unique to the American way of life

12.____

Questions 13-15.

DIRECTIONS: The management study of employee absence due to sickness is an effective tool in planning. Answer Questions 13 through 15 SOLELY on the data given below.

Number of days absent per worker (sickness)	1	2	3	4	5	6	7	8 or Over
Number of workers	76	23	6	3	1	0	1	0

Total Number of Workers: 400
Period Covered: January 1 - December 31

13. The total number of man days lost due to illness was

    A. 110   B. 137   C. 144   D. 164

13.____

14. What percent of the workers had 4 or more days absence due to sickness?

    A. .25%   B. 2.5%   C. 1.25%   D. 12.5%

14.____

15. Of the 400 workers studied, the number who lost no days due to sickness was

    A. 190   B. 236   C. 290   D. 346

15.____

Questions 16-18.

DIRECTIONS: In the graph below, the lines labeled "A" and "B" represent the cumulative progress in the work of two file clerks, each of whom was given 500 consecutively numbered applications to file in the proper cabinets over a five-day work week. Answer Questions 16 through 18 SOLELY upon the data provided in the graph.

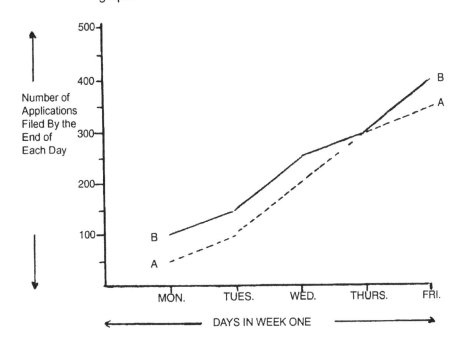

6

16. The day during which the LARGEST number of applications was filed by both clerks was   16.____

    A. Monday   B. Tuesday   C. Wednesday   D. Friday

17. At the end of the second day, the percentage of applications STILL to be filed was   17.____

    A. 25%   B. 50%   C. 66%   D. 75%

18. Assuming that the production pattern is the same the following week as the week shown in the chart, the day on which the file clerks will FINISH this assignment will be   18.____

    A. Monday   B. Tuesday   C. Wednesday   D. Friday

Questions 19-21.

DIRECTIONS: The following chart shows the differences between the rates of production of employees in Department D in 1996 and 2006. Answer Questions 19 through 21 SOLELY on the basis of the information given in the chart.

Number of Employees Producing Work-Units Within Range in 1996	Number of Work-Units Produced	Number of Employees Producing Work-Units Within Range in 2006
7	500 - 1000	4
14	1001 - 1500	11
26	1501 - 2000	28
22	2001 - 2500	36
17	2501 - 3000	39
10	3001 - 3500	23
4	3501 - 4000	9

19. Assuming that within each range of work-units produced the average production was at the mid-point at that range (e.g., category 500 - 1000 = 750), then the AVERAGE number of work-units produced per employee in 1996 fell into the range   19.____

    A. 1001 - 1500   B. 1501 - 2000
    C. 2001 - 2500   D. 2501 - 3000

20. The ratio of the number of employees producing more than 2000 work-units in 1996 to the number of employees producing more than 2000 work-units in 2006 is *most nearly*   20.____

    A. 1:2   B. 2:3   C. 3:4   D. 4:5

21. In Department D, which of the following were GREATER in 2006 than in 1996?   21.____
    I.   Total number of employees
    II. Total number of work-units produced
    III. Number of employees producing 2000 or fewer work-units
The CORRECT answer is:

    A. I, II, III   B. I, II
    C. I, III   D. II, III

22. Unit S's production fluctuated substantially from one year to another. In 2004, Unit S's production was 100% greater than in 2003. In 2005, production decreased by 25% from 2004. In 2006, Unit S's production was 10% greater than in 2005.
On the basis of this information, it is CORRECT to conclude that Unit S's production in 2006 exceeded Unit S's production in 2003 by

22.____

    A. 65%   B. 85%   C. 95%   D. 135%

23. Agency "X" is moving into a new building. It has 1500 employees presently on its staff and does not contemplate much variance from this level. The new building contains 100 available offices, each with a maximum capacity of 30 employees. It has been decided that only 2/3 of the maximum capacity of each office will be utilized. The TOTAL number of offices that will be occupied by Agency "X" is

23.____

    A. 30   B. 66   C. 75   D. 90

24. One typist completes a form letter every 5 minutes and another typist completes one every 6 minutes.
If the two typists start together, they will again start typing new letters simultaneously _____ minutes later and will have completed _____ letters by that time.

24.____

    A. 11; 30   B. 12; 24   C. 24; 12   D. 30; 11

25. During one week, a machine operator produces 10 fewer pages per hour of work than he usually does. If it ordinarily takes him six hours to produce a 300-page report, it will take him____hours LONGER to produce that same 300-page report during the week when he produces MORE slowly.

25.____

    A. $1\frac{1}{2}$ B. $1\frac{2}{3}$ C. 2   D. $2\frac{3}{4}$

KEY (CORRECT ANSWERS)

		Incorrect Words
1.	A	stability
2.	D	obsolete
3.	D	freeze
4.	D	abrogated
5.	C	preclude

6.	C	16.	C
7.	C	17.	D
8.	B	18.	B
9.	A	19.	C
10.	D	20.	A
11.	D	21.	B
12.	C	22.	A
13.	D	23.	C
14.	C	24.	D
15.	C	25.	A

READING COMPREHENSION
UNDERSTANDING AND INTERPRETING WRITTEN MATERIAL
EXAMINATION SECTION
TEST 1

DIRECTIONS: Each question or incomplete statement is followed by several suggested answers or completions. Select the one that BEST answers the question or completes the statement. *PRINT THE LETTER OF THE CORRECT ANSWER IN THE SPACE AT THE RIGHT.*

Questions 1-5.

DIRECTIONS: Questions 1 through 5 are to be answered SOLELY on the basis of the following passage.

The most effective control mechanism to prevent gross incompetence on the part of public employees is a good personnel program. The personnel officer in the line departments and the central personnel agency should exert positive leadership to raise levels of performance. Although the key factor is the quality of the personnel recruited, staff members other than personnel officers can make important contributions to efficiency. Administrative analysts, now employed in many agencies, make detailed studies of organization and procedures, with the purpose of eliminating delays, waste, and other inefficiencies. Efficiency is, however, more than a question of good organization and procedures; it is also the product of the attitudes and values of the public employees. Personal motivation can provide the will to be efficient. The best management studies will not result in substantial improvement of the performance of those employees who feel no great urge to work up to their abilities.

1.   The above passage indicates that the KEY factor in preventing gross incompetence of public employees is the

    A.   hiring of administrative analysts to assist personnel people
    B.   utilization of effective management studies
    C.   overlapping of responsibility
    D.   quality of the employees hired

1.____

2.   According to the above passage, the central personnel agency staff SHOULD

    A.   work more closely with administrative analysts in the line departments than with personnel officers
    B.   make a serious effort to avoid jurisdictional conflicts with personnel officers in line departments
    C.   contribute to improving the quality of work of public employees
    D.   engage in a comprehensive program to change the public's negative image of public employees

2.____

3.   The above passage indicates that efficiency in an organization can BEST be brought about by

    A.   eliminating ineffective control mechanisms
    B.   instituting sound organizational procedures

3.____

    C.   promoting competent personnel
    D.   recruiting people with desire to do good work

4. According to the above passage, the purpose of administrative analysis in a public   4._____
    agency is to

    A.   prevent injustice to the public employee
    B.   promote the efficiency of the agency
    C.   protect the interests of the public
    D.   ensure the observance of procedural due process

5. The above passage implies that a considerable rise in the quality of work of public   5._____
    employees can be brought about by

    A.   encouraging positive employee attitudes toward work
    B.   controlling personnel officers who exceed their powers
    C.   creating warm personal associations among public employees in an agency
    D.   closing loopholes in personnel organization and procedures

Questions 6-8.

DIRECTIONS: Questions 6 through 8 are to be answered SOLELY on the basis of the following passage on Employee Needs.

EMPLOYEE NEEDS

The greatest waste in industry and in government may be that of human resources. This waste usually derives not from employees' unwillingness or inability, but from management's ineptness to meet the maintenance and motivational needs of employees. Maintenance needs refer to such needs as providing employees with safe places to work, written work rules, job security, adequate salary, employer-sponsored social activities, and with knowledge of their role in the overall framework of the organization. However, of greatest significance to employees are the motivational needs of job growth, achievement, responsibility, and recognition.

Although employee dissatisfaction may stem from either poor maintenance or poor motivation factors, the outward manifestation of the dissatisfaction may be very much alike, i.e., negativism, complaints, deterioration of performance, and so forth. The improvement in the lighting of an employee's work area or raising his level of pay won't do much good if the source of the dissatisfaction is the absence of a meaningful assignment. By the same token, if an employee is dissatisfied with what he considers inequitable pay, the introduction of additional challenge in his work may simply make matters worse.

It is relatively easy for an employee to express frustration by complaining about pay, washroom conditions, fringe benefits, and so forth; but most people cannot easily express resentment in terms of the more abstract concepts concerning job growth, responsibility, and achievement.

It would be wrong to assume that there is no interaction between maintenance and motivational needs of employees. For example, conditions of high motivation often overshadow poor maintenance conditions. If an organization is in a period of strong growth and expansion, opportunities for job growth, responsibility, recognition, and achievement are usually abundant, but the rapid growth may have outrun the upkeep of maintenance factors. In this situation, motivation may be high, but only if employees recognize the poor maintenance conditions as unavoidable and temporary. The subordination of maintenance factors cannot go on indefinitely, even with the highest motivation.

Both maintenance and motivation factors influence the behavior of all employees, but employees are not identical and, furthermore, the needs of any individual do not remain constant. However, a broad distinction can be made between employees who have a basic orientation toward maintenance factors and those with greater sensitivity toward motivation factors.

A highly maintenance-oriented individual, preoccupied with the factors peripheral to his job rather than the job itself, is more concerned with comfort than challenge. He does not get deeply involved with his work but does with the condition of his work area, toilet facilities, and his time for going to lunch. By contrast, a strongly motivation-oriented employee is usually relatively indifferent to his surroundings and is caught up in the pursuit of work goals.

Fortunately, there are few people who are either exclusively maintenance-oriented or purely motivation-oriented. The former would be deadwood in an organization, while the latter might trample on those around him in his pursuit to achieve his goals.

6. With respect to employee motivational and maintenance needs, the management policies of an organization which is growing rapidly will probably result   6._____

    A. more in meeting motivational needs rather than maintenance needs
    B. more in meeting maintenance needs rather than motivational needs
    C. in meeting both of these needs equally
    D. in increased effort to define the motivational and maintenance needs of its employees

7. In accordance with the above passage, which of the following CANNOT be considered as an example of an employee maintenance need for railroad clerks?   7._____

    A. Providing more relief periods
    B. Providing fair salary increases at periodic intervals
    C. Increasing job responsibilities
    D. Increasing health insurance benefits

8. Most employees in an organization may be categorized as being interested in   8._____

    A. maintenance needs *only*
    B. motivational needs *only*
    C. both motivational and maintenance needs
    D. money only, to the exclusion of all other needs

Questions 9-11.

DIRECTIONS: Questions 9 through 11 are to be answered SOLELY on the basis of the following passage on Good Employee Practices.

GOOD EMPLOYEE PRACTICES

As a city employee, you will be expected to take an interest in your work and perform the duties of your job to the best of your ability and in a spirit of cooperation. Nothing shows an interest in your work more than coming to work on time, not only at the start of the day but also when returning from lunch. If it is necessary for you to keep a personal appointment at lunch hour which might cause a delay in getting back to work on time, you should explain the situation to your supervisor and get his approval to come back a little late before you leave for lunch.

You should do everything that is asked of you willingly and consider important even the small jobs that your supervisor gives you. Although these jobs may seem unimportant, if you forget to do them or if you don't do them right, trouble may develop later.

Getting along well with your fellow workers will add much to the enjoyment of your work. You should respect your fellow workers and try to see their side when a disagreement arises. The better you get along with your fellow workers and your supervisor, the better you will like your job and the better you will be able to do it.

9. According to the above passage, in your job as a city employee, you are expected to   9._____

    A.   show a willingness to cooperate on the job
    B.   get your supervisor's approval before keeping any personal appointments at lunch hour
    C.   avoid doing small jobs that seem unimportant
    D.   do the easier jobs at the start of the day and the more difficult ones later on

10. According to the above passage, getting to work on time shows that you   10._____

    A.   need the job
    B.   have an interest in your work
    C.   get along well with your fellow workers
    D.   like your supervisor

11. According to the above passage, the one of the following statements that is NOT true is   11._____

    A.   if you do a small job wrong, trouble may develop
    B.   you should respect your fellow workers
    C.   if you disagree with a fellow worker, you should try to see his side of the story
    D.   the less you get along with your supervisor, the better you will be able to do your job

Questions 12-15.

DIRECTIONS: Questions 12 through 15 are to be answered SOLELY on the basis of the following passage on Employee Suggestions.

EMPLOYEE SUGGESTIONS

To increase the effectiveness of the city government, the city asks its employees to offer suggestions when they feel an improvement could be made in some government operation. The Employees' Suggestions Program was started to encourage city employees to do this.

Through this Program, which is only for city employees, cash awards may be given to those whose suggestions are submitted and approved. Suggestions are looked for not only from supervisors but from all city employees as any city employee may get an idea which might be approved and contribute greatly to the solution of some problem of city government

Therefore, all suggestions for improvement are welcome, whether they be suggestions on how to improve working conditions, or on how to increase the speed with which work is done, or on how to reduce or eliminate such things as waste, time losses, accidents or fire hazards. There are, however, a few types of suggestions for which cash awards cannot be given. An example of this type would be a suggestion to increase salaries or a suggestion to change the regulations about annual leave or about sick leave. The number of suggestions sent in has increased sharply during the past few years. It is hoped that it will keep increasing in the future in order to meet the city's needs for more ideas for improved ways of doing things.

12. According to the above passage, the MAIN reason why the city asks its employees for suggestions about government operations is to

    A. increase the effectiveness of the city government
    B. show that the Employees' Suggestion Program is working well
    C. show that everybody helps run the city government
    D. have the employee win a prize

12.____

13. According to the above passage, the Employees' Suggestion Program can approve awards ONLY for those suggestions that come from

    A. city employees
    B. city employees who are supervisors
    C. city employees who are not supervisors
    D. experienced employees of the city

13.____

14. According to the above passage, a cash award cannot be given through the Employees' Suggestion Program for a suggestion about

    A. getting work done faster
    B. helping prevent accidents on the job
    C. increasing the amount of annual leave for city employees
    D. reducing the chance of fire where city employees work

14.____

15. According to the above passage, the suggestions sent in during the past few years have

    A. all been approved
    B. generally been well written
    C. been mostly about reducing or eliminating waste
    D. been greater in number than before

15.____

Questions 16-18.

DIRECTIONS: Questions 16 through 18 are to be answered SOLELY on the basis of the following passage.

The supervisor will gain the respect of the members of his staff and increase his influence over them by controlling his temper and avoiding criticizing anyone publicly. When a mistake is made, the good supervisor will talk it over with the employee quietly and privately. The supervisor will listen to the employee's story, suggest the better way of doing the job, and offer help so the mistake won't happen again. Before closing the discussion, the supervisor should try to find something good to say about other parts of the employee's work. Some praise and appreciation, along with instruction, is more likely to encourage an employee to improve in those areas where he is weakest.

16. A good title that would show the meaning of the above passage would be   16._____

    A.   HOW TO CORRECT EMPLOYEE ERRORS
    B.   HOW TO PRAISE EMPLOYEES
    C.   MISTAKES ARE PREVENTABLE
    D.   THE WEAK EMPLOYEE

17. According to the above passage, the work of an employee who has made a mistake is   17._____
more likely to improve if the supervisor

    A.   avoids criticizing him
    B.   gives him a chance to suggest a better way of doing the work
    C.   listens to the employee's excuses to see if he is right
    D.   praises good work at the same time he corrects the mistake

18. According to the above passage, when a supervisor needs to correct an employee's mis-   18._____
take, it is important that he

    A.   allow some time to go by after the mistake is made
    B.   do so when other employees are not present
    C.   show his influence with his tone of voice
    D.   tell other employees to avoid the same mistake

Questions 19-23.

DIRECTIONS: Questions 19 through 23 are to be answered SOLELY on the basis of the following passage.

In studying the relationships of people to the organizational structure, it is absolutely nec-essary to identify and recognize the informal organizational structure. These relationships are necessary when coordination of a plan is attempted. They may be with *the boss,* line supervi-sors, staff personnel, or other representatives of the formal organization's hierarchy, and they may include the *liaison men* who serve as the leaders of the informal organization. An acquaintanceship with the people serving in these roles in the organization, and its formal counterpart, permits a supervisor to recognize sensitive areas in which it is simple to get a conflict reaction. Avoidance of such areas, plus conscious efforts to inform other people of his own objectives for various plans, will usually enlist their aid and support. Planning *without people* can lead to disaster because the individuals who must act together to make any plan a success are more important than the plans themselves.

19. Of the following titles, the one that MOST clearly describes the above passage is   19._____

    A.   COORDINATION OF A FUNCTION
    B.   AVOIDANCE OF CONFLICT
    C.   PLANNING WITH PEOPLE
    D.   PLANNING OBJECTIVES

20. According to the above passage, attempts at coordinating plans may fail unless   20.____

    A. the plan's objectives are clearly set forth
    B. conflict between groups is resolved
    C. the plans themselves are worthwhile
    D. informal relationships are recognized

21. According to the above passage, conflict   21.____

    A. may, in some cases, be desirable to secure results
    B. produces more heat than light
    C. should be avoided at all costs
    D. possibilities can be predicted by a sensitive supervisor

22. The above passage implies that   22.____

    A. informal relationships are more important than formal structure
    B. the weakness of a formal structure depends upon informal relationships
    C. liaison men are the key people to consult when taking formal and informal structures into account
    D. individuals in a group are at least as important as the plans for the group

23. The above passage suggests that   23.____

    A. some planning can be disastrous
    B. certain people in sensitive areas should be avoided
    C. the supervisor should discourage acquaintanceships in the organization
    D. organizational relationships should be consciously limited

Questions 24-25.

DIRECTIONS: Questions 24 and 25 are to be answered SOLELY on the basis of the following passage.

    Good personnel relations of an organization depend upon mutual confidence, trust, and good will. The basis of confidence is understanding. Most troubles start with people who do not understand each other. When the organization's intentions or motives are misunderstood, or when reasons for actions, practices, or policies are misconstrued, complete cooperation from individuals is not forthcoming. If management expects full cooperation from employees, it has a responsibility of sharing with them the information which is the foundation of proper understanding, confidence, and trust. Personnel management has long since outgrown the days when it was the vogue to *treat them rough and tell them nothing.* Up-to-date personnel management provides all possible information about the activities, aims, and purposes of the organization. It seems altogether creditable that a desire should exist among employees for such information which the best-intentioned executive might think would not interest them and which the worst-intentioned would think was none of their business.

24. The above passage implies that one of the causes of the difficulty which an organization   24.____
might have with its personnel relations is that its employees

    A. have not expressed interest in the activities, aims, and purposes of the organization
    B. do not believe in the good faith of the organization

C. have not been able to give full cooperation to the organization
D. do not recommend improvements in the practices and policies of the organization

25. According to the above passage, in order for an organization to have good personnel relations, it is NOT essential that   25.____

A. employees have confidence in the organization
B. the purposes of the organization be understood by the employees
C. employees have a desire for information about the organization
D. information about the organization be communicated to employees

---

KEY (CORRECT ANSWERS)

1. D		11. D	
2. C		12. A	
3. D		13. A	
4. B		14. C	
5. A		15. D	
6. A		16. A	
7. C		17. D	
8. C		18. B	
9. A		19. C	
10. B		20. D	

21. D
22. D
23. A
24. B
25. C

TEST 2

Questions 1-8.

DIRECTIONS: Questions 1 through 8 are to be answered SOLELY on the basis of the following passage.

Important figures in education and in public affairs have recommended development of a private organization sponsored in part by various private foundations which would offer installment payment plans to full-time matriculated students in accredited colleges and universities in the United States and Canada. Contracts would be drawn to cover either tuition and fees, or tuition, fees, room and board in college facilities, from one year up to and including six years. A special charge, which would vary with the length of the contract, would be added to the gross repayable amount. This would be in addition to interest at a rate which would vary with the income of the parents. There would be a 3% annual interest charge for families with total income, before income taxes, of $50,000 or less. The rate would increase by 1/10 of 1% for every $1,000 of additional net income in excess of $50,000 up to a maximum of 10% interest. Contracts would carry an insurance provision on the life of the parent or guardian who signs the contract; all contracts must have the signature of a parent or guardian. Payment would be scheduled in equal monthly installments.

1. Which of the following students would be eligible for the payment plan described in the above passage? A

    A. matriculated student taking six semester hours toward a graduate degree
    B. matriculated student taking seventeen semester hours toward an undergraduate degree
    C. graduate matriculated at the University of Mexico taking eighteen semester hours toward a graduate degree
    D. student taking eighteen semester hours in a special pre-matriculation program

1.____

2. According to the above passage, the organization described would be sponsored in part by

    A. private foundations
    B. colleges and universities
    C. persons in the field of education
    D. persons in public life

2.____

3. Which of the following expenses could NOT be covered by a contract with the organization described in the above passage?

    A. Tuition amounting to $20,000 per year
    B. Registration and laboratory fees
    C. Meals at restaurants near the college
    D. Rent for an apartment in a college dormitory

3.____

4. The total amount to be paid would include ONLY the

    A. principal
    B. principal and interest
    C. principal, interest, and special charge
    D. principal, interest, special charge, and fee

4.____

5. The contract would carry insurance on the   5._____

    A. life of the student
    B. life of the student's parents
    C. income of the parents of the student
    D. life of the parent who signed the contract

6. The interest rate for an annual loan of $25,000 from the organization described in the   6._____
    above passage for a student whose family's net income was $55,000 should be

    A. 3%   B. 3.5%   C. 4%   D. 4.5%

7. The interest rate for an annual loan of $35,000 from the organization described in the   7._____
    above passage for a student whose family's net income was $100,000 should be

    A. 5%   B. 8%   C. 9%   D. 10%

8. John Lee has submitted an application for the installment payment plan described in the   8._____
    above passage. John's mother and father have a store which grossed $500,000 last
    year, but the income which the family received from the store was $90,000 before taxes.
    They also had $5,000 income from stock dividends. They paid $10,000 in income taxes.
    The amount of income upon which the interest should be based is

    A. $85,000   B. $90,000   C. $95,000   D. $105,000

Questions 9-13.

DIRECTIONS: Questions 9 through 13 are to be answered SOLELY on the basis of the follow-
              ing passage.

    Since an organization chart is pictorial in nature, there is a tendency for it to be drawn in
an artistically balanced and appealing fashion, regardless of the realities of actual organizational structure. In addition to being subject to this distortion, there is the difficulty of commu-
nicating in any organization chart the relative importance or the relative size of various
component parts of an organizational structure. Furthermore, because of the need for sim-
plicity of design, an organization chart can never indicate the full extent of the interrelation-
ships among the component parts of an organization.

    These interrelationships are often just as vital as the specifications which an organization
chart endeavors to indicate. Yet, if an organization chart were to be drawn with all the wide
variety of criss-crossing communication and cooperation networks existent within a typical
organization, the chart would probably be much more confusing than informative. It is also
obvious that no organization chart as such can prove or disprove that the organizational
structure it represents is effective in realizing the objectives of the organization. At best, an
organization chart can only illustrate some of the various factors to be taken into consideration in understanding, devising, or altering organizational arrangements.

9. According to the above passage, an organization chart can be expected to portray the   9._____

    A. structure of the organization along somewhat ideal lines
    B. relative size of the organizational units quite accurately
    C. channels of information distribution within the organization graphically
    D. extent of the obligation of each unit to meet the organizational objectives

10. According to the above passage, those aspects of internal functioning which are NOT   10._____
    shown on an organization chart

    A. can be considered to have little practical application in the operations of the organization

    B. might well be considered to be as important as the structural relationships which a chart does present

    C. could be the cause of considerable confusion in the operations of an organization which is quite large

    D. would be most likely to provide the information needed to determine the overall effectiveness of an organization

11. In the above passage, the one of the following conditions which is NOT implied as being   11._____
    a defect of an organization chart is that an organization chart may

    A. present a picture of the organizational structure which is different from the structure that actually exists

    B. fail to indicate the comparative size of various organizational units

    C. be limited in its ability to convey some of the meaningful aspects of organizational relationships

    D. become less useful over a period of time during which the organizational facts which it illustrated have changed

12. The one of the following which is the MOST suitable title for the above passage is   12._____

    A. THE DESIGN AND CONSTRUCTION OF AN ORGANIZATION CHART
    B. THE INFORMAL ASPECTS OF AN ORGANIZATION CHART
    C. THE INHERENT DEFICIENCIES OF AN ORGANIZATION CHART
    D. THE UTILIZATION OF A TYPICAL ORGANIZATION CHART

13. It can be INFERRED from the above passage that the function of an organization chart is   13._____
    to

    A. contribute to the comprehension of the organization form and arrangements
    B. establish the capabilities of the organization to operate effectively
    C. provide a balanced picture of the operations of the organization
    D. eliminate the need for complexity in the organization's structure

Questions 14-16.

DIRECTIONS: Questions 14 through 16 are to be answered SOLELY on the basis of the following passage.

    In dealing with visitors to the school office, the school secretary must use initiative, tact, and good judgment. All visitors should be greeted promptly and courteously. The nature of their business should be determined quickly and handled expeditiously. Frequently, the secretary should be able to handle requests, receipts, deliveries, or passes herself. Her judgment should determine when a visitor should see members of the staff or the principal. Serious problems or doubtful cases should be referred to a supervisor.

14. In general, visitors should be handled by the   14.____

    A. school secretary   B. principal
    C. appropriate supervisor   D. person who is free

15. It is wise to obtain the following information from visitors: 15.____

    A. Name   B. Nature of business
    C. Address   D. Problems they have

16. All visitors who wish to see members of the staff should   16.____

    A. be permitted to do so
    B. produce identification
    C. do so for valid reasons only
    D. be processed by a supervisor

Questions 17-19.

DIRECTIONS: Questions 17 through 19 are to be answered SOLELY on the basis of the following passage.

Information regarding payroll status, salary differentials, promotional salary increments, deductions, and pension payments should be given to all members of the staff who have questions regarding these items. On occasion, if the secretary is uncertain regarding the information, the staff member should be referred to the principal or the appropriate agency. No question by a staff member regarding payroll status should be brushed aside as immaterial or irrelevant. The school secretary must always try to handle the question or pass it on to the person who can handle it.

17. If a teacher is dissatisfied with information regarding her salary status, as given by the   17.____
school secretary, the matter should be

    A. dropped
    B. passed on to the principal
    C. passed on by the secretary to proper agency or the principal
    D. made a basis for grievance procedures

18. The following is an adequate summary of the above passage: 18.____

    A. The secretary must handle all payroll matters
    B. The secretary must handle all payroll matters or know who can handle them
    C. The secretary or the principal must handle all payroll matters
    D. Payroll matters too difficult to handle must be followed up until they are solved

19. The above passage implies that   19.____

    A. many teachers ask immaterial questions regarding payroll status
    B. few teachers ask irrelevant pension questions
    C. no teachers ask immaterial salary questions
    D. no question regarding salary should be considered irrelevant

Questions 20-22:

DIRECTIONS: Questions 20 through 22 are to be answered SOLELY on the basis of the following passage.

The necessity for good speech on the part of the school secretary cannot be overstated. The school secretary must deal with the general public, the pupils, the members of the staff, and the school supervisors. In every situation which involves the general public, the secretary serves as a representative of the school. In dealing with pupils, the secretary's speech must serve as a model from which students may guide themselves. Slang, colloquialisms, malapropisms, and local dialects must be avoided.

20. The above passage implies that the speech pattern of the secretary must be

    A. perfect
    B. very good
    C. average
    D. on a level with that of the pupils

20._____

21. The last sentence indicates that slang

    A. is acceptable
    B. occurs in all speech
    C. might be used occasionally
    D. should be shunned

21._____

22. The above passage implies that the speech of pupils

    A. may be influenced   B. does not change readily
    C. is generally good   D. is generally poor

22._____

Questions 23-25.

DIRECTIONS: Questions 23 through 25 are to be answered SOLELY on the basis of the following passage.

The school secretary who is engaged in the task of filing records and correspondence should follow a general set of rules. Items which are filed should be available to other secretaries or to supervisors quickly and easily by means of the application of a modicum of common sense and good judgment. Items which, by their nature, may be difficult to find should be cross-indexed. Folders and drawers should be neatly and accurately labeled. There should never be a large accumulation of papers which have not been filed.

23. A good general rule to follow in filing is that materials should be

    A. placed in folders quickly
    B. neatly stored
    C. readily available
    D. cross-indexed

23._____

24. Items that are filed should be available to

    A. the secretary charged with the task of filing
    B. secretaries and supervisors
    C. school personnel
    D. the principal

24._____

25. A modicum of common sense means _____ common sense.

    A. an average amount of   B. a great deal of
    C. a little   D. no

25.____

KEY (CORRECT ANSWERS)

1.	B		11.	D
2.	A		12.	C
3.	C		13.	A
4.	C		14.	A
5.	D		15.	B
6.	B		16.	C
7.	B		17.	C
8.	C		18.	B
9.	A		19.	D
10.	B		20.	B

21.	D
22.	A
23.	C
24.	B
25.	C

TEST 3

Questions 1-4.

DIRECTIONS: Questions 1 through 4 are to be answered SOLELY on the basis of the following passage.

The proposition that administrative activity is essentially the same in all organizations appears to underlie some of the practices in the administration of private higher education. Although the practice is unusual in public education, there are numerous instances of industrial, governmental, or military administrators being assigned to private institutions of higher education and, to a lesser extent, of college and university presidents assuming administrative positions in other types of organizations. To test this theory that administrators are interchangeable, there is a need for systematic observation and classification. The myth that an educational administrator must first have experience in the teaching profession is firmly rooted in a long tradition that has historical prestige. The myth is bound up in the expectations of the public and personnel surrounding the administrator. Since administrative success depends significantly on how well an administrator meets the expectations others have of him, the myth may be more powerful than the special experience in helping the administrator attain organizational and educational objectives. Educational administrators who have risen through the teaching profession have often expressed nostalgia for the life of a teacher or scholar, but there is no evidence that this nostalgia contributes to administrative success

1. Which of the following statements as completed is MOST consistent with the above passage? The greatest number of administrators has moved from   1.____

   A. industry and the military to government and universities
   B. government and universities to industry and the military
   C. government, the armed forces, and industry to colleges and universities
   D. colleges and universities to government, the armed forces, and industry

2. Of the following, the MOST reasonable inference from the above passage is that a specific area requiring further research is the   2.____

   A. place of myth in the tradition and history of the educational profession
   B. relative effectiveness of educational administrators from inside and outside the teaching profession
   C. performance of administrators in the administration of public colleges
   D. degree of reality behind the nostalgia for scholarly pursuits often expressed by educational administrators

3. According to the above passage, the value to an educational administrator of experience in the teaching profession   3.____

   A. lies in the firsthand knowledge he has acquired of immediate educational problems
   B. may lie in the belief of his colleagues, subordinates, and the public that such experience is necessary
   C. has been supported by evidence that the experience contributes to administrative success in educational fields
   D. would be greater if the administrator were able to free himself from nostalgia for his former duties

4. Of the following, the MOST suitable title for the above passage is   4.____
   A. EDUCATIONAL ADMINISTRATION, ITS PROBLEMS
   B. THE EXPERIENCE NEEDED FOR EDUCATIONAL ADMINISTRATION
   C. ADMINISTRATION IN HIGHER EDUCATION
   D. EVALUATING ADMINISTRATIVE EXPERIENCE

Questions 5-6.

DIRECTIONS: Questions 5 and 6 are to be answered SOLELY on the basis of the following
              passage.

Management by objectives (MBO) may be defined as the process by which the superior
and the subordinate managers of an organization jointly define its common goals, define
each individual's major areas of responsibility in terms of the results expected of him and use
these measures as guides for operating the unit and assessing the contribution of each of its
members.

The MBO approach requires that after organizational goals are established and communicated, targets must be set for each individual position which are congruent with organizational goals. Periodic performance reviews and a final review using the objectives set as
criteria are also basic to this approach.

Recent studies have shown that MBO programs are influenced by attitudes and percep-
tions of the boss, the company, the reward-punishment system, and the program itself. In
addition, the manner in which the MBO program is carried out can influence the success of
the program. A study done in the late sixties indicates that the best results are obtained when
the manager sets goals which deal with significant problem areas in the organizational unit,
or with the subordinate's personal deficiencies. These goals must be clear with regard to
what is expected of the subordinate. The frequency of feedback is also important in the success of a management-by-objectives program. Generally, the greater the amount of feedback, the more successful the MBO program.

5. According to the above passage, the expected output for individual employees should be   5.____
   determined

   A. after a number of reviews of work performance
   B. after common organizational goals are defined
   C. before common organizational goals are defined
   D. on the basis of an employee's personal qualities

6. According to the above passage, the management-by-objectives approach requires   6.____

   A. less feedback than other types of management programs
   B. little review of on-the-job performance after the initial setting of goals
   C. general conformance between individual goals and organizational goals
   D. the setting of goals which deal with minor problem areas in the organization

Questions 7-10.

DIRECTIONS: Questions 7 through 10 are to be answered SOLELY on the basis of the follow-
              ing passage.

Management, which is the function of executive leadership, has as its principal phases the planning, organizing, and controlling of the activities of subordinate groups in the accomplishment of organizational objectives. Planning specifies the kind and extent of the factors, forces, and effects, and the relationships among them, that will be required for satisfactory accomplishment. The nature of the objectives and their requirements must be known before determinations can be made as to what must be done, how it must be done and why, where actions should take place, who should be responsible, and similar problems pertaining to the formulation of a plan. Organizing, which creates the conditions that must be present before the execution of the plan can be undertaken successfully, cannot be done intelligently without knowledge of the organizational objectives. Control, which has to do with the constraint and regulation of activities entering into the execution of the plan, must be exercised in accordance with the characteristics and requirements of the activities demanded by the plan.

7. The one of the following which is the MOST suitable title for the above passage is   7._____

    A. THE NATURE OF SUCCESSFUL ORGANIZATION
    B. THE PLANNING OF MANAGEMENT FUNCTIONS
    C. THE IMPORTANCE OF ORGANIZATIONAL FUNCTIONS
    D. THE PRINCIPLE ASPECTS OF MANAGEMENT

8. It can be inferred from the above passage that the one of the following functions whose   8._____
   existence is essential to the existence of the other three is the

    A. regulation of the work needed to carry out a plan
    B. understanding of what the organization intends to accomplish
    C. securing of information of the factors necessary for accomplishment of objectives
    D. establishment of the conditions required for successful action

9. The one of the following which would NOT be included within any of the principal phases   9._____
   of the function of executive leadership as defined in the above passage is

    A. determination of manpower requirements
    B. procurement of required material
    C. establishment of organizational objectives
    D. scheduling of production

10. The conclusion which can MOST reasonably be drawn from the above passage is that   10._____
    the control phase of managing is most directly concerned with the

    A. influencing of policy determinations
    B. administering of suggestion systems
    C. acquisition of staff for the organization
    D. implementation of performance standards

Questions 11-12.

DIRECTIONS: Questions 11 and 12 are to be answered SOLELY on the basis of the following
              passage.

Under an open-and-above-board policy, it is to be expected that some supervisors will gloss over known shortcomings of subordinates rather than face the task of discussing them face-to-face. It is also to be expected that at least some employees whose job performance is below par will reject the supervisor's appraisal as biased and unfair. Be that as it may, these are inescapable aspects of any performance appraisal system in which human beings are involved. The supervisor who shies away from calling a spade a spade, as well as the employee with a chip on his shoulder, will each in his own way eventually be revealed in his true light--to the benefit of the organization as a whole.

11. The BEST of the following interpretations of the above passage is that 11._____

    A. the method of rating employee performance requires immediate revision to improve employee acceptance
    B. substandard performance ratings should be discussed with employees even if satisfactory ratings are not
    C. supervisors run the risk of being called unfair by their subordinates even though their appraisals are accurate
    D. any system of employee performance rating is satisfactory if used properly

12. The BEST of the following interpretations of the above passage is that 12._____

    A. supervisors generally are not open-and-above-board with their subordinates
    B. it is necessary for supervisors to tell employees objectively how they are performing
    C. employees complain when their supervisor does not keep them informed
    D. supervisors are afraid to tell subordinates their weaknesses

Questions 13-15.

DIRECTIONS: Questions 13 through 15 are to be answered SOLELY on the basis of the following passage.

During the last decade, a great deal of interest has been generated around the phenomenon of *organizational development,* or the process of developing human resources through conscious organization effort. Organizational development (OD) stresses improving interpersonal relationships and organizational skills, such as communication, to a much greater degree than individual training ever did. The kind of training that an organization should emphasize depends upon the present and future structure of the organization. If future organizations are to be unstable, shifting coalitions, then individual skills and abilities, particularly those emphasizing innovativeness, creativity, flexibility, and the latest technological knowledge, are crucial and individual training is most appropriate.

But if there is to be little change in organizational structure, then the main thrust of training should be group-oriented or organizational development. This approach seems better designed for overcoming hierarchical barriers, for developing a degree of interpersonal relationships which make communication along the chain of command possible, and for retaining a modicum of innovation and/or flexibility.

13. According to the above passage, group-oriented training is MOST useful in 13._____

    A. developing a communications system that will facilitate understanding through the chain of command
    B. highly flexible and mobile organizations
    C. preventing the crossing of hierarchical barriers within an organization
    D. saving energy otherwise wasted on developing methods of dealing with rigid hierarchies

14. The one of the following conclusions which can be drawn MOST appropriately from the above passage is that   14.____

    A. behavioral research supports the use of organizational development training methods rather than individualized training
    B. it is easier to provide individualized training in specific skills than to set up sensitivity training programs
    C. organizational development eliminates innovative or flexible activity
    D. the nature of an organization greatly influences which training methods will be most effective

15. According to the above passage, the one of the following which is LEAST important for large-scale organizations geared to rapid and abrupt change is   15.____

    A. current technological information
    B. development of a high degree of interpersonal relationships
    C. development of individual skills and abilities
    D. emphasis on creativity

Questions 16-18.

DIRECTIONS: Questions 16 through 18 are to be answered SOLELY on the basis of the following passage.

The increase in the extent to which each individual is personally responsible to others is most noticeable in a large bureaucracy. No one person *decides* anything; each decision of any importance, is the product of an intricate process of brokerage involving individuals inside and outside the organization who feel some reason to be affected by the decision, or who have special knowledge to contribute to it. The more varied the organization's constituency, the more outside *veto-groups* will need to be taken into account. But even if no outside consultations were involved, sheer size would produce a complex process of decision. For a large organization is a deliberately created system of tensions into which each individual is expected to bring work-ways, viewpoints, and outside relationships markedly different from those of his colleagues. It is the administrator's task to draw from these disparate forces the elements of wise action from day to day, consistent with the purposes of the organization as a whole.

16. The above passage is essentially a description of decision making as   16.____

    A. an organization process
    B. the key responsibility of the administrator
    C. the one best position among many
    D. a complex of individual decisions

17. Which one of the following statements BEST describes the responsibilities of an administrator?   17.____

    A. He modifies decisions and goals in accordance with pressures from within and outside the organization.
    B. He creates problem-solving mechanisms that rely on the varied interests of his staff and *veto-groups.*
    C. He makes determinations that will lead to attainment of his agency's objectives.
    D. He obtains agreement among varying viewpoints and interests.

18. In the context of the operations of a central public personnel agency, a *veto group* would LEAST likely consist of   18.____

   A. employee organizations
   B. professional personnel societies
   C. using agencies
   D. civil service newspapers

Questions 19-25.

DIRECTIONS: Questions 19 through 25 are to be answered SOLELY on the basis of the following passage, which is an extract from a report prepared for Department X, which outlines the procedure to be followed in the case of transfers of employees.

Every transfer, regardless of the reason therefore, requires completion of the record of transfer, Form DT 411. To denote consent to the transfer, DT 411 should contain the signatures of the transferee and the personnel officer(s) concerned, except that, in the case of an involuntary transfer, the signatures of the transferee's present and prospective supervisors shall be entered in Boxes 8A and 8B, respectively, since the transferee does not consent. Only a permanent employee may request a transfer; in such cases, the employee's attendance record shall be duly considered with regard to absences, latenesses, and accrued overtime balances. In the case of an inter-district transfer, the employee's attendance record must be included in Section 8A of the transfer request, Form DT 410, by the personnel officer of the district from which the transfer is requested. The personnel officer of the district to which the employee requested transfer may refuse to accept accrued overtime balances in excess of ten days.

An employee on probation shall be eligible for transfer. If such employee is involuntarily transferred, he shall be credited for the period of time already served on probation. However, if such transfer is voluntary, the employee shall be required to serve the entire period of his probation in the new position. An employee who has occurred a disability which prevents him from performing his normal duties may be transferred during the period of such disability to other appropriate duties. A disability transfer requires the completion of either Form DT 414 if the disability is job-connected, or Form DT 415 if it is not a job-connected disability. In either case, the personnel officer of the district from which the transfer is made signs in Box 6A of the first two copies and the personnel officer of the district to which the transfer is made signs in Box 6B of the last two copies, or, in the case of an intra-district disability transfer, the personnel officer must sign in Box 6A of the first two copies and Box 6B of the last two copies.

19. When a personnel officer consents to an employee's request for transfer from his district, this procedure requires that the personnel officer sign Form(s)   19.____

   A. DT 411
   B. DT 410 and DT 411
   C. DT 411 and either Form DT 414 or DT 415
   D. DT 410 and DT 411, and either Form DT 414 or DT 415

20. With respect to the time record of an employee transferred against his wishes during his probationary period, this procedure requires that   20.____

   A. he serve the entire period of his probation in his present office
   B. he lose his accrued overtime balance

C. his attendance record be considered with regard to absences and latenesses
D. he be given credit for the period of time he has already served on probation

21. Assume you are a supervisor and an employee must be transferred into your office
against his wishes. According to the this procedure, the box you must sign on the record
of transfer is

    A. 6A   B. 8A   C. 6B   D. 8B

21.____

22. Under this procedure, in the case of a disability transfer, when must Box 6A on Forms DT
414 and DT 415 be signed by the personnel officer of the district to which the transfer is
being made?

    A. In all cases when either Form DT 414 or Form DT 415 is used
    B. In all cases when Form DT 414 is used and only under certain circumstances
       when Form DT 415 is used
    C. In all cases when Form DT 415 is used and only under certain circumstances
       when Form DT 414 is used
    D. Only under certain circumstances when either Form DT 414 or Form DT 415 is
       used

22.____

23. From the above passage, it may be inferred MOST correctly that the number of copies of
Form DT 414 is

    A. no more than 2
    B. at least 3
    C. at least 5
    D. more than the number of copies of Form DT 415

23.____

24. A change in punctuation and capitalization only which would change one sentence into
two and possibly contribute to somewhat greater ease of reading this report extract
would be MOST appropriate in the

    A. 2nd sentence, 1st paragraph
    B. 3rd sentence, 1st paragraph
    C. next to he last sentence, 2nd paragraph
    D. 2nd sentence, 2nd paragraph

24.____

25. In the second paragraph, a word that is INCORRECTLY used is

    A. *shall* in the 1st sentence
    B. *voluntary* in the 3rd sentence
    C. *occurred* in the 4th sentence
    D. *intra-district* in the last sentence

25.____

KEY (CORRECT ANSWERS)

1. C	11. C
2. B	12. B
3. B	13. A
4. B	14. D
5. B	15. B
6. C	16. A
7. D	17. C
8. B	18. B
9. C	19. A
10. D	20. D

21. D
22. D
23. B
24. B
25. C

PREPARING WRITTEN MATERIAL

PARAGRAPH REARRANGEMENT
COMMENTARY

The sentences which follow are in scrambled order. You are to rearrange them in proper order and indicate the letter choice containing the correct answer at the space at the right.

Each group of sentences in this section is actually a paragraph presented in scrambled order. Each sentence in the group has a place in that paragraph; no sentence is to be left out. You are to read each group of sentences and decide upon the best order in which to put the sentences so as to form as well-organized paragraph.

The questions in this section measure the ability to solve a problem when all the facts relevant to its solution are not given.

More specifically, certain positions of responsibility and authority require the employee to discover connections between events sometimes, apparently, unrelated. In order to do this, the employee will find it necessary to correctly infer that unspecified events have probably occurred or are likely to occur. This ability becomes especially important when action must be taken on incomplete information.

Accordingly, these questions require competitors to choose among several suggested alternatives, each of which presents a different sequential arrangement of the events. Competitors must choose the MOST logical of the suggested sequences.

In order to do so, they may be required to draw on general knowledge to infer missing concepts or events that are essential to sequencing the given events. Competitors should be careful to infer only what is essential to the sequence. The plausibility of the wrong alternatives will always require the inclusion of unlikely events or of additional chains of events which are NOT essential to sequencing the given events.

It's very important to remember that you are looking for the best of the four possible choices, and that the best choice of all may not even be one of the answers you're given to choose from.

There is no one right way to solve these problems. Many people have found it helpful to first write out the order of the sentences, as they would have arranged them, on their scrap paper before looking at the possible answers. If their optimum answer is there, this can save them some time. If it isn't, this method can still give insight into solving the problem. Others find it most helpful to just go through each of the possible choices, contrasting each as they go along. You should use whatever method feels comfortable, and works, for you.

While most of these types of questions are not that difficult, we've added a higher percentage of the difficult type, just to give you more practice. Usually there are only one or two questions on this section that contain such subtle distinctions that you're unable to answer confidently, and you then may find yourself stuck deciding between two possible choices, neither of which you're sure about.

EXAMINATION SECTION
TEST 1

DIRECTIONS: The following groups of sentences need to be arranged in an order that makes sense. Select the letter preceding the sequence that represents the BEST sentence order. *PRINT THE LETTER OF THE CORRECT ANSWER IN THE SPACE AT THE RIGHT.*

1. I. The keyboard was purposely designed to be a little awkward to slow typists down.
   II. The arrangement of letters on the keyboard of a typewriter was not designed for the convenience of the typist.
   III. Fortunately, no one is suggesting that a new keyboard be designed right away.
   IV. If one were, we would have to learn to type all over again.
   V. The reason was that the early machines were slower than the typists and would jam easily.

   A. I, III, IV, II, V   B. II, V, I, IV, III
   C. V, I, II, III, IV   D. II, I, V, III, IV

   1.____

2. I. The majority of the new service jobs are part-time or low-paying.
   II. According to the U.S. Bureau of Labor Statistics, jobs in the service sector constitute 72% of all jobs in this country.
   III. If more and more workers receive less and less money, who will buy the goods and services needed to keep the economy going?
   IV. The service sector is by far the fastest growing part of the United States economy.
   V. Some economists look upon this trend with great concern.

   A. II, IV, I, V, III   B. II, III, IV, I, V
   C. V, IV, II, III, I   D. III, I, II, IV, V

   2.____

3. I. They can also affect one's endurance.
   II. This can stabilize blood sugar levels, and ensure that the brain is receiving a steady, constant supply of glucose, so that one is *hitting on all cylinders* while taking the test.
   III. By food, we mean real food, not junk food or unhealthy snacks.
   IV. For this reason, it is important not to skip a meal, and to bring food with you to the exam.
   V. One's blood sugar levels can affect how clearly one is able to think and concentrate during an exam.

   A. V, IV, II, III, I   B. V, II, I, IV, III
   C. V, I, IV, III, II   D. V, IV, I, III, II

   3.____

4. I. Those who are the embodiment of desire are absorbed in material quests, and those who are the embodiment of feeling are warriors who value power more than possession.
   II. These qualities are in everyone, but in different degrees.
   III. But those who value understanding yearn not for goods or victory, but for knowledge.
   IV. According to Plato, human behavior flows from three main sources: desire, emotion, and knowledge,

   4.____

V. In the perfect state, the industrial forces would produce but not rule, the military would protect but not rule, and the forces of knowledge, the philosopher kings, would reign.

A. IV, V, I, II, III   B. V, I, II, III, IV
C. IV, III, II, I, V   D. IV, II, I, III, V

5.   I. Of the more than 26,000 tons of garbage produced daily in New York City, 12,000 tons arrive daily at Fresh Kills.
     II. In a month, enough garbage accumulates there to fill the Empire State Building.
     III. In 1937, the Supreme Court halted the practice of dumping the trash of New York City into the sea.
     IV. Although the garbage is compacted, in a few years the mounds of garbage at Fresh Kills will be the highest points south of Maine's Mount Desert Island on the Eastern Seaboard.
     V. Instead, tugboats now pull barges of much of the trash to Staten Island and the largest landfill in the world, Fresh Kills.

5.____

A. III, V, IV, I, II   B. III, V, II, IV, I
C. III, V, I, II, IV   D. III, II, V, IV, I

6.   I. Communists rank equality very high, but freedom very low.
     II. Unlike communists, conservatives place a high value on freedom and a very low value on equality.
     III. A recent study demonstrated that one way to classify people's political beliefs is to look at the importance placed on two words: freedom and equality.
     IV. Thus, by demonstrating how members of these groups feel about the two words, the study has proved to be useful for political analysts in several European countries.
     V. According to the study, socialists and liberals rank both freedom and equality very high, while fascists rate both very low.

6.____

A. III, V, I, II, IV   B. III, IV, V, I, II
C. III, V, IV, II, I   D. III, I, II, IV, V

7.   I. "Can there be anything more amazing than this?"
     II. If the riddle is successfully answered, his dead brothers will be brought back to life.
     III. "Even though man sees those around him dying every day," says Dharmaraj, "he still believes and acts as if he were immortal."
     IV. "What is the cause of ceaseless wonder?" asks the Lord of the Lake.
     V. In the ancient epic, The Mahabharata, a riddle is asked of one of the Pandava brothers.

7.____

A. V, II, I, IV, III   B. V, IV, III, I, II
C. V, II, IV, III, I   D. V, II, IV, I, III

8.
 I. On the contrary, the two main theories — the cooperative (neoclassical) theory and the radical (labor theory) — clearly rest on very different assumptions, which have very different ethical overtones.
 II. The distribution of income is the primary factor in determining the relative levels of material well-being that different groups or individuals attain.
 III. Of all issues in economics, the distribution of income is one of the most controversial.
 IV. The neoclassical theory tends to support the existing income distribution (or minor changes), while the labor theory tends to support substantial changes in the way income is distributed.
 V. The intensity of the controversy reflects the fact that different economic theories are not purely neutral, *detached* theories with no ethical or moral implications.

8.____

   A. II, I, V, IV, III   B. III, II, V, I, IV
   C. III, V, II, I, IV   D. III, V, IV, I, II

9.
 I. The pool acts as a broker and ensures that the cheapest power gets used first.
 II. Every six seconds, the pool's computer monitors all of the generating stations in the state and decides which to ask for more power and which to cut back.
 III. The buying and selling of electrical power is handled by the New York Power Pool in Guilderland, New York.
 IV. This is to the advantage of both the buying and selling utilities.
 V. The pool began operation in 1970, and consists of the state's eight electric utilities.

9.____

   A. V, I, II, III, IV   B. IV, II, I, III, V
   C. III, V, I, IV, II   D. V, III, IV, II, I

10.
 I. Modern English is much simpler grammatically than Old English.
 II. Finnish grammar is very complicated; there are some fifteen cases, for example.
 III. Chinese, a very old language, may seem to be the exception, but it is the great number of characters/ words that must be mastered that makes it so difficult to learn, not its grammar.
 IV. The newest literary language — that is, written as well as spoken — is Finnish, whose literary roots go back only to about the middle of the nineteenth century.
 V. Contrary to popular belief, the longer a language is been in use the simpler its grammar — not the reverse.

10.____

   A. IV, I, II, III, V   B. V, I, IV, II, III
   C. I, II, IV, III, V   D. IV, II, III, I, V

KEY (CORRECT ANSWERS)

1.	D	6.	A
2.	A	7.	C
3.	C	8.	B
4.	D	9.	C
5.	C	10.	B

TEST 2

DIRECTIONS: This type of question tests your ability to recognize accurate paraphrasing, well-constructed paragraphs, and appropriate style and tone. It is important that the answer you select contains only the facts or concepts given in the original sentences. It is also important that you be aware of incomplete sentences, inappropriate transitions, unsupported opinions, incorrect usage, and illogical sentence order. Paragraphs that do not include all the necessary facts and concepts, that distort them, or that add new ones are not considered correct.

The format for this section may vary. Sometimes, long paragraphs are given, and emphasis is placed on style and organization. Our first five questions are of this type. Other times, the paragraphs are shorter, and there is less emphasis on style and more emphasis on accurate representation of information. Our second group of five questions are of this nature.

For each of Questions 1 through 10, select the paragraph that BEST expresses the ideas contained in the sentences above it. *PRINT THE LETTER OF THE CORRECT ANSWER IN THE SPACE AT THE RIGHT.*

1.   I.   Listening skills are very important for managers.   1.____
    II.   Listening skills are not usually emphasized.
   III.   Whenever managers are depicted in books, manuals or the media, they are always talking, never listening.
   IV.   We'd like you to read the enclosed handout on listening skills and to try to consciously apply them this week.
    V.   We guarantee they will improve the quality of your interactions.

   A.   Unfortunately, listening skills are not usually emphasized for managers. Managers are always depicted as talking, never listening. We'd like you to read the enclosed handout on listening skills. Please try to apply these principles this week. If you do, we guarantee they will improve the quality of your interactions.

   B.   The enclosed handout on listening skills will be important improving the quality of your interactions. We guarantee it. All you have to do is take some time this week to read it and to consciously try to apply the principles. Listening skills are very important for managers, but they are not usually emphasized. Whenever managers are depicted in books, manuals or the media, they are always talking, never listening.

   C.   Listening well is one of the most important skills a manager can have, yet it's not usually given much attention. Think about any representation of managers in books, manuals, or in the media that you may have seen. They're always talking, never listening. We'd like you to read the enclosed handout on listening skills and consciously try to apply them the rest of the week. We guarantee you will see a difference in the quality of your interactions.

   D.   Effective listening, one very important tool in the effective manager's arsenal, is usually not emphasized enough. The usual depiction of managers in books, manuals or the media is one in which they are always talking, never listening. We'd like you to read the enclosed handout and consciously try to apply the information contained therein throughout the rest of the week. We feel sure that you will see a marked difference in the quality of your interactions.

2. I. Chekhov wrote three dramatic masterpieces which share certain themes and for-   2._____
        mats: <u>Uncle Vanya</u>, <u>The Cherry Orchard</u>, and <u>The Three Sisters</u>.
    II. They are primarily concerned with the passage of time and how this erodes
        human aspirations.
    III. The plays are haunted by the ghosts of the wasted life.
    IV. The characters are concerned with life's lesser problems; however, such as the
        inability to make decisions, loyalty to the wrong cause, and the inability to be
        clear.
    V. This results in a sweet, almost aching, type of a sadness referred to as Chek-
        hovian.

    A. Chekhov wrote three dramatic masterpieces: Uncle <u>Vanya</u>, <u>The Cherry Orchard,</u>
        and <u>The Three Sisters</u>. These masterpieces share certain themes and formats: the
        passage of time, how time erodes human aspirations, and the ghosts of wasted
        life. Each masterpiece is characterized by a sweet, almost aching, type of sadness
        that has become known as Chekhovian. The sweetness of this sadness hinges on
        the fact that it is not the great tragedies of life which are destroying these charac-
        ters, but their minor flaws: indecisiveness, misplaced loyalty, unclarity.
    B. <u>The Cherry Orchard</u>, <u>Uncle Vanya</u>, and <u>The Three Sisters</u> are three dramatic mas-
        terpieces written by Chekhov that use similar formats to explore a common theme.
        Each is primarily concerned with the way that passing time wears down human
        aspirations, and each is haunted by the ghosts of the wasted life. The characters
        are shown struggling futilely with the lesser problems of life: indecisiveness, loyalty
        to the wrong cause, and the inability to be clear. These struggles create a mood of
        sweet, almost aching, sadness that has become known as Chekhovian.
    C. Chekhov's dramatic masterpieces are, along with <u>The Cherry Orchard</u>, <u>Uncle </u>
        <u>Vanya</u>, and The Three Sisters. These plays share certain thematic and formal simi-
        larities. They are concerned most of all with the passage of time and the way in
        which time erodes human aspirations. Each play is haunted by the specter of the
        wasted life. Chekhov's characters are caught, however, by life's lesser snares:
        indecisiveness, loyalty to the wrong cause, and unclarity. The characteristic mood
        is a sweet, almost aching type of sadness that has come to be known as Chek-
        hovian.
    D. A Chekhovian mood is characterized by sweet, almost aching, sadness. The term
        comes from three dramatic tragedies by Chekhov which revolve around the sad-
        ness of a wasted life. The three masterpieces (<u>Uncle Vanya</u>, <u>The Three Sisters</u>,
        and <u>The Cherry Orchard)</u> share the same theme and format. The plays are con-
        cerned with how the passage of time erodes human aspirations. They are peopled
        with characters who are struggling with life's lesser problems. These are people
        who are indecisive, loyal to the wrong causes, or are unable to make themselves
        clear.

3.   I.   Movie previews have often helped producers decide what parts of movies they should take out or leave in.

      II. The first 1933 preview of <u>King Kong</u> was very helpful to the producers because many people ran screaming from the theater and would not return when four men first attacked by Kong were eaten by giant spiders.

     III. The 1950 premiere of Sunset Boulevard resulted in the filming of an entirely new beginning, and a delay of six months in the film's release.

     IV. In the original opening scene, William Holden was in a morgue talking with thirty-six other "corpses" about the ways some of them had died.

     V. When he began to tell them of his life with Gloria Swanson, the audience found this hilarious, instead of taking the scene seriously.

3. _____

A. Movie previews have often helped producers decide what parts of movies they should leave in or take out. For example, the first preview of <u>King Kong</u> in 1933 was very helpful. In one scene, four men were first attacked by Kong and then eaten by giant spiders. Many members of the audience ran screaming from the theater and would not return. The premiere of the 1950 film <u>Sunset Boulevard</u> was also very helpful. In the original opening scene, William Holden was in a morgue with thirty-six other "corpses," discussing the ways some of them had died. When he began to tell them of his life with Gloria Swanson, the audience found this hilarious. They were supposed to take the scene seriously. The result was a delay of six months in the release of the film while a new beginning was added.

B. Movie previews have often helped producers decide whether they should change various parts of a movie. After the 1933 preview of <u>King Kong,</u> a scene in which four men who had been attacked by Kong were eaten by giant spiders was taken out as many people ran screaming from the theater and would not return. The 1950 premiere of <u>Sunset Boulevard</u> also led to some changes. In the original opening scene, William Holden was in a morgue talking with thirty-six other "corpses" about the ways some of them had died. When he began to tell them of his life with Gloria Swanson, the audience found this hilarious, instead of taking the scene seriously.

C. What do <u>Sunset Boulevard</u> and <u>King Kong</u> have in common? Both show the value of using movie previews to test audience reaction. The first 1933 preview of <u>King Kong</u> showed that a scene showing four men being eaten by giant spiders after having been attacked by Kong was too frightening for many people. They ran screaming from the theater and couldn't be coaxed back. The 1950 premiere of <u>Sunset Boulevard</u> was also a scream, but not the kind the producers intended. The movie opens with William Holden lying in a morgue discussing the ways they had died with thirty-six other "corpses." When he began to tell them of his life with Gloria Swanson, the audience couldn't take him seriously. Their laughter caused a six-month delay while the beginning was rewritten.

D. Producers very often use movie previews to decide if changes are needed. The premiere of <u>Sunset Boulevard</u> in 1950 led to a new beginning and a six-month delay in film release. At the beginning, William Holden and thirty-six other "corpses" discuss the ways some of them died. Rather than taking this seriously, the audience thought it was hilarious when he began to tell them of his life with Gloria Swanson. The first 1933 preview of <u>King Kong</u> was very helpful for its producers because one scene so terrified the audience that many of them ran screaming from the theater and would not return. In this particular scene, four men who had first been attacked by Kong were being eaten by giant spiders.

4.	I.	It is common for supervisors to view employees as "things" to be manipulated.	4.____
	II.	This approach does not motivate employees, nor does the carrot-and-stick approach because employees often recognize these behaviors and resent them.
	III.	Supervisors can change these behaviors by using self-inquiry and persistence.
	IV.	The best managers genuinely respect those they work with, are supportive and helpful, and are interested in working as a team with those they supervise.
	V.	They disagree with the Golden Rule that says "he or she who has the gold makes the rules."

	A.	Some managers act as if they think the Golden Rule means "he or she who has the gold makes the rules." They show disrespect to employees by seeing them as "things" to be manipulated. Obviously, this approach does not motivate employees any more than the carrot-and-stick approach motivates them. The employees are smart enough to spot these behaviors and resent them. On the other hand, the managers genuinely respect those they work with, are supportive and helpful, and are interested in working as a team. Self-inquiry and persistence can change even the former type of supervisor into the latter.

	B.	Many supervisors fall into the trap of viewing employees as "things" to be manipulated, or try to motivate them by using a earrot-and-stick approach. These methods do not motivate employees, who often recognize the behaviors and resent them. Supervisors can change these behaviors, however, by using self-inquiry and persistence. The best managers are supportive and helpful, and have genuine respect for those with whom they work. They are interested in working as a team with those they supervise. To them, the Golden Rule is not "he or she who has the gold makes the rules."

	C.	Some supervisors see employees as "things" to be used or manipulated using a carrot-and-stick technique. These methods don't work. Employees often see through them and resent them. A supervisor who wants to change may do so. The techniques of self-inquiry and persistence can be used to turn him or her into the type of supervisor who doesn't think the Golden Rule is "he or she who has the gold makes the rules." They may become like the best managers who treat those with whom they work with respect and give them help and support. These are the managers who know how to build a team.

	D.	Unfortunately, many supervisors act as if their employees are objects whose movements they can position at will. This mistaken belief has the same result as another popular motivational technique—the carrot-and-stick approach. Both attitudes can lead to the same result — resentment from those employees who recognize the behaviors for what they are. Supervisors who recognize these behaviors can change through the use of persistence and the use of self-inquiry. It's important to remember that the best managers respect their employees. They readily give necessary help and support and are interested in working as a team with those they supervise. To these managers, the Golden Rule is not "he or she who has the gold makes the rules."

5.　　I.　The first half of the nineteenth century produced a group of pessimistic poets —　　5.____
　　　　　　Byron, De Musset, Heine, Pushkin, and Leopardi.
　　　II.　It also produced a group of pessimistic composers—Schubert, Chopin, Schu-
　　　　　　mann, and even the later Beethoven.
　　　III.　Above all, in philosophy, there was the profoundly pessimistic philosopher,
　　　　　　Schopenhauer.
　　　IV.　The Revolution was dead, the Bourbons were restored, the feudal barons were
　　　　　　reclaiming their land, and progress everywhere was being suppressed, as the
　　　　　　great age was over.
　　　V.　"I thank God," said Goethe, "that I am not young in so thoroughly finished a
　　　　　　world."

　　　A.　"I thank God," said Goethe, "that I am not young in so thoroughly finished a world."
　　　　　　The Revolution was dead, the Bourbons were restored, the feudal barons were
　　　　　　reclaiming their land, and progress everywhere was being suppressed. The first
　　　　　　half of the nineteenth century produced a group of pessimistic poets: Byron, De
　　　　　　Musset, Heine, Pushkin, and Leopardi. It also produced pessimistic composers:
　　　　　　Schubert, Chopin, Schumann. Although Beethoven came later, he fits into this
　　　　　　group, too. Finally and above all, it also produced a profoundly pessimistic philoso-
　　　　　　pher, Schopenhauer. The great age was over.
　　　B.　The first half of the nineteenth century produced a group of pessimistic poets:
　　　　　　Byron, De Musset, Heine, Pushkin, and Leopardi. It produced a group of pessimis-
　　　　　　tic composers: Schubert, Chopin, Schumann, and even the later Beethoven.
　　　　　　Above all, it produced a profoundly pessimistic philosopher, Schopenhauer. For
　　　　　　each of these men, the great age was over. The Revolution was dead, and the
　　　　　　Bourbons were restored. The feudal barons were reclaiming their land, and
　　　　　　progress everywhere was being suppressed.
　　　C.　The great age was over. The Revolution was dead—the Bourbons were restored,
　　　　　　and the feudal barons were reclaiming their land. Progress everywhere was being
　　　　　　suppressed. Out of this climate came a profound pessimism. Poets, like Byron, De
　　　　　　Musset, Heine, Pushkin, and Leopardi; composers, like Schubert, Chopin, Schu-
　　　　　　mann, and even the later Beethoven; and, above all, a profoundly pessimistic phi-
　　　　　　losopher, Schopenauer. This pessimism which arose in the first half of the
　　　　　　nineteenth century is illustrated by these words of Goethe, "I thank God that I am
　　　　　　not young in so thoroughly finished a world."
　　　D.　The first half of the nineteenth century produced a group of pessimistic poets,
　　　　　　Byron, De Musset, Heine, Pushkin, and Leopardi — and a group of pessimistic
　　　　　　composers, Schubert, Chopin, Schumann, and the later Beethoven. Above all, it
　　　　　　produced a profoundly pessimistic philosopher, Schopenhauer. The great age was
　　　　　　over. The Revolution was dead, the Bourbons were restored, the feudal barons
　　　　　　were reclaiming their land, and progress everywhere was being suppressed. "I
　　　　　　thank God," said Goethe, "that I am not young in so thoroughly finished a world."

6.　　I.　A new manager sometimes may feel insecure about his or her competence in the　　6.____
　　　　　　new position.
　　　II.　The new manager may then exhibit defensive or arrogant behavior towards
　　　　　　those one supervises, or the new manager may direct overly flattering behavior
　　　　　　toward one's new supervisor.

A. Sometimes, a new manager may feel insecure about his or her ability to perform well in this new position. The insecurity may lead him or her to treat others differently. He or she may display arrogant or defensive behavior towards those he or she supervises, or be overly flattering to his or her new supervisor.

B. A new manager may sometimes feel insecure about his or her ability to perform well in the new position. He or she may then become arrogant, defensive, or overly flattering towards those he or she works with.

C. There are times when a new manager may be insecure about how well he or she can perform in the new job. The new manager may also behave defensive or act in an arrogant way towards those he or she supervises, or overly flatter his or her boss.

D. Sometimes, a new manager may feel insecure about his or her ability to perform well in the new position. He or she may then display arrogant or defensive behavior towards those they supervise, or become overly flattering towards their supervisors.

7. I. It is possible to eliminate unwanted behavior by bringing it under stimulus control — tying the behavior to a cue, and then never, or rarely, giving the cue.
    II. One trainer successfully used this method to keep an energetic young porpoise from coming out of her tank whenever she felt like it, which was potentially dangerous.
    III. Her trainer taught her to do it for a reward, in response to a hand signal, and then rarely gave the signal.

7.____

A. Unwanted behavior can be eliminated by tying the behavior to a cue, and then never, or rarely, giving the cue. This is called stimulus control. One trainer was able to use this method to keep an energetic young porpoise from coming out of her tank by teaching her to come out for a reward in response to a hand signal, and then rarely giving the signal.

B. Stimulus control can be used to eliminate unwanted behavior. In this method, behavior is tied to a cue, and then the cue is rarely, if ever, given. One trainer was able to successfully use stimulus control to keep an energetic young porpoise from coming out of her tank whenever she felt like it — a potentially dangerous practice. She taught the porpoise to come out for a reward when she gave a hand signal, and then rarely gave the signal.

C. It is possible to eliminate behavior that is undesirable by bringing it under stimulus control by tying behavior to a signal, and then rarely giving the signal. One trainer successfully used this method to keep an energetic young porpoise from coming out of her tank, a potentially dangerous situation. Her trainer taught the porpoise to do it for a reward, in response to a hand signal, and then would rarely give the signal.

D. By using stimulus control, it is possible to eliminate unwanted behavior by tying the behavior to a cue, and then rarely or never give the cue. One trainer was able to use this method to successfully stop a young porpoise from coming out of her tank whenever she felt like it. To curb this potentially dangerous practice, the porpoise was taught by the trainer to come out of the tank for a reward, in response to a hand signal, and then rarely given the signal.

8. I.   There is a great deal of concern over the safety of commercial trucks, caused by
         their greatly increased role in serious accidents since federal deregulation in 1981.
    II. Recently, 60 percent of trucks in New York and Connecticut and 70 percent of
         trucks in Maryland randomly stopped by state troopers failed safety inspections.
    III. Sixteen states in the United States require no training at all for truck drivers.

8.____

    A.   Since federal deregulation in 1981, there has been a great deal of concern over the
         safety of commercial trucks, and their greatly increased role in serious accidents.
         Recently, 60 percent of trucks in New York and Connecticut, and 70 percent of
         trucks in Maryland failed safety inspections. Sixteen states in the United States
         require no training at all for truck drivers.
    B.   There is a great deal of concern over the safety of commercial trucks since federal
         deregulation in 1981. Their role in serious accidents has greatly increased.
         Recently, 60 percent of trucks randomly stopped in Connecticut and New York, and
         70 percent in Maryland failed safety inspections conducted by state troopers. Six-
         teen states in the United States provide no training at all for truck drivers.
    C.   Commercial trucks have a greatly increased role in serious accidents since federal
         deregulation in 1981. This has led to a great deal of concern. Recently, 70 percent
         of trucks in Maryland and 60 percent of trucks in New York and Connecticut failed
         inspection of those that were randomly stopped by state troopers. Sixteen states in
         the United States require no training for all truck drivers.
    D.   Since federal deregulation in 1981, the role that commercial trucks have played in
         serious accidents has greatly increased, and this has led to a great deal of con-
         cern. Recently, 60 percent of trucks in New York and Connecticut, and 70 percent
         of trucks in Maryland randomly stopped by state troopers failed safety inspections.
         Sixteen states in the U.S. don't require any training for truck drivers.

9. I.   No matter how much some people have, they still feel unsatisfied and want more,
         or want to keep what they have forever.
    II. One recent television documentary showed several people flying from New York
         to Paris for a one-day shopping spree to buy platinum earrings, because they
         were bored.
    III. In Brazil, some people are ordering coffins that cost a minimum of $45,000 and
         are equipping them with deluxe stereos, televisions and other graveyard neces-
         sities.

9.____

    A.   Some people, despite having a great deal, still feel unsatisfied and want more, or
         think they can keep what they have forever. One recent documentary on television
         showed several people enroute from Paris to New York for a one day shopping
         spree to buy platinum earrings, because they were bored. Some people in Brazil
         are even ordering coffins equipped with such graveyard necessities as deluxe ste-
         reos and televisions. The price of the coffins start at $45,000.
    B.   No matter how much some people have, they may feel unsatisfied. This leads them
         to want more, or to want to keep what they have forever. Recently, a television doc-
         umentary depicting several people flying from New York to Paris for a one day
         shopping spree to buy platinum earrings. They were bored. Some people in Brazil
         are ordering coffins that cost at least $45,000 and come equipped with deluxe tele-
         visions, stereos and other necessary graveyard items.
    C.   Some people will be dissatisfied no matter how much they have. They may want
         more, or they may want to keep what they have forever. One recent television doc-
         umentary showed several people, motivated by boredom, jetting from New York to

Paris for a one-day shopping spree to buy platinum earrings. In Brazil, some people are ordering coffins equipped with deluxe stereos, televisions and other graveyard necessities. The minimum price for these coffins - $45,000.

D. Some people are never satisfied. No matter how much they have they still want more, or think they can keep what they have forever. One television documentary recently showed several people flying from New York to Paris for the day to buy platinum earrings because they were bored. In Brazil, some people are ordering coffins that cost $45,000 and are equipped with deluxe stereos, televisions and other graveyard necessities.

10.
I. A television signal or Video signal has three parts.

II. Its parts are the black-and-white portion, the color portion, and the synchronizing (sync) pulses, which keep the picture stable.

III. Each video source, whether it's a camera or a video-cassette recorder, contains its own generator of these synchronizing pulses to accompany the picture that it's sending in order to keep it steady and straight.

IV. In order to produce a clean recording, a video-cassette recorder must "lock-up" to the sync pulses that are part of the video it is trying to record, and this effort may be very noticeable if the device does not have genlock.

A. There are three parts to a television or video signal: the black-and-white part, the color part, and the synchronizing (sync) pulses, which keep the picture stable. Whether it's a video-cassette recorder or a camera, each each video source contains its own pulse that synchronizes and generates the picture it's sending in order to keep it straight and steady. A video-cassette recorder must "lock up" to the sync pulses that are part of the video it's trying to record. If the device doesn't have genlock, this effort must be very noticeable.

B. A video signal or television is comprised of three parts: the black-and-white portion, the color portion, and the the sync (synchronizing) pulses, which keep the picture stable. Whether it's a camera or a video-cassette recorder, each video source contains its own generator of these synchronizing pulses. These accompany the picture that it's sending in order to keep it straight and steady. A video-cassette recorder must "lock up" to the sync pulses that are part of the video it is trying to record in order to produce a clean recording. This effort may be very noticeable if the device does not have genlock.

C. There are three parts to a television or video signal: the color portion, the black-and-white portion, and the sync (synchronizing pulses). These keep the picture stable. Each video source, whether it's a video-cassette recorder or a camera, generates these synchronizing pulses accompanying the picture it's sending in order to keep it straight and steady. If a clean recording is to be produced, a video-cassette recorder must store the sync pulses that are part of the video it is trying to record. This effort may not be noticeable if the device does not have genlock.

D. A television signal or video signal has three parts: the black-and-white portion, the color portion, and the synchronizing (sync) pulses. It's the sync pulses which keep the picture stable, which accompany it and keep it steady and straight. Whether it's a camera or a video-cassette recorder, each video source contains its own generator of these synchronizing pulses. To produce a clean recording, a video-cassette recorder must "lock-up" to the sync pulses that are part of the video it is trying to record. If the device does not have genlock, this effort may be very noticeable.

KEY (CORRECT ANSWERS)

1.	C	6.	A
2.	B	7.	B
3.	A	8.	D
4.	B	9.	C
5.	D	10.	D

———

PREPARING WRITTEN MATERIAL
EXAMINATION SECTION
TEST 1

DIRECTIONS: The following groups of sentences need to be arranged in an order that makes sense. Select the letter preceding the sequence that represents the *BEST sentence order. PRINT THE LETTER OF THE CORRECT ANSWER IN THE SPACE AT THE RIGHT.*

1.

      1._____

   I.   A large Naval station on Alameda Island, near Oakland, held many warships in port, and the War Department was worried that if the bridge were to be blown up by the enemy, passage to and from the bay would be hopelessly blocked.

   II.   Though many skeptics were opposed to the idea of building such an enormous bridge, the most vocal opposition came from a surprising source: the United States War Department.

   III.   The War Department's concerns led to a showdown at San Francisco City Hall between Strauss and the Secretary of War, who demanded to know what would happen if a military enemy blew up the bridge.

   IV.   In 1933, by submitting a construction cost estimate of $17 million, an engineer named Joseph Strauss won the contract to build the Golden Gate Bridge of San Francisco, which would then become one of the world's largest bridges.

   V.   Strauss quickly ended the debate by explaining that the Golden Gate Bridge was to be a suspension bridge, whose roadway would hang in the air from cables strung between two huge towers, and would immediately sink into three hundred feet of water if it were destroyed.

The best order is
A.   II, III, I, IV, V
B.   I, II, III, V, IV
C.   IV, II, I, III, V
D.   IV, I, III, V, II

2.

I. Plastic surgeons have already begun to use virtual reality to map out the complex nerve and tissue structures of a particular patient's face, in order to prepare for delicate surgery.

II. A virtual reality program responds to these movements by adjusting the Images that a person sees on a screen or through goggles, thereby creating an "interactive" world in which a person can see and touch three-dimensional graphic objects.

III. No more than a computer program that is designed to build and display graphic images, the virtual reality program takes graphic programs a step further by sensing a person's head and body movements.

IV. The computer technology known as virtual reality, now in its very first stages of development, is already revolutionizing some aspects of contemporary life.

V. Virtual reality computers are also being used by the space program, most recently to simulate conditions for the astronauts who were launched on a repair mission to the Hubble telescope.

The best order is
A. IV, II, I, V, III
B. III, I, V, II, IV
C. IV, III, II, I, V
D. III, I, II, IV, V

3.

I. Before you plant anything, the soil in your plant bed should be carefully raked level, a small section at a time, and any clods or rocks that can't be broken up should be removed.

II. Your plant should be placed in a hole that will position it at the same level it was at the nursery, and a small indentation should be pressed into the soil around the plant in order to hold water near it roots.

III. Before placing the plant in the soil, lightly separate any roots that may have been matted together in the container, cutting away any thick masses that can't be separated, so that the remaining roots will be able to grow outward.

IV. After the bed is ready, remove your plant from its container by turning it upside down and tapping or pushing on the bottom — never remove it by pulling on the plant.

V. When you bring home a small plant in an individual container from the nursery, there are several things to remember while preparing to plant it in your own garden.

The best order is
A. V, IV, III, II, I
B. V, I, IV, III, II
C. I, IV, II, III, V
D. I, IV, V, II, III

4.   4._____

    I.   The motte and its tower were usually built first, so that sentries could use it as a lookout to warn the castle workers of any danger that might approach the castle.

    II. Though the moat and palisade offered the bailey a good deal of protection, it was linked to the motte by a set of stairs that led to a retractable drawbridge at the motte's gate, to enable people to evacuate and retreat onto the motte in case of an attack.

    III. The *motte* of these early castles was a fortified hill, sometimes as high as one hundred feet, on which stood a palisade and tower.

    IV. The *bailey* was a clear, level spot below the motte, also enclosed by a palisade, which in turn was surrounded by a large trench or moat.

    V. The earliest castles built in Europe were not the magnificent stone giants that still tower over much of the European landscape, but simpler wooden constructions called motte-and-bailey castles.

The best order is
A. V, III, I, IV, II
B. V, IV, I, II, III
C. I, IV, IIII, II, V
D. I, III, II, IV, V

5.   5._____

    I.   If an infant is left alone or abandoned for a short while, its immediate response is to cry loudly, accompanying its screams with aggressive flailing of its legs and limbs.

    II. If a child has been abandoned for a longer period of time, it becomes completely still and quiet, as if realizing that now its only chance for survival is to shut its mouth and remain motionless.

    III. Along with their intense fear of the dark, the crying behavior of human infants offers insights into how prehistoric newborn children might have evolved instincts that would prevent them from becoming victims of predators.

    IV. This behavior often surprises people who enter a hospital's maternity ward for the first time and encounter total silence from a roomful of infants.

    V. This violent screaming response is quite different from an infant's cries of discomfort or hunger, and seems to serve as either the child's first line of defense against an unwanted intruder, or a desperate attempt to communicate its position to the mother.

The best order is
A. III, II, IV, I, V
B. III, I, V, II, IV
C. I, V, IV, II, III
D. II, IV, I, V, III

6.

   I.   When two cats meet who are strangers, their first actions and gestures determine who the "dominant" cat will be, at least for the time being.

   II.   Unlike dogs, cats are typically a solitary animal species who avoid social interaction, but they do display specific social responses to each other upon meeting.

   III. This is unlikely, however; before such a point of open hostility is reached, one of the cats will usually take the "submissive" position of crouching down while looking away from the other cat.

   IV. If a cat desires dominance or sees the other cat as a threat to its territory, it will stare directly at the intruder with a lowered tail.

   V.   If the other cat responds with a similar gesture, or with the strong defensive posture of an arched back, laid-back ears and raised tail, a fight or chase is likely if neither cat gives in.

The best order is
A. IV, II, I, V, III
B. I, II, IV, V, III
C. I, IV, V, III, II
D. II, I, IV, V, III

7.

   I.   A star or planet's gravitational force can best be explained in this way: anything passing through this "dent" in space will veer toward the star or planet as if it were rolling into a hole.

   II.   Objects that are massive or heavy, such as stars or planets, "sink" into this surface, creating a sort of dent or concavity in the surrounding space.

   III. Black holes, the most massive objects known to exist in space, create dents so large and deep that the space surrounding them actually folds in on itself, preventing anything that falls in — even light — from ever escaping again.

   IV. The sort of dent a star or planet makes depends on how massive it is; planets generally have weak gravitational pulls, but stars, which are larger and heavier, make a bigger "dent" that will attract more matter.

   V.   In outer space, the force of gravity works as if the surrounding space is a soft, flat surface.

The best order is
A. III, V, II, I, IV
B. III, IV, I, V, II
C. V, II, I, IV, III
D. I, V, II, IV, III

8.   8._____

    I.   Eventually, the society of Kyoto gave the world one of its first and greatest
          novels when Japan's most prominent writer, Lady Murasaki Shikibu, wrote
          her chronicle of Kyoto's society, *The Tale of Genji*, which preceded the first
          European novels by more than 500 years.

    II.   The society of Kyoto was dedicated to the pleasures of art; the courtiers
          experimented with new and colorful methods of sculpture, painting, writing,
          decorative gardening, and even making clothes.

    III. Japanese culture began under the powerful authority of Chinese Buddhism,
          which influenced every aspect of Japanese life from religion to politics and art.

    IV. This new, vibrant culture was so sophisticated that all the people in Kyoto's
          imperial court considered themselves poets, and the line between life and art
          hardly existed — lovers corresponded entirely through written verses, and even
          government officials communicated by writing poems to each other.

    V.   In the eighth century, when the emperor established the town of Kyoto as the
          capital of the Japanese empire, Japanese society began to develop its own
          distinctive style.

The best order is
A. V, II, IV, I, III
B. II, I, V, IV, III
C. V, III, IV, I, II
D. III, V, II, IV, I

9.   9._____

    I.   Instead of wheels, the HSST uses two sets of magnets, one which sits on the
          track, and another that is carried by the train; these magnets generate an
          identical magnetic field which forces the two sets apart.

    II.   In the last few decades, railway travel has become less popular throughout the
          world, because it is much slower than travel by airplane, and not much less
          expensive.

    III. The HSST's designers say that the train can take passengers from one town
          to another as quickly as a jet plane — while consuming less than half the energy.

    IV. This repellent effect is strong enough to lift the entire train above the trackway,
          and the train, literally traveling on air, rockets along at speeds of up to 300 miles
          per hour.

    V.   The revolutionary technology of magnetic levitation, currently being tested by
          Japan's experimental HSST (High Speed Surface Transport), may yet bring
          passenger trains back from the dead.

The best order is
A. II, V, I, IV, III
B. II, I, IV, III, V
C. V, II, III, I, IV
D. V, I, III, IV, II

10.   10._____

   I.   When European countries first began to colonize the African continent, their impression of the African people was of a vast group of loosely organized tribal societies, without any great centralized source of power or wealth.

   II.   The legend of Timbuktu persisted until the nineteenth century, when a French adventurer visited Timbuktu and found that raids by neighboring tribesmen had made the city a shadow of its former self.

   III.   In the fifteenth century, when the stories of travelers who had traveled Africa's Sudan region began circulating around Europe, this impression began to change.

   IV.   In 1470, an Italian merchant named Benedetto Dei traveled to Timbuktu and confirmed these rumors, describing a thriving metropolis where rich and poor people worshipped together in the city's many ornate mosques — there was even a university in Timbuktu, much like its European counterparts, where African scholars pursued their studies in the arts and sciences.

   V.   The travelers' legends told of an enormous city in the western Sudan, Timbuktu, where the streets were crowded with goods brought by faraway caravans, and where there was a stone palace as large as any in Europe.

The best order is
A. III, V, I, IV, II
B. I, II, IV, III, V
C. I, III, V, IV, II
D. II, I, III, IV, V

11.   11._____

   I.   Also, our reference points in sighting the moon may make us believe that its size is changing; when the moon is rising through the trees, it seems huge, because our brains unconsciously compare the size of the moon with the size of the trees in the foreground.

   II.   To most people, the sky itself appears more distant at the horizon than directly overhead, and if the moon's size — which remains constant — is projected from the horizon, the apparent distance of the horizon makes the moon look bigger.

   III.   Up higher in the sky, the moon is set against tiny stars in the background, which will make the moon seem smaller.

   IV.   People often wonder why the moon becomes bigger when it approaches the horizon, but most scientists agree that this is a complicated optical illusion, produced by at least three factors.

   V.   The moon illusion may also be partially explained by a phenomenon that has nothing to do with errors in our perception — light that enters the earth's atmosphere is sometimes refracted, and so the atmosphere may act as a kind of magnifying glass for the moon's image.

The best order is
A. IV, III, V, II, I
B. IV, II, I, III, V
C. V, II, I, III, IV
D. II, I, III, IV, V

12.

  I.   When the Native Americans were introduced to the horses used by white explorers, they were amazed at their new alternative — here was an animal that was strong and swift, would patiently carry a person or other loads on its back, and, they later discovered, was right at home on the plains.

  II.   Before the arrival of European explorers to North America, the natives of the American plains used large dogs to carry their travois-long lodgepoles loaded with clothing, gear, and food.

  III.   These horses, it is now known, were not really strangers to North America; the very first horses originated here, on this continent, tens of thousands of years ago, and migrated into Asia across the Bering Land Bridge, a strip of land that used to link our continent with the Eastern world.

  IV.   At first, the natives knew so little about horses that at least one tribe tried to feed their new animals pieces of dried meat and animal fat, and were surprised when the horses turned their heads away and began to eat the grass of the prairie.

  V.   The American horse eventually became extinct, but its Asian cousins were reintroduced to the New World when the European explorers brought them to live among the Native Americans.

The best order is
A. II, I, IV, III, V
B. II, IV, I, III, V
C. I, II, IV, III, V
D. I, III, V, II, IV

13.

  I.   The dress worn by the dancer is believed to have been adorned in the past by shells which would strike each other as the dancer performed, creating a lovely sound.

  II.   Today's jingle-dress is decorated with the tin lids of snuff cans, which are rolled into cones and sewn onto the dress.

  III.   During the jingle-dress dance, the dancer must blend complicated footwork with a series of gentle hops that cause the cones to jingle in rhythm to a drumbeat.

  IV.   When contemporary Native American tribes meet for a pow-wow, one of the most popular ceremonies to take place is the women's jingle-dress dance.

  V.   Besides being more readily available than shells, the lids are thought by many dancers to create a softer, more subtle sound.

The best order is
A. II, IV, V, I, III
B. IV, II, I, III, V
C. II, I, III, V, IV
D. IV, I, II, V, III

14.

    14._____

    I.   If a homeowner lives where seasonal climates are extreme, deciduous shade trees — which will drop their leaves in the winter and allow sunlight to pass through the windows — should be planted near the southern exposure in order to keep the house cool during the summer.

    II.   This trajectory is shorter and lower in the sky than at any other time of year during the winter, when a house most requires heating; the northern-facing parts of a house do not receive any direct sunlight at all.

    III.   In designing an energy-efficient house, especially in colder climates, it is important to remember that most of the house's windows should face south.

    IV.   Though the sun always rises in the east and sets in the west, the sun of the northern hemisphere is permanently situated in the southern portion of the sky.

    V.   The explanation for why so many architects and builders want this "southern exposure"
is related to the path of the sun in the sky.

The best order is
A. III, I, V, IV, II
B. III, V, IV, II, I
C. I, III, IV, II, V
D. I, II, V, IV, III

15.

    15._____

    I.   His journeying lasted twenty-four years and took him over an estimated 75,000 miles, a distance that would not be surpassed by anyone other than Magellan — who sailed around the world — for another six hundred years.

    II.   Perhaps the most far-flung of these lesser-known travelers was Ibn Batuta, an African Moslem who left his birthplace of Tangier in the summer of 1325.

    III.   Ibn Batuta traveled all over Africa and Asia, from Niger to Peking, and to the islands of Maldive and Indonesia.

    IV.   However, a few explorers of the Eastern world logged enough miles and adventures to make Marco Polo's voyage look like an evening stroll.

    V.   In America, the most well-known of the Old World's explorers are usually Europeans such as Marco Polo, the Italian who brought many elements of Chinese culture to the Western world.

The best order is
A. V, IV, II, III, I
B. V, IV, III, II, I
C. III, II, I, IV, V
D. II, III, I, IV, V

16.

16._____

I. In the rain forests of South America, a rare species of frog practices a reproductive method that is entirely different from this standard process.

II. She will eventually carry each of the tadpoles up into the canopy and drop each into its own little pool, where it will be easy to locate and safe from most predators.

III. After fertilization, the female of the species, who lives almost entirely on the forest floor, lays between 2 and 16 eggs among the leaf litter at the base of a tree, and stands watch over these eggs until they hatch.

IV. Most frogs are pond-dwellers who are able to deposit hundreds of eggs in the water and then leave them alone, knowing that enough eggs have been laid to insure the survival of some of their offspring.

V. Once the tadpoles emerge, the female backs in among them, and a tadpole will wriggle onto her back to be carried high into the forest canopy, where the female will deposit it in a little pool of water cupped in the leaf of a plant.

The best order is
A. I, IV, III, II, V
B. I, III, V, II, IV
C. IV, III, II, V, I
D. IV, I, III, V, II

17.

17._____

I. Eratosthenes had heard from travelers that at exactly noon on June 21, in the ancient city of Aswan, Egypt, the sun cast no shadow in a well, which meant that the sun must be directly overhead.

II. He knew the sun always cast a shadow in Alexandria, and so he figured that if he could measure the length of an Alexandria shadow at the time when there was no shadow in Aswan, he could calculate the angle of the sun, and therefore the circumference of the earth.

III. The evidence for a round earth was not new in 1492; in fact, Eratosthenes, an Alexandrian geographer who lived nearly sixteen centuries before Columbus's voyage (275-195 B.C.), actually developed a method for calculating the circumference of the earth that is still in use today.

IV. Eratosthenes's method was correct, but his result — 28,700 miles — was about 15 percent too high, probably because of the inaccurate ancient methods of keeping time, and because Aswan was not due south of Alexandria, as Eratosthenes had believed.

V. When Christopher Columbus sailed across the Atlantic Ocean for the first time in 1492, there were still some people in the world who ignored scientific evidence and believed that the earth was flat, rather than round.

The best order is
A. I, II, V, III, IV
B. V, III, IV, I, II
C. V, III, I, II, IV
D. III, V, I, II, IV

18.

I. The first name for the child is considered a trial naming, often impersonal and neutral, such as the Ngoni name *Chabwera*, meaning "it has arrived."

II. This sort of name is not due to any parental indifference to the child, but is a kind of silent recognition of Africa's sometimes high infant death rate; most parents ease the pain of losing a child with the belief that it is not really a person until it has been given a final name.

III. In many tribal African societies, families often give two different names to their children, at different periods in time.

IV. After the trial naming period has subsided and it is clear that the child will survive, the parents choose a final name for the child, an act that symbolically completes the act of birth.

V. In fact, some African first-given names are explicitly uncomplimentary, translating as "I am dead" or "I am ugly," in order to avoid the jealousy of ancestral spirits who might wish to take a child that is especially healthy or attractive.

The best order is
A. III, I, II, V, IV
B. III, IV, II, I, V
C. IV, III, I, II, V
D. IV, V, III, I, II

19.

I. Though uncertain of the definite reasons for this behavior, scientists believe the birds digest the clay in order to counteract toxins contained in the seeds of certain fruits that are eaten by macaws.

II. For example, all macaws flock to riverbanks at certain times of the year to eat the clay that is found in river mud.

III. The macaws of South America are not only among the largest and most beautifully colored of the world's flying birds, but they are also one of the smartest.

IV. It is believed that macaws are forced to resort to these toxic fruits during the dry season, when foods are more scarce.

V. The macaw's intelligence has led to intense study by scientists, who have discovered some macaw behaviors that have not yet been explained.

The best order is
A. III, IV, I, II, V
B. III, V, II, I, IV
C. V, II, I, IV, III
D. IV, I, II, III, V

20.   20._____

    I.   Although Maggie Kuhn has since passed away, the Gray Panthers are still waging a campaign to reinstate the historical view of the elderly as people whose experience allows them to make their greatest contribution in their later years.

    II.   In 1972, an elderly woman named Maggie Kuhn responded to this sort of treatment by forming a group called the Gray Panthers, an organization of both old and young adults with the common goal of creating change.

    III.   This attitude is reflected strongly in the way elderly people are treated by our society; many are forced into early retirement, or are placed in rest homes in which they are isolated from their communities.

    IV.   Unlike most other cultures around the world, Americans tend to look upon old age with a sense of dread and sadness.

    V.   Kuhn believed that when the elderly are forced to withdraw into lives that lack purpose, society loses one of its greatest resources: people who have a lifetime of experience and wisdom to offer their communities.

The best order is
A. IV, III, II, V, I
B. IV, II, I, III, V
C. II, IV, III, V, I
D. II, I, IV, III, V

21.   21._____

    I.   The current theory among most anthropologists is that humans evolved from apes who lived in trees near the grasslands of Africa.

    II.   Still, some anthropologists insist that such an invention was necessary for the survival of early humans, and point to the Kung Bushmen of central Africa as a society in which the sling is still used in this way.

    III.   Two of these inventions — fire, and weapons such as spears and clubs — were obvious defenses against predators, and there is archaeological evidence to support the theory of their use.

    IV.   Once people had evolved enough to leave the safety of trees and walk upright, they needed the protection of several inventions in order to survive.

    V.   But another invention, a leather or fiber sling that allowed mothers to carry children while leaving their hands free to gather roots or berries, would certainly have decomposed and left behind no trace of itself.

The best order is
A. I, II, III, V, IV
B. IV, I, II, III, V
C. I, IV, III, V, II
D. IV, III, V, II, I

22.

22._____

   I.   The person holding the bird should keep it in hot water up to its neck, and the person cleaning should work a mild solution of dishwashing liquid into the bird's plumage, paying close attention to the head and neck.

   II.   When rinsing the bird, after all the oil has been removed, the running water should be directed against the lay of its feathers, until water begins to bead off the surface of the feathers — a sign that all the detergent has been rinsed out.

   III. If you have rescued a sea bird from an oil spill and want to restore it to clean and normal living, you need a large sink, a constant supply of running hot water (a little over 100° F), and regular dishwashing liquid.

   IV. This cleaning with detergent solution should be repeated as many times as it takes to remove all traces of oil from the bird's feathers, sometimes over a period of several days.

   V.   But before you begin to clean the bird, you must first find a partner, because cleaning an oiled bird is a two-person job.

The best order is
A. III, I, II, IV, V
B. III, V, I, IV, II
C. III, I, IV, V, II
D. III, IV, V, I, II

23.

23._____

   I.   The most difficult time of year for the Tsaatang is the spring calving, when the reindeer leave their wintering ground and rush to their accustomed calving place, without stopping by night or by day.

   II.   Reindeer travel in herds, and though some animals are tamed by the Tsaatang for riding or milking, the herds are allowed to roam free.

   III. This journey is hard for the Tsaatang, who carry all their possessions with them, but once it's over it proves worthwhile; the Tsaatang can immediately begin to gather milk from reindeer cows who have given birth.

   IV. The Tsaatang, a small tribe who live in the far northwest corner of Mongolia, practice a lifestyle that is completely dependent on the reindeer, their main resource for food, clothing, and transport.

   V.   The people must follow their yearly migrations, living in portable shelters that resemble Native American tepees.

The best order is
A. I, III, II, V, IV
B. I, IV, II, V, III
C. IV, I, III, V, II
D. IV, II, V, I, III

24.

   I.   The Romans later improved this system by installing these heated pipe networks throughout walls and ceilings, supplying heat to even the uppermost floors of a building — a system that, to this day, hasn't been much improved.

   II. Air-conditioning, the method by which humans control indoor temperatures, was practiced much earlier than most people think.

  III. The earliest heating devices other than open fires were used in 350 B.C. by the ancient Greeks, who directed air that had been heated by underground fires into baked clay pipes that ran under the floor.

  IV. Ironically, the first successful cooling system, patented in England in 1831, used fire as its main energy source — fires were lit in the attic of a building, creating an updraft of air that drew cool air into the building through ducts that had underground openings near the river Thames.

   V. Cooling buildings was more of a challenge, and wasn't attempted until 1500: a water-based system, designed by Leonardo da Vinci, does not appear to have been successful, since it was never used again.

The best order is
A. III, V, IV, I, II
B. III, I, II, V, IV
C. II, III, I, V, IV
D. IV, II, III, I, V

25.

   I.   Cold, dry air from Canada passes over the Rocky Mountains and sweeps down onto the plains, where it collides with warm, moist air from the waters of the Gulf of Mexico, and when the two air masses meet, the resulting disturbance sometimes forms a violent funnel cloud that strikes the earth and destroys virtually everything in its path.

   II. Hurricanes, storms which are generally not this violent and last much longer, are usually given names by meteorologists, but this tradition cannot be applied to tornados, which have a life span measured in minutes and disappear in the same way as they are born — unnamed.

  III. A tornado funnel forms rotating columns of air whose speed reaches three hundred miles an hour — a speed that can only be estimated, because no wind-measuring devices in the direct path of a storm have ever survived.

  IV. The natural phenomena known as tornados occur primarily over the midwestern grasslands of the United States.

   V. It is here, meteorologists tell us, that conditions for the formation of tornados are sometimes perfect during the spring months.

The best order is
A. II, IV, V, I, III
B. II, III, I, V, IV
C. IV, V, I, III, II
D. IV, III, I, V, II

KEY (CORRECT ANSWERS)

1.	C		11.	B
2.	C		12.	A
3.	B		13.	D
4.	A		14.	B
5.	B		15.	A
6.	D		16.	D
7.	C		17.	C
8.	D		18.	A
9.	A		19.	B
10.	C		20.	A

21.	C
22.	B
23.	D
24.	C
25.	C

PREPARING WRITTEN MATERIAL

EXAMINATION SECTION
TEST 1

DIRECTIONS : Each of the sentences in the tests that follow may be classified under one of the following four categories:

    A. *Incorrect* because of faulty grammar or sentence structure
    B. *Incorrect* because of faulty punctuation
    C. *Incorrect* because of faulty capitalization
    D. *Correct*

       Examine each sentence carefully to determine under which of the above four options it is best classified. Then, in the space on the right, print the capital letter preceding the option which is the *BEST* of the four suggested above.
       (Each incorrect sentence contains but one type of error. Consider a sentence to be correct if it contains none of the types of errors mentioned, even though there may be other correct ways of expressing the same thought.)

1. This fact, together with those brought out at the previous meeting, prove that the schedule is satisfactory to the employees.   1._____

2. Like many employees in scientific fields, the work of bookkeepers and accountants requires accuracy and neatness.   2._____

3. "What can I do for you," the secretary asked as she motioned to the visitor to take a seat.   3._____

4. Our representative, Mr. Charles will call on you next week to determine whether or not your claim has merit.   4._____

5. We expect you to return in the spring; please do not disappoint us.   5._____

6. Any supervisor, who disregards the just complaints of his subordinates, is remiss in the performance of his duty.   6._____

7. Because she took less than an hour for lunch is no reason for permitting her to leave before five o'clock.   7._____

8. "Miss Smith," said the supervisor, "Please arrange a meeting of the staff for two o'clock on Monday."   8._____

9. A private company's vacation and sick leave allowance usually differs considerably from a public agency.   9._____

10. Therefore, in order to increase the efficiency of operations in the department, a report on the recommended changes in procedures was presented to the departmental committee in charge of the program.   10._____

11. We told him to assign the work to whoever was available.   11._____

12. Since John was the most efficient of any other employee in the bureau, he received the highest service rating.   12._____

13. Only those members of the national organization who resided in the middle West attended the conference in Chicago.

13._____

14. The question of whether the office manager has as yet attained, or indeed can ever hope to secure professional status is one which has been discussed for years.

14._____

15. No one knew who to blame for the error which, we later discovered, resulted in a considerable loss of time.

15._____

KEY (CORRECT ANSWERS)

1.	A		6.	B
2.	A		7.	A
3.	B		8.	C
4.	B		9.	A
5.	D		10.	D

11.	D
12.	A
13.	C
14.	B
15.	A

TEST 2

DIRECTIONS : Each of the sentences in the tests that follow may be classified under one of the following four categories:

        A. *Incorrect* because of faulty grammar or sentence structure
        B. *Incorrect* because of faulty punctuation
        C. *Incorrect* because of faulty capitalization
        D. *Correct*

1. The National alliance of Businessmen is trying to persuade private businesses to hire youth in the summertime.   1._____

2. The supervisor who is on vacation, is in charge of processing vouchers.   2._____

3. The activity of the committee at its conferences is always stimulating.   3._____

4. After checking the addresses again, the letters went to the mailroom.   4._____

5. The director, as well as the employees, are interested in sharing the dividends.   5._____

KEY (CORRECT ANSWERS)

1. C
2. B
3. D
4. A
5. A

TEST 3

DIRECTIONS: In each of the following groups of sentences, one of the four sentences is faulty in grammar, punctuation, or capitalization. Select the incorrect sentence in each case.

1. A. Sailing down the bay was a thrilling experience for me.
    B. He was not consulted about your joining the club.
    C. This story is different than the one I told you yesterday.
    D. There is no doubt about his being the best player.

    1._____

2. A. He maintains there is but one road to world peace.
    B. It is common knowledge that a child sees much he is not supposed to see.
    C. Much of the bitterness might have been avoided if arbitration had been resorted to earlier in the meeting.
    D. The man decided it would be advisable to marry a girl somewhat younger than him.

    2._____

3. A. In this book, the incident I liked least is where the hero tries to put out the forest fire.
    B. Learning a foreign language will undoubtedly give a person a better understanding of his mother tongue.
    C. His actions made us wonder what he planned to do next.
    D. Because of the war, we were unable to travel during the summer vacation.

    3._____

4. A. The class had no sooner become interested in the lesson than the dismissal bell rang.
    B. There is little agreement about the kind of world to be planned at the peace conference.
    C. "Today," said the teacher, "we shall read 'The Wind in the Willows.' I am sure you'll like it.
    D. The terms of the legal settlement of the family quarrel handicapped both sides for many years.

    4._____

5. A. I was so suprised that I was not able to say a word.
    B. She is taller than any other member of the class.
    C. It would be much more preferable if you were never seen in his company.
    D. We had no choice but to excuse her for being late.

    5._____

KEY (CORRECT ANSWERS)

1. C
2. D
3. A
4. C
5. C

———————

TEST 4

DIRECTIONS: In each of the following groups of sentences, one of the four sentences is faulty in grammar, punctuation, or capitalization. Select the incorrect sentence in each case.

1. A. Please send me these data at the earliest opportunity.   1._____
   B. The loss of their material proved to be a severe handicap.
   C. My principal objection to this plan is that it is impracticable.
   D. The doll had laid in the rain for an hour and was ruined.

2. A. The garden scissors, left out all night in the rain, were in a badly rusted condition.   2._____
   B. The girls felt bad about the misunderstanding which had arisen.
   C. Sitting near the campfire, the old man told John and I about many exciting adventures he had had.
   D. Neither of us is in a position to undertake a task of that magnitude.

3. A. The general concluded that one of the three roads would lead to the besieged city.   3._____
   B. The children didn't, as a rule, do hardly anything beyond what they were told to do.
   C. The reason the girl gave for her negligence was that she had acted on the spur of the moment.
   D. The daffodils and tulips look beautiful in that blue vase.

4. A. If I was ten years older, I should be interested in this work.   4._____
   B. Give the prize to whoever has drawn the best picture.
   C. When you have finished reading the book, take it back to the library.
   D. My drawing is as good as or better than yours.

5. A. He asked me whether the substance was animal or vegetable.   5._____
   B. An apple which is unripe should not be eaten by a child.
   C. That was an insult to me who am your friend.
   D. Some spy must of reported the matter to the enemy.

6. A. Limited time makes quoting the entire message impossible.   6._____
   B. Who did she say was going?
   C. The girls in your class have dressed more dolls this year than we.
   D. There was such a large amount of books on the floor that I couldn't find a place for my rocking chair.

7. A. What with his sleeplessness and his ill health, he was unable to assume any responsibility for the success of the meeting.   7._____
   B. If I had been born in February, I should be celebrating my birthday soon.
   C. In order to prevent breakage, she placed a sheet of paper between each of the plates when she packed them.
   D. After the spring shower, the violets smelled very sweet.

8. A. He had laid the book down very reluctantly before the end of the lesson.   8._____
   B. The dog, I am sorry to say, had lain on the bed all night.
   C. The cloth was first lain on a flat surface; then it was pressed with a hot iron.
   D. While we were in Florida, we lay in the sun until we were noticeably tanned.

9. A. If John was in New York during the recent holiday season, I have no doubt he spent most of his time with his parents. 9.____
    B. How could he enjoy the television program; the dog was barking and the baby was crying.
    C. When the problem was explained to the class, he must have been asleep.
    D. She wished that her new dress were finished so that she could go to the party.

10. A. The engine not only furnishes power but light and heat as well. 10.____
    B. You're aware that we've forgotten whose guilt was established, aren't you?
    C. Everybody knows that the woman made many sacrifices for her children.
    D. A man with his dog and gun is a familiar sight in this neighborhood.

KEY (CORRECT ANSWERS)

1.	D	6.	D
2.	C	7.	B
3.	B	8.	C
4.	A	9.	B
5.	D	10.	A

TEST 5

DIRECTIONS: Each of Questions 1 to 15 consists of a sentence which may be classified appropriately under one of the following four categories:
A. *Incorrect* because of faulty grammar
B. *Incorrect* because of faulty punctuation
C. *Incorrect* because of faulty spelling
D. *Correct*

Examine each sentence carefully. Then, print, in the space on the right, the letter preceding the category which is the best of the four suggested above.

(Note: Each incorrect sentence contains only one type of error. Consider a sentence correct if it contains no errors, although there may be other correct ways of writing the sentence.)

1. Of the two employees, the one in our office is the most efficient. 1.____

2. No one can apply or even understand, the new rules and regulations. 2.____

3. A large amount of supplies were stored in the empty office. 3.____

4. If an employee is occassionally asked to work overtime, he should do so willingly. 4.____

5. It is true that the new procedures are difficult to use but, we are certain that you will learn them quickly. 5.____

6. The office manager said that he did not know who would be given a large allotment under the new plan. 6.____

7. It was at the supervisor's request that the clerk agreed to postpone his vacation. 7.____

8. We do not believe that it is necessary for both he and the clerk to attend the conference. 8.____

9. All employees, who display perseverance, will be given adequate recognition. 9.____

10. He regrets that some of us employees are dissatisfied with our new assignments. 10.____

11. "Do you think that the raise was merited," asked the supervisor? 11.____

12. The new manual of procedure is a valuable supplament to our rules and regulations. 12.____

13. The typist admitted that she had attempted to pursuade the other employees to assist her in her work. 13.____

14. The supervisor asked that all amendments to the regulations be handled by you and I. 14.____

15. The custodian seen the boy who broke the window. 15.____

2 (#5)

KEY (CORRECT ANSWERS)

1.	A		6.	D
2.	B		7.	D
3.	A		8.	A
4.	C		9.	B
5.	B		10.	D

11. B
12. C
13. C
14. A
15. A

INTERPRETING STATISTICAL DATA
GRAPHS, CHARTS AND TABLES
TEST 1

DIRECTIONS: Each question or incomplete statement is followed by several suggested answers or completions. Select the one that BEST answers the question or completes the statement. *PRINT THE LETTER OF THE CORRECT ANSWER IN THE SPACE AT THE RIGHT.*

Questions 1-5.

DIRECTIONS: Questions 1 through 5 are to be answered SOLELY on the basis of the following chart.

JOB. NO.	DATES			PROCESS	NO. OF ORIGINALS	NO. OF COPIES OF EACH ORIGINAL	REQUEST-ING UNIT
	Submitted	Required	Completed				
324	6/22	6/25	6/25	Xerox	14	25	Research
325	6/25	6/27	6/28	Kodak	10	125	Training
326	6/25	6/25	6/25	Xerox	12	11	Budget
327	6/25	6/27	6/26	Press	17	775	Admin. Div. H
328	6/28	ASAP*	6/25	Press	5	535	Personnel
329	6/26	6/26	6/27	Xerox	15	8	Admin. Div. G

DUPLICATION JOBS

*ASAP - As soon as possible

1. The unit whose job was to be xeroxed but was NOT completed by the date required is   1.____

   A. Administrative Division H
   B. Administrative Division G
   C. Research
   D. Training

2. The job with the LARGEST number of original pages to be xeroxed is job number   2.____

   A. 324   B. 326   C. 327   D. 329

3. Jobs were completed AFTER June 26, for   3.____

    A. Training and Administrative Division G
    B. Training and Administrative Division H
    C. Research and Budget
    D. Administrative Division G *only*

4. Which one of the following units submitted a job which was completed SOONER than   4.____
required?

    A. Training
    B. Administrative Division H
    C. Personnel
    D. Administrative Division G

5. The jobs which were submitted on different days but were completed on the SAME day   5.____
and used the SAME process had job numbers

    A. 324 and 326   B. 327 and 328
    C. 324, 326, and 328   D. 324, 326, and 329

KEY (CORRECT ANSWERS)

1. B
2. D
3. A
4. B
5. A

TEST 2

Questions 1-10.

DIRECTIONS: Questions 1 through 10 are to be answered SOLELY on the basis of the Production Record table shown below for the Information Unit in Agency X for the work week ended Friday, December 6. The table shows, for each employee, the quantity of each type of work performed and the percentage of the work week spent in performing each type of work.

NOTE: Assume that each employee works 7 hours a day and 5 days a week, making a total of 35 hours for the work week.

PRODUCTION RECORD - INFORMATION UNIT IN AGENCY X
(For the work week ended Friday, December 6)

	NUMBER OF			
	Papers Filed	Sheets Proofread	Visitors Received	Envelopes Addressed
Miss Agar	3120	33	178	752
Mr. Brun	1565	59	252	724
Miss Case	2142	62	214	426
Mr. Dale	4259	29	144	1132
Miss Earl	2054	58	212	878
Mr. Farr	1610	69	245	621
Miss Glen	2390	57	230	790
Mr. Hope	3425	32	176	805
Miss Iver	3726	56	148	650
Mr. Joad	3212	55	181	495

	PERCENTAGE OF WORK WEEK SPENT ON				
	Filing Papers	Proof-reading	Receiving Visitors	Addressing Envelopes	Performing Miscellaneous Work
Miss Agar	30%	9%	34%	11%	16%
Mr. Brun	13%	15%	52%	10%	10%
Miss Case	23%	18%	38%	6%	15%
Mr. Dale	50%	7%	17%	16%	10%
Miss Earl	24%	14%	37%	14%	11%
Mr. Farr	16%	19%	48%	8%	9%
Miss Glenn	27%	12%	42%	12%	7%
Mr. Hope	38%	8%	32%	13%	9%
Miss Iver	43%	13%	24%	9%	11%
Mr. Joad	33%	11%	36%	7%	13%

1. For the week, the average amount of time which the employees spent in proofreading was MOST NEARLY _____ hours.

   A. 3.1 B. 3.6 C. 4.4 D. 5.1

   1._____

2. The average number of visitors received daily by an employee was MOST NEARLY

   A. 40 B. 57 C. 198 D. 395

   2._____

3. Of the following employees, the one who addressed envelopes at the FASTEST rate was

   A. Miss Agar B. Mr. Brun C. Miss Case D. Mr. Dale

   3._____

4. Mr. Farr's rate of filing papers was MOST NEARLY _____ pages per minute.

   A. 2 B. 1.7 C. 5 D. 12

   4._____

5. The average number of hours that Mr. Brun spent daily on receiving visitors exceeded the average number of hours that Miss Iver spent daily on the same type of work by MOST NEARLY _____ hours.

   A. 2 B. 3 C. 4 D. 5

   5._____

6. Miss Earl worked at a FASTER rate than Miss Glen in

   A. filing papers B. proofreading sheets
   C. receiving visitors D. addressing envelopes

   6._____

7. Mr. Joad's rate of filing papers _____ Miss Iver's rate of filing papers by APPROXI-MATELY _____ .

   A. was less than; 10% B. exceeded; 33%
   C. was less than; 16% D. exceeded; 12%

   7._____

8. Assume that in the following week Miss Case is instructed to increase the percentage of her time spent on filing papers to 35%.
   If she continued to file papers at the same rate as she did for the week ended December 6, the number of additional papers that she filed the following week was MOST NEARLY

   A. 3260 B. 5400 C. 250 D. 1120

   8._____

9. Assume that in the following week Mr. Hope increased his weekly total of envelopes addressed to 1092.
   If he continued to spend the same amount of time on this assignment as he did for the week ended December 6, the increase in his rate of addressing envelopes the following week was MOST NEARLY _____ envelopes per hour.

   A. 15 B. 65 C. 155 D. 240

   9._____

10. Assume that in the following week Miss Agar and Mr. Dale spent 3 and 9 hours less, respectively, on filing papers than they had spent for the week ended December 6, without changing their rates of work.
The total number of papers filed during the following week by both Miss Agar and Mr. Dale was MOST NEARLY

    A. 4235   B. 4295   C. 4315   D. 4370

10.____

KEY (CORRECT ANSWERS)

    1. C
    2. A
    3. B
    4. C
    5. A
    6. C
    7. D
    8. D
    9. B
  10. B

TEST 3

Questions 1-6.

DIRECTIONS: Questions 1 through 6 are to be answered SOLELY on the basis of the chart below.

EMPLOYMENT ERRORS

	Allan	Barry	Cary	David
July	5	4	1	7
Aug.	8	3	9	8
Sept.	7	8	7	5
Oct.	3	6	5	3
Nov.	2	4	4	6
Dec.	5	2	8	4

1. The clerk with the HIGHEST number of errors for the 6-month period was   1.____

   A. Allan   B. Barry   C. Cary   D. David

2. If the number of errors made by Allan in the six months shown represented one-eighth of   2.____
   the total errors made by the unit during the entire year, what was the TOTAL number of
   errors made by the unit for the year?

   A. 124   B. 180   C. 240   D. 360

3. The number of errors made by David in November was what fraction of the total errors   3.____
   made in November?

   A. 1/3   B. 1/6   C. 378   D. 3/16

4. The average number of errors made per month per clerk was MOST NEARLY   4.____

   A. 4   B. 5   C. 6   D. 7

5. Of the total number of errors made during the six-month period, the percentage made in   5.____
   August was MOST NEARLY

   A. 2%   B. 4%   C. 23%   D. 44%

6. If the number of errors in the unit were to decrease in the next six months by 30%, what   6.____
   would be MOST NEARLY the total number of errors for the unit for the next six months?

   A. 87   B. 94   C. 120   D. 137

KEY (CORRECT ANSWERS)

1. C
2. C
3. C
4. B
5. C
6. A

TEST 4

Questions 1-5.

DIRECTIONS: Questions 1 through 5 are to be answered SOLELY on the basis of the data given below. These data show the performance rates of the employees in a particular division for a period of six months.

Employee	Jan.	Feb.	Mar.	April	May	June
A	96	53	64	48	76	72
B	84	58	69	56	67	79
C	73	68	71	54	59	62
D	98	74	79	66	86	74
E	89	78	67	74	75	77

1. According to the above data, the average monthly performance for a worker is MOST NEARLY

    A. 66   B. 69   C. 72   D. 75

1.____

2. According to the above data, the mean monthly performance for the division is MOST NEARLY

    A. 350   B. 358   C. 387   D. 429

2.____

3. According to the above data, the employee who shows the LEAST month-to-month variation in performance is

    A. A   B. B   C. C   D. D

3.____

4. According to the above data, the employee who shows the GREATEST range in performance is

    A. A   B. B   C. C   D. D

4.____

5. According to the above data, the median employee with respect to performance for the six-month period is

    A. A   B. B   C. C   D. D

5.____

KEY (CORRECT ANSWERS)

1. C
2. B
3. C
4. A
5. B

TEST 5

Questions 1-5.

DIRECTIONS: Questions 1 through 5 are to be answered SOLELY on the basis of the chart below, which shows the absences in Unit A for the period November 1 through November 15.

	ABSENCE RECORD - UNIT A														
	November 1-15														
Date:	1	2	3	4	5	6	7	8	9	10	11	12	13	14	15
Employee:															
Ames	X	s	H					X			H			X	X
Bloom	X		H			X	X	S	s	H	S	S			X
Deegan	X	J	H	J	J	J	X	X			H				X
Howard	X		H					X			H			X	X
Jergens	X	M	H	M	M	M		X			H			X	X
Lange	X		H			S	X	X							X
Morton	X						X	X	V	V	H				X
O'Shea	X		H			0		X			H	X		X	X

CODE FOR TYPES OF ABSENCE

X - Saturday or Sunday
H - Legal Holiday
P - Leave without pay
M - Military Leave
J - Jury duty
V - Vacation
S - Sick Leave
O - Other leave of absence

NOTE: If there is no entry against an employee's name under a date, the employee worked on that date.

1. According to the above chart, NO employee in Unit A was absent on   1.____

    A. leave without pay   B. military leave
    C. other leave of absence   D. vacation

2. According to the above chart, all but one of the employees in Unit A were present on the   2.____

    A. 3rd   B. 5th   C. 9th   D. 13th

3. According to the above chart, the ONLY employee who worked on a legal holiday when   3.____
the other employees were absent are

    A. Deegan and Morton   B. Howard and O'Shea
    C. Lange and Morton   D. Morton and O'Shea

4. According to the above chart, the employee who was absent ONLY on a day that was a   4.____
Saturday, Sunday, or legal holiday was

   A. Bloom   B. Howard   C. G. Morton   D. O'Shea

5. The employees who had more absences than anyone else are   5.____

   A. Bloom and Deegan
   B. Bloom, Deegan, and Jergens
   C. Deegan and Jergens
   D. Deegan, Jergens, and O'Shea

KEY (CORRECT ANSWERS)

1. A
2. D
3. C
4. B
5. B

TEST 6

Questions 1-7.

DIRECTIONS: Questions 1 through 7 are to be answered SOLELY on the basis of the time sheet and instructions given below.

	MON.	TUBS.	WED.	THURS .	FRI.
	IN OUT	IN OUT	IN OUT	IN OUT	IN OUT
Walker	8:45 5:02	9:20 5:00	9:00 5:02	Annual Lv.	9:04 5:05
Jones	9:01 5:00	9:03 5:02	9:08 5:01	8:55 5:04	9:00 5:00
Rubins	8:49 5:04	Sick Lv.	9:05 5:04	9:03 5:03	9:04 3:30(PB)
Brown	9:00 5:01	8:55 5:03	9:00 5:05	9:04 5:07	9:05 5:03
Roberts	9:30 5:08 (PA)	8:43 5:07	9:05 5:05	9:09 12:30 (PB)	8:58 5:04

The above time sheet indicates the arrival and leaving times of five telephone operators who punched a time clock in a city agency for the week of April 14. The times they arrived at work in the mornings are indicated in the columns labeled *IN* and the times they left work are indicated in the columns labeled *OUT.* The letters (PA) mean prearranged lateness, and the letters (PB) mean personal business. Time lost for these purposes is charged to annual leave.

The operators are scheduled to arrive at 9:00. However, they are not considered late unless they arrive after 9:05. If they prearrange a lateness, they are not considered late. Time lost through lateness is charged to annual leave. A full day's work is eight hours, from 9:00 to 5:00.

1. Which operator worked the entire week WITHOUT using any annual leave or sick leave time?

   A. Jones
   C. Roberts
   B. Brown
   D. None of the above

   1.____

2. On which days was NONE of the operators considered late?

   A. Monday and Wednesday
   C. Wednesday and Thursday
   B. Monday and Friday
   D. Wednesday and Friday

   2.____

3. Which operator clocked out at a different time each day of the week?

   A. Roberts   B. Jones   C. Rubins   D. Brown

   3.____

4. How many of the operators were considered late on Wednesday?

   A. 0   B. 1   C. 2   D. 3

   4.____

5. What was the TOTAL number of charged latenesses for the week of April 14?

   A. 1   B. 3   C. 5   D. 7

   5.____

6. Which day shows the MOST time charged to all types of leave by all the operators?

   A. Monday   B. Tuesday   C. Wednesday   D. Thursday

   6.____

7. What operators were considered ON TIME all week? 7.____

    A. Jones and Rubins   B. Rubins and Brown
    C. Brown and Roberts   D. Walker and Brown

KEY (CORRECT ANSWERS)

    1. B
    2. B
    3. A
    4. B
    5. B
    6. D
    7. B

TEST 7

Questions 1-10.

DIRECTIONS: Questions 1 through 10 are to be answered SOLELY on the basis of the information and code tables given below.

In accordance with these code tables, each employee in the department is assigned a code number consisting of ten digits arranged from left to right in the following order:

    I.   Division in Which Employed
    II.   Title of Position
    III. Annual Salary
    IV.   Age
    V.   Number of Years Employed in Department

EXAMPLE: A clerk is 21 years old, has been employed in the department for three years, and is working in the Supply Division at a yearly salary of $25,000. His code number is 90-115-13-02-2.

DEPARTMENTAL CODE

TABLE I		TABLE II		TABLE III		TABLE IV		TABLE V	
Code	Division No. in Which Employed	Code	Title No. of Position	Code	Annual No. Salary	Code	No. Age	Code	No. of No. Years Employee in Dept.
10	Accounting	115	Clerk	11	$18,000 or less	01	Under 20 yrs.	1	Less than 1 yr.
20	Construction	155	Typist	12	$18,001 to $24,000	02	20 to 29 yrs.	2	1 to 5 yrs.
30	Engineering	175	Stenographer	13	$24,001 to $30,000	03	30 to 39 yrs.	3	6 to 10 yrs.
40	Information	237	Bookkeeper	14	$30,001 to $36,000	04	40 to 49 yrs.	4	11 to 15 yrs.
50	Maintenance	345	Statistician	15	$36,001 to $45,000	05	50 to 59 yrs.	5	16 to 25 yrs.
60	Personnel	545	Storekeeper	16	$45,001 to $60,000	06	60 to 69 yrs.	6	26 to 35 yrs.
70	Record	633	Draftsman	17	$60,001 to $70,000	07	70 yrs. or over	7	36 yrs. or over
80	Research	665	Civil Engineer	18	$70,001 or over				
90	Supply	865	Machinist						
		915	Porter						

1. A draftsman employed in the Engineering Division at a yearly salary of $34,800 is 36 years old and has been employed in the department for 9 years.
He should be coded

    A. 20-633-13-04-3   B. 30-865-13-03-4
    C. 20-665-14-04-4   D. 30-633-14-03-3

1.____

2. A porter employed in the Maintenance Division at a yearly salary of $28,800 is 52 years old and has been employed in the department for 6 years.
He should be coded

    A. 50-915-12-03-3   B. 90-545-12-05-3
    C. 50-915-13-05-3   D. 90-545-13-03-3

2.____

3. Richard White, who has been employed in the department for 12 years, receives $50,000 a year as a civil engineer in the Construction Division. He is 38 years old.
He should be coded

    A. 20-665-16-03-4   B. 20-665-15-02-1
    C. 20-633-14-04-2   D. 20-865-15-02-5

3.____

4. An 18-year-old clerk appointed to the department six months ago is assigned to the Record Division. His annual salary is $21,600.
He should be coded

    A. 70-115-11-01-1   B. 70-115-12-01-1
    C. 70-115-12-02-1   D. 70-155-12-01-1

4.____

5. An employee has been coded 40-155-12-03-3.
Of the following statements regarding this employee, the MOST accurate one is that he is

    A. a clerk who has been employed in the department for at least 6 years
    B. a typist who receives an annual salary which does not exceed $24,000
    C. under 30 years of age and has been employed in the department for at least 11 years
    D. employed in the Supply Division at a salary which exceeds $18,000 per annum

5.____

6. Of the following statements regarding an employee who is coded 60-175-13-01-2, the LEAST accurate statement is that this employee

    A. is a stenographer in the Personnel Division
    B. has been employed in the department for at least one year
    C. receives an annual salary which exceeds $24,000
    D. is more than 20 years of age

6.____

7. The following are the names of four employees of the department with their code numbers:

                James Black, 80-345-15-03-4
                William White, 30-633-14-03-4
                Sam Green, 80-115-12-02-3
                John Jones, 10-237-13-04-5

If a salary increase is to be given to the employees who have been employed in the department for 11 years or more and who earn less than $36,001 a year, the two of the above employees who will receive a salary increase are

7.____

A. John Jones and William White
B. James Black and Sam Green
C. James Black and William White
D. John Jones and Sam Green

8. Code number 50-865-14-02-6, which has been assigned to a machinist, contains an   8.____
    obvious inconsistency.
    This inconsistency involves the figures

    A. 50-865   B. 865-14   C. 14-02   D. 02-6

9. Ten employees were awarded merit prizes for outstanding service during the year. Their   9.____
    code numbers were:

80-345-14-04-4	40-155-12-02-2
40-155-12-04-4	10-115-12-02-2
10-115-13-03-2	80-115-13-02-2
80-175-13-05-5	10-115-13-02-3
10-115-12-04-3	30-633-14-04-4

    Of these outstanding employees, the number who were clerks employed in the
    Accounting Division at a salary ranging from $24,001 to $30,000 per annum is

    A. 1   B. 2   C. 3   D. 4

10. The MOST accurate of the following statements regarding the ten outstanding employ-   10.____
    ees listed in the previous question is that

    A. fewer than half of the employees were under 40 years of age
    B. there were fewer typists than stenographers
    C. four of the employees were employed in the department 11 years or more
    D. two of the employees in the Research Division receive annual salaries ranging
        from $30,001 to $36,000

KEY (CORRECT ANSWERS)

1. D
2. C
3. A
4. B
5. B
6. D
7. A
8. D
9. B
10. C

INTERPRETING STATISTICAL DATA
GRAPHS, CHARTS AND TABLES

TEST 1

DIRECTIONS: Each question or incomplete statement is followed by several suggested answers or completions. Select the one that BEST answers the question or completes the statement. *PRINT THE LETTER OF THE CORRECT ANSWER IN THE SPACE AT THE RIGHT.*

Questions 1-5.

DIRECTIONS: Questions 1 through 5 are to be answered SOLELY on the basis of the following table.

ANNUAL SALARIES PAID TO SELECTED CLERICAL TITLES IN FIVE MAJOR CITIES IN 2012 AND 2014					
2014					
	Clerk	Typist	Steno	Legal Steno	Computer Operator
Newton	$33,900	$34,800	$36,300	$43,800	$35,400
Barton	$32,400	$34,200	$35,400	$43,500	$34,200
Phelton	$32,400	$32,400	$34,200	$42,000	$33,000
Washburn	$33,600	$34,800	$35,400	$43,800	$34,800
Biltmore	$33,000	$34,200	$35,100	$43,500	$34,500
2012					
	Clerk	Typist	Steno	Legal Steno	Computer Operator
Newtown	$31,800	$33,600	$35,400	$41,400	$34,500
Barton	$30,000	$31,500	$33,000	$39,600	$31,500
Phelton	$29,400	$30,600	$31,800	$37,800	$31,200
Washburn	$30,600	$32,400	$33,600	$40,200	$32,400
Biltmore	$30,000	$31,800	$33,000	$39,600	$32,100

1. Assume that the value of the fringe benefits offered to clerical employees in 2014 amounted to 14% of their annual salaries in Newton, 17% in Barton, 18% in Phelton, 15% in Washburn, and 16% in Biltmore.
The total cost of employing a computer operator for 2014 was GREATEST in

   A. Newtown   B. Barton   C. Phelton   D. Washburn

1.____

2. During negotiations for their 2015 contract, the stenographers of Biltmore are demanding that their rate of pay be fixed at 85% of the legal stenographer salary.
If this demand is granted and if the legal stenographer salary increases by 7% in 2015, the 2015 stenographer salary will be MOST NEARLY

   A. $36,972   B. $37,560   C. $39,564   D. $40,020

2.____

3. Of the following, the GREATEST percentage increase in salary from 2012 to 2014 was gained by   3.____

    A.   clerks in Newtown
    B.   stenographers in Barton
    C.   legal stenographers in Washburn
    D.   computer operators in Biltmore

4. The title which achieved the SMALLEST average percentage increase in salary from 2012 to 2014 was   4.____

    A.   clerk   B.   typist
    C.   stenographer   D.   legal stenographer

5. Assume that, in 2014, clerks accounted for 60% of the clerical work force in Barton. The clerical work force consists of 140 employees. In 2012, the clerks accounted for 65% of the clerical work force in Barton. The clerical work force then consisted of 120 employees.   5.____
The difference between the 2012 and 2014 payroll for clerks in Barton is MOST NEARLY

    A. $120,000   B. $240,000   C. $360,000   D. $480,000

KEY (CORRECT ANSWERS)

    1.   A
    2.   C
    3.   C
    4.   C
    5.   C

TEST 2

Questions 1-9.

DIRECTIONS: Questions 1 through 9 are to be answered SOLELY on the basis of the facts given in the table below, which contains certain information about employees in a city bureau.

NAME	TITLE	AGE	ANNUAL SALARY	YEARS OF SERVICE	EXAMINATION RATING
Jones	Clerk	34	$20,400	10	82
Smith	Stenographer	25	19,200	2	72
Black	Typist	19	14,400	1	71
Brown	Stenographer	36	25,200	12	88
Thomas	Accountant	49	41,200	21	91
Gordon	Clerk	31	30,000	8	81
Johnson	Stenographer	26	26,400	5	75
White	Accountant	53	36,000	30	90
Spencer	Clerk	42	27,600	19	85
Taylor	Typist	24	21,600	5	74
Simpson	Accountant	37	50,000	11	87
Reid	Typist	20	12,000	2	72
Fulton	Accountant	55	55,000	31	100
Chambers	Clerk	22	15,600	4	75
Calhoun	Stenographer	48	28,800	16	80

RECORD OF EMPLOYEES IN A CITY BUREAU

1. The name of the employee whose salary would be the middle one if all the salaries were ranked in order of magnitude is

   A. White   B. Johnson   C. Brown   D. Spencer

   1.____

2. The combined monthly salary of all the stenographers EXCEEDS the combined monthly salary of all the clerks by

   A. $6,000   B. $500   C. $22,800   D. $600

   2.____

3. The age of the employee who received the HIGHEST rating in the examination among those who have less than 10 years of service is _____ years.

   A. 22   B. 31   C. 55   D. 34

   3.____

4. The average examination rating of those employees who had 15 years of service or more as compared with the average examination rating of those employees who had 5 years of service or less is MOST NEARLY _____ points _____.

   A. 16; greater   B. 7; greater
   C. 10; less   D. 25; greater

   4.____

5. The name of the youngest employee whose monthly salary is more than $1,000 per month and who has more than one year of service is

   A. Reid   B. Black   C. Chambers   D. Taylor

   5.____

6. The name of the employee who received an examination rating of over 85%, who has more than 15 years of service, and who earns a yearly salary of more than $25,000 but less than $40,000 is

   A. Thomas   B. Spencer   C. Calhoun   D. White

   6.____

7. The annual salary of the HIGHEST paid stenographer is

    A. more than twice as great as the salary of the youngest employee

    B. greater than the salary of the oldest typist but not as great as the salary of the oldest clerk

    C. greater than the salary of the highest paid typist but not as great as the salary of the lowest paid accountant

    D. less than the combined salaries of the two youngest typists

7.____

8. The number of employees whose annual salary is more than $15,600 but less than $28,800 and who have at least 5 years of service is

    A. 11   B. 8   C. 6   D. 5

8.____

9. Of the following, it would be MOST accurate to state that the

    A. youngest employee is lowest with respect to number of years of service, examination rating, and salary

    B. oldest employee is highest with respect to number of years of service, examination rating, but not with respect to salary

    C. annual salary of the youngest clerk is $1,200 more than the annual salary of the youngest typist and $2,400 less than the annual salary of the youngest stenographer

    D. difference in age between the youngest and oldest typist is less than one-fourth the difference in age between the youngest and oldest stenographer

9.____

KEY (CORRECT ANSWERS)

1. B
2. B
3. B
4. A
5. C
6. D
7. C
8. D
9. D

TEST 3

Questions 1-10.

DIRECTIONS: Questions 1 through 10 are to be answered SOLELY on the basis of the Personnel Record of Division X shown below.

Employee	Bureau In Which Employed	Title	Annual Salary	No. of Days Absent On Vacation	No. of Days Absent On Sick Leave	No. of Times Late
Abbott	Mail	Clerk	$31,200	18	0	1
Barnes	Mail	Clerk	25,200	25	3	7
Davis	Mail	Typist	24,000	21	9	2
Adams	Payroll	Accountant	42,500	10	0	2
Bell	Payroll	Bookkeeper	31,200	23	2	5
Duke	Payroll	Clerk	27,600	24	4	3
Gross	Payroll	Clerk	21,600	12	5	7
Lane	Payroll	Stenographer	26,400	19	16	20
Reed	Payroll	Typist	22,800	15	11	11
Arnold	Record	Clerk	32,400	6	15	9
Cane	Record	Clerk	24,500	14	3	4
Fay	Record	Clerk	21,100	20	0	4
Hale	Record	Typist	25,200	18	2	7
Baker	Supply	Clerk	30,000	20	3	2
Clark	Supply	Clerk	27,600	25	6	5
Ford	Supply	Typist	22,800	25	4	22

Table title: DIVISION X — PERSONNEL RECORD - CURRENT YEAR

1. The percentage of the total number of employees who are clerks is MOST NEARLY   1._____

   A. 25%   B. 33%   C. 38%   D. 56%

2. Of the following employees, the one who receives a monthly salary of $2,100 is   2._____

   A. Barnes   B. Gross   C. Reed   D. Clark

3. The difference between the annual salary of the highest paid clerk and that of the lowest   3._____
   paid clerk is

   A. $6,000   B. $8,400   C. $11,300   D. $20,900

4. The number of employees receiving more than $25,000 a year but less than $40,000 a   4._____
   year is

   A. 6   B. 9   C. 12   D. 15

5. The TOTAL annual salary of the employees of the Mail Bureau is _____ the total annual   5._____
   salary of the employees of the _____.

   A. one-half of; Payroll Bureau
   B. less than; Record Bureau by $21,600
   C. equal to; Supply Bureau
   D. less than; Payroll Bureau by $71,600

6. The average annual salary of the employees who are not clerks is MOST NEARLY   6.____

    A. $23,700   B. $25,450   C. $26,800   D. $27,850

7. If all the employees were given a 10% increase in pay, the annual salary of Lane would   7.____
then be

    A. *greater* than that of Barnes by $1,320
    B. *less* than that of Bell by $4,280
    C. *equal* to that of Clark
    D. *greater* than that of Ford by $3,600

8. Of the clerks who earned less than $30,000 a year, the one who was late the FEWEST   8.____
number of times was late _____ time(s).

    A. 1   B. 2   C. 3   D. 4

9. The bureau in which the employees were late the FEWEST number of times on an aver-   9.____
age is the _____ Bureau.

    A. Mail   B. Payroll   C. Record   D. Supply

10. The MOST accurate of the following statements is that   10.____

    A. Reed was late more often than any other typist
    B. Bell took more time off for vacation than any other employee earning $30,000 or
       more annually
    C. of the typists, Ford was the one who was absent the fewest number of times
       because of sickness
    D. three clerks took no time off because of sickness

KEY (CORRECT ANSWERS)

1. D
2. A
3. C
4. B
5. C
6. D
7. A
8. C
9. A
10. B

TEST 4

Questions 1-10.

DIRECTIONS: Questions 1 through 10 are to be answered SOLELY on the basis of the Weekly Payroll Record shown below of Bureau X in a public agency. In answering these questions, note that gross weekly salary is the salary before deductions have been made; take-home pay is the amount remaining after all indicated weekly deductions have been made from the gross weekly salary. In answering questions involving annual amounts, compute on the basis of 52 weeks per year.

Unit In Which Employed	Employee	Title	Gross Weekly Salary (Before Deductions)	Weekly Deductions From Gross Salary		
				Medical Insurance	Income Tax	Pension System
Accounting	Allen	Accountant	$950	$14.50	$125.00	$53.20
Accounting	Barth	Bookkeeper	720	19.00	62.00	40.70
Accounting	Keller	Clerk	580	6.50	82.00	33.10
Accounting	Peters	Typist	560	6.50	79.00	35.30
Accounting	Simons	Stenographer	610	14.50	64.00	37.80
Information	Brown	Clerk	560	13.00	56.00	42.20
Information	Smith	Clerk	590	14.50	61.00	58.40
Information	Turner	Typist	580	13.00	59.00	62.60
Information	Williams	Stenographer	620	19.00	44.00	69.40
Mail	Conner	Clerk	660	13.00	74.00	55.40
Mail	Farrell	Typist	540	6.50	75.00	34.00
Mail	Johnson	Stenographer	580	19.00	36.00	37.10
Records	Dillon	Clerk	640	6.50	94.00	58.20
Records	Martin	Clerk	540	19.00	29.00	50.20
Records	Standish	Typist	620	14.50	67.00	60.10
Records	Wilson	Stenographer	690	6.50	101.00	75.60

1. Dillon's annual take-home pay is MOST NEARLY

    A. $25,000   B. $27,000   C. $31,000   D. $33,000

1.____

2. The difference between Turner's gross annual salary and his annual take-home pay is MOST NEARLY

    A. $3,000   B. $5,000   C. $7,000   D. $9,000

2.____

3. Of the following, the employee whose weekly take-home pay is CLOSEST to that of Keller's is

    A. Peters   B. Brown   C. Smith   D. Turner

3.____

4. The average gross annual salary of the typists is

    A. less than $27,500
    B. more than $27,500 but less than $30,000
    C. more than $30,000 but less than $32,500
    D. more than $32,500

4.____

5. The average gross weekly salary of the stenographers EXCEEDS the gross weekly salary of the clerks by

    A. $20   B. $30   C. $40   D. $50

5.____

6. Of the following employees in the Accounting Unit, the one who pays the HIGHEST percentage of his gross weekly salary for the Pension System is

    A. Barth   B. Keller   C. Peters   D. Simons

6.____

7. For all of the Accounting Unit employees, the total annual deductions for Medical Insurance are less than the total annual deductions for the Pension System by MOST NEARLY

    A. $6,000   B. $7,000   C. $8,000   D. $9,000

7.____

8. Of the following, the employee whose total weekly deductions are MOST NEARLY 27% of his gross weekly salary is

    A. Barth   B. Brown   C. Martin   D. Wilson

8.____

9. The total amount of the gross weekly salaries of all the employees in the Records Unit is MOST NEARLY

    A. 95% of the total amount of the gross weekly salaries of all the employees in the Information Unit
    B. 10% greater than the total amount of the gross weekly salaries of all the employees in the Mail Unit
    C. 75% of the total amount of the gross weekly salaries of all the employees in the Accounting Unit
    D. four times as great as the total amount deducted weekly for tax for all the employees in the Records Unit

9.____

10. For the employees in the Information Unit, the AVERAGE weekly deductions for Income Tax _____ the average weekly deduction for _____.

    A. exceeds; Income Tax for the employees in the Records Unit
    B. is less than; the Pension System for the employees in the Mail Unit
    C. exceeds; Income Tax for the employees in the Accounting Unit
    D. is less than; the Pension System for the employees in the Records Unit

10.____

KEY (CORRECT ANSWERS)

1. A
2. C
3. C
4. B
5. B
6. C
7. B
8. D
9. C
10. D

TEST 5

Questions 1-9.

DIRECTIONS: Questions 1 through 9 are to be answered SOLELY on the basis of the following information.

Assume that the following rules for computing service ratings are to be used experimentally in determining the service ratings of seven permanent city employees. (Note that these rules are hypothetical and are NOT to be confused with the existing method of computing service ratings for city employees.) The personnel record of each of these seven employees is given in Table II. You are to determine the answer to each of the questions on the basis of the rules given below for computing service ratings and the data contained in the personnel records of these seven employees.

All computations should be made as of the close of the rating period ending March 31, 2017.

Service Rating
The service rating of each permanent competitive class employee shall be computed by adding the following three scores: (1) a basic score, (2) the employee's seniority score, and (3) the employee's efficiency score.

Seniority Score
An employee's seniority score shall be computed by crediting him with 1/2% per year for each year of service starting with the date of the employee's entrance as a permanent employee into the competitive class, up to a maximum of 15 years (7 1/2%).

A residual fractional period of eight months or more shall be considered as a full year and credited with 1/2%. A residual fraction of from four to, but not including, eight months shall be considered as a half-year and credited with 1/4%. A residual fraction of less than four months shall receive no credit in the seniority score.

For example, a person who entered the competitive class as a permanent employee on August 1, 2014 would, as of March 31, 2017, be credited with a seniority score of 1 1/2% for his 2 years and 8 months of service.

Efficiency Score
An employee's efficiency score shall be computed by adding the annual efficiency ratings received by him during his service in his present position. (Where there are negative efficiency ratings, such ratings shall be subtracted from the sum of the positive efficiency ratings.) An employee's annual efficiency rating shall be based on the grade he receives from his supervisor for his work performance during the annual efficiency rating period.

Basic Score
A basic score of 70% shall be given to each employee upon permanent appointment to a competitive class position.

An employee shall receive a grade of A for performing work of the highest quality and shall be credited with an efficiency rating of plus (+) 3%. An employee shall receive a grade of F for performing work of the lowest quality and shall receive an efficiency rating of minus (-) 2%. Table I, entitled BASIS FOR DETERMINING ANNUAL EFFICIENCY RATINGS, lists the six grades of work performance with their equivalent annual efficiency ratings. Table I also lists the efficiency ratings to be assigned for service in a position for less than a year during the annual efficiency rating period.

The annual efficiency rating period shall run from April 1 to March 31, inclusive.

TABLE I – BASIS FOR DETERMINING ANNUAL EFFICIENCY RATINGS				
		Annual Efficiency Rating for Service in a Position For:		
Quality of Work Per-formed	Grade Assigned	8 months to a full year	At least 4 months but less than 8 months	Less than 4 months
Highest	A	+3%	+1 1/2%	0%
Good	B	+2%	+1%	0%
Standard	C	+1%	+1/2%	0%
Substandard	D	0%	0%	0%
Poor	E	-1%	-4%	0%
Lowest	F	-2%	-1%	0%

Appointment or Promotion During an Efficiency Rating Period

An employee who has been appointed or promoted during an efficiency rating period shall receive for that period an efficiency rating only for work performed by him during the portion of the period that he served in the position to which he was appointed or promoted. His efficiency rating for the period shall be determined in accordance with Table I.

Sample Computation of Service Rating

John Smith entered the competitive class as a permanent employee on December 1, 2012 and was promoted to his present position as a Clerk, Grade 3, on November 1, 2015. As a Clerk, Grade 3, he received a grade of B for work performed during the five-month period extending from November 1, 2015 to March 31, 2016 and a grade of C for work performed during the full annual period extending from April 1, 2016 to March 31, 2017.

On the basis of the RULES FOR COMPUTING SERVICE RATINGS, John Smith should be credited with:

    70%   Basic Score
    2 1/4%. Seniority Score - for 4 years and 4 months of service (from 12/1/12 to 3/31/17)
    2%   Efficiency Score - for 5 months of B service and a full _____ year of C service
    74 1/4%

TABLE II
PERSONNEL RECORD OF SEVEN PERMANENT
COMPETITIVE CLASS EMPLOYEES

Employee	Present Position	Date of Appointment or Promotion To Present Position	Date of Entry as Permanent Employee in Competitive Class
Allen	Clerk, Gr. 5	6-1-13	7-1-00
Brown	Clerk, Gr. 4	1-1-15	7-1-17
Cole	Clerk, Gr. 3	9-1-13	11-1-10
Fox	Clerk, Gr. 3	10-1-13	9-1-08
Green	Clerk, Gr. 2	12-1-11	12-1-11
Hunt	Clerk, Gr. 2	7-1-12	7-1-12
Kane	Steno, Gr. 3	11-16-14	3-1-11

GRADES RECEIVED ANNUALLY FOR WORK
PERFORMED IN PRESENT POSITION

Employee	4-1-11 to 3-31-12	4-1-12 to 3-31-13	4-1-13 to 3-31-14	4-1-14 to 3-31-15	4-1-15 to 3-31-16	4-1-16 to 3-31-17
Allen			C*	C	B	C
Brown				C*	C	B
Cole			A*	B	C	C
Fox			C*	C	D	C
Green	C*	D	C	D	C	C
Hunt		C*	C	E	C	C
Kane				B*	B	C

EXPLANATORY NOTES:

* Served in present position for less than a full year during this rating period. (Note date of appointment, or promotion, to present position.)

All seven employees have served continuously as permanent employees since their entry into the competitive class.

Questions 1 through 9 refer to the employees listed in Table II. You are to answer these questions SOLELY on the basis of the preceding RULES FOR COMPUTING SERVICE RATINGS and on the information concerning these seven employees given in Table II. You are reminded that all computations are to be made as of the close of the rating period ending March 31, 2017. Candidates may find it helpful to arrange their computations on their scratch paper in an orderly manner since the computations for one question may also be utilized in answering another question.

1. The seniority score of Allen is

    A. 7 1/2%　　　B. 8 1/2%　　　C. 8%　　　D. 8 1/4%

2. The seniority score of Fox EXCEEDS that of Cole by

    A. 1 1/2%　　　B. 2%　　　C. 1%　　　D. 3/4%

3. The seniority score of Brown is

    A. *equal* to Hunt's
    C. *move* than Hunt's by 1 1/2%
    B. *twice* Hunt's
    D. *less* than by Hunt's by 1/2%

4. Green's efficiency score is 4.____

    A. *twice* that of Kane
    B. *equal* to that of Kane
    C. *less* than Kane's by 1/2%
    D. *less* than Kane's by 1%

5. Of the following employees, the one who has the LOWEST efficiency score is 5.____

    A. Brown   B. Fox   C. Hunt   D. Kane

6. A comparison of Hunt's efficiency score with his seniority score reveals that his efficiency score is 6.____

    A. *less* than his seniority score by 1/2%
    B. *less* than his seniority score by 3/4%
    C. *equal* to his seniority score
    D. *greater* than his seniority score by 1/2%

7. Fox's service rating is 7.____

    A. 72 1/2%   B. 74%   C. 76 1/2%   D. 76 3/4%

8. Brown's service rating is 8.____

    A. less than 78%   B. 78%
    C. 78 1/4%   D. more than 78 1/4%

9. Cole's service rating EXCEEDS Kane's by 9.____

    A. less than 2%   B. 2%
    C. 2 1/4%   D. more than 2 1/4%

KEY (CORRECT ANSWERS)

1. A
2. C
3. B
4. C
5. B
6. D
7. D
8. B
9. A

GLOSSARY OF PERSONNEL TERMS

CONTENTS

GLOSSARY OF PERSONNEL TERMS

A

Abandonment of Position—When an employee quits work without resigning. (715)

Absence Without Leave (AWOL) Absence — without prior approval, therefore without pay, that may be subject to disciplinary action. See also, *Leave Without Pay,* which is an approved absence. (630)

Administrative Workweek— A period of seven consecutive calendar days designated in advance by the head of the agency. Usually an administrative workweek coincides with a calendar week. (610)

Admonishment— Informal reproval of an employee by a supervisor; usually oral, but some agencies require written notice. (751)

Adverse Action— A removal, suspension, furlough without pay for 30 days or less, or reduction-in-grade or pay. An adverse action may be taken against an employee for disciplinary or non-disciplinary reasons. However, if the employee is covered by FPM part 752, the action must be in accordance with those procedures. Removals or reductions-in-grade based solely on unacceptable performance are covered by Part 432. Actions taken for reductions-in-force reasons are covered by Part 351. (752)

Affirmative Action — A policy followed closely by the Federal civil service that requires agencies to take positive steps to insure equal opportunity in employment, development, advancement, and treatment of all employees and applicants for employment regardless of race, color, sex, religion, national origin, or physical or mental handicap. Affirmative action also requires that specific actions be directed at the special problems and unique concerns in assuring equal employment opportunity for minorities, women and other disadvantaged groups.

Agreement—See *Collective Bargaining.*

Annuitant—A retired Federal civil service employee or a survivor (spouse or children) being paid an annuity from the Retirement Fund. (831)

Annuity—Payments to a former employee who retired, or to the surviving spouse or children. It is computed as an annual rate but paid monthly. (831)

Appeal—A request by an employee for review of an agency action by an outside agency: The right to such review-is provided by law or regulation and may include an adversary-type hearing and a written decision in which a finding of facts is made and applicable law, Executive order and regulations are applied.

Appointing Officer—A person having power by law or lawfully delegated authority to make appointments. (210, 311)

Appointment, Noncompetitive— Employment without competing with others, in the sense that it is done without regard to civil service registers, etc. Includes reinstatements, transfers, reassignments, demotions, and promotion. (335)

Appointment, Superior Qualifications—Appointment of a candidate to a position in grade 11 or above of the General Schedule at a rate above the minimum because of the candidate's superior qualifications. A rate above the minimum for the grade must be justified by the applicant's unusually high or unique qualifications, a special need of the Government for the candidate's services, or because the candidate's current pay is higher than the minimum for the grade which he or she is offered. (338, 531)

Appointment, TAPER—Abbreviation for "temporary appointment pending establishment of a register." Employment made under an OPM authority granted to an agency when there are insufficient eligibles on a register appropriate to fill the position involved. (316)

Appointment, Temporary Limited—Nonpermanent appointment of an employee hired for a specified time of one year or less, or for seasonal or intermittent positions. (316)

Appointment, Term—Nonpermanent appointment of an employee hired to work on a project expected to last over one year, but less than four years. (316)

Appropriate Unit —A group of employees which a labor organization seeks to represent for the purpose of negotiating agreements; an aggregation of employees which has a clear and identifiable community of interest and which promotes effective dealings and efficiency of operations. It may be established on a plant or installation, craft, functional or other basis. (Also known as bargaining unit, appropriate bargaining unit.) (711)

Arbitration—Final step of the negotiated grievance procedure which may be invoked by the agency or the union (not the employee) if the grievance has not been resolved. Involves use of an impartial arbitrator selected by the agency and union to render a binding award to resolve the grievance. (711)

Arbitrator—An impartial third party to whom disputing parties submit their differences for decision (award). An *ad hoc* arbitrator is one selected to act in a specific case or a limited group of cases. A permanent arbitrator is one selected to serve for the life of the agreement or a stipulated term, hearing all disputes that arise during this period. (711)

Area Office (OPM)—Forcal point for administering and implementing all OPM programs, except investigations, in the geographic area assigned. Provides personnel management advice and assistance to agencies, and personnel evaluation, recruiting and examining and special program leadership. Principal source of employment information for agencies and the public.

Audit, Work—Visit to an employee or his supervisor to verify or gather information about a position. Sometimes called "desk audit."

B

Bargaining Rights—Legally recognized right of the labor organization to represent employees in negotiations with employers. (711)

Bargaining Unit—An appropriate grouping of employees represented on an exclusive basis by a labor organization. "Appropriate" for this purpose means that it is a grouping of employees who share a community of interest and which promotes effective union and agency dealings and efficient agency operations. (711)

Basic Workweek—For a full-time employee, the 40-hour non overtime work schedule within an administrative workweek. The usual workweek consists of five 8-hour days, Monday through Friday. (610)

Break in Service—The time between separation and reemployment that may cause a loss of rights or privileges. For transfer purposes, it means not being on an agency payroll for one working day or more. For the three-year career conditional period or for reinstatement purposes, it means not being on an agency payroll for over 30 calendar days. (315)

Bumping—During reduction-in-force, the displacement of one employee by another employee in a higher group or subgroup. (351)

C

Career—Tenure of a permanent employee in the competitive service who has completed three years of substantially continuous creditable Federal service. (315)

Career-Conditional—Tenure of a permanent employee in the competitive service who *has not* completed three years of substantially continuous creditable Federal service. (315)

Career Counseling—Service available to employees to assist them in: (1) assessing their skills, abilities, interests, and aptitudes; (2) determining qualifications required for occupations within the career system and how the requirements relate to their individual capabilities; (3) defining their career goals and developing plans for reaching the goals; (4) identifying and assessing education and training opportunities and enrollment procedures; (5) identifying factors which may impair career development; and (6) learning about resources, inside or outside the agency, where additional help is available. (250)

Career Development—Systematic development designed to increase an employee's potential for advancement and career change. It may include classroom training, reading, work experience, etc. (410)

Career Ladder—A career ladder is a series of developmental positions of increasing difficulty in the same line of work, through which an employee may progress to a journeyman level on his or her personal development and performance in that series.

Career Reserved Position—A position within SES that has a specific requirement for impartiality. May be filled" only by career appointment. (920)

Ceiling, Personnel—The maximum number of employees authorized at a given time. (312)

Certification—The process by which eligibles are ranked, according to regulations, for appointment or promotion consideration. (332, 335)

Certification, Selective—Certifying only the names of eligibles who have special qualifications required to fill particular vacant positions. (332)

Certification, Top of the Register—Certifying in regular order, beginning with the eligibles at the top of the register. (332)

Change in Duty Station—A personnel action that changes an employee from one geographical location to another in the same agency. (296)

Change to Lower Grade—Downgrading a position or reducing an employee's grade. See *Demotion.* (296)

Class of Positions—All positions sufficiently similar in: (1) kind or subject matter of work; (2) level of difficulty and responsibility; and (3) qualification requirements, so as to warrant similar treatment in personnel and pay administration. For example, all Grade GS-3 Clerk-Typist positions. (511)

Classified Service—See *Competitive Service* (212)

Collective Bargaining—Performance of the mutual obligation of the employer and the exclusive (employee) representative to meet at reasonable times, to confer and negotiate in good faith, and to execute a written agreement with respect to conditions of employment, except that by any such obligation neither party shall be compelled to agree to proposals, or be required to make concessions. (Also known as collective negotiations, negotiations, and negotiation of agreement.) (711)

Collective Bargaining Agreement—A written agreement between management and a labor-organization which is usually for a definite term, and usually defines conditions of employment, and includes grievance and arbitration procedures. The terms "collective bargaining agreement" and "contract" are synonymous. (711)

Collective Bargaining Unit—A group of employees recognized as appropriate for representation by a labor organization for collective bargaining. (See *Appropriate Unit)* (711)

Compensatory Time Off—Time off (hour-for-hour) granted an employee in lieu of overtime pay. (550)

Competitive Area—For reduction-in-force, that part of an agency within which employees are in competition for retention. Generally, it is that part of an agency covered by a single appointing office. (351)

Competitive Service—Federal positions normally filled through open competitive examination (hence the term "competitive service") under civil service rules and regulations. About 86 percent of all Federal positions are in the competitive service. (212)

Competitive Status—Basic eligibility of a person to be selected to fill a position in the competitive service without open competitive examination. Competitive status may be acquired by career-conditional or career appointment through open competitive examination, or may be granted by statute, executive order, or civil service rules without competitive examination. A person with competitive status may be promoted, transferred, reassigned, reinstated, or demoted subject to the conditions prescribed by civil service rules and regulations. (212)

Consultant—An advisor to an officer or instrumentality of the Government, as distinguished from an officer or employee who carries out the agency's duties and responsibilities. (304)

Consultation—The obligation of an agency to consult the labor organization on particular personnel issues. The process of consultation lies between notification to the labor organization, which may amount simply to providing information, and negotiation, which implies agreement on the part of the labor organization. (711)

Conversion—The process of changing a person's tenure from one type of appointment to another (e.g., conversion from temporary to career-conditional). (315)

D

Demotion—A change of an employee, while serving continuously with the same agency:
(a) To a lower grade when both the old and the new positions are in the General Schedule or under the same type graded wage schedule; or
(b) To a position with a lower rate of pay when both the old and the new positions are under the same type ungraded wage schedule, or are in different pay method categories. (335, 752)

Detail—A temporary assignment of an employee to different duties or to a different position for a specified time, with the employee returning to his/her regular duties at the end of the detail. (300)

Differentials—Recruiting incentives in the form of compensation adjustments justified by: (1) extraordinarily difficult living conditions; (2) excessive physical hardship; or (3) notably unhealthful conditions. (591)

Disciplinary Action—Action taken to correct the conduct of an employee; may range from an admonishment through reprimand, suspension, reduction in grade or pay, to removal from the service. (751, 752)

Displaced Employee Program—(DEP)— A system to help find jobs for career and career-conditional employees displaced either through reduction-in-force or by an inability to accept assignment to another commuting area. (330)

Downgrading—Change of a position to a lower grade. (511, 532)

Dual Compensation—When an employee receives compensation for more than one Federal position if he/she worked more than 40 hours during the week. The term is also used in connection with compensation from a full-time Federal position as well as a retirement annuity for prior military service. (550)

Duty Station—The specific geographical area in which an employee is permanently assigned. (296)

E

Eligible—Any applicant for appointment or promotion who meets the minimum qualification requirements. (337)

Employee Development—A term which may include *career development* and *upward mobility*. It may be oriented toward development for better performance on an employee's current job, for learning a new policy or procedure, or for enhancing an employee's potential for advancement. (410, 412)

Employee, Exempt—An employee exempt from the overtime provisions of the Fair Labor Standards Act. (551)

Employee, Nonexempt—An employee subject to the overtime provision of the Fair Labor Standards Act. (551)

Employee Organization— See *Labor Organization.*

Employee Relations—The personnel function which centers upon the relationship between the supervisor and individual employees. (711)

Entrance Level Position—A position in an occupation at the beginning level grade. (511)

Environmental Differential—Additional pay authorized for a duty involving unusually severe hazards or working conditions. (532, 550)

Equal Employment Opportunity—Federal policy to provide equal employment opportunity for all; to prohibit discrimination on the grounds of age, race, color, religion, sex, national origin, or physical or mental handicap; and to promote the full realization of employees' potential through a continuing affirmative action program in each executive department and agency. (713)

Equal Employment Opportunity Commission—Regulates and enforces the Federal program for insuring equal employment opportunity, and oversees the development and implementation of Federal agencies' affirmative action programs.

Equal Pay for Substantially Equal Work—An underlying principle that provides the same pay level for work at the same level of difficulty and responsibility. (271)

Examination, Assembled—An examination which includes as one of its parts a written or performance test for which applicants are required to assemble at appointed times and places. (337)

Examination— A means of measuring, in a practical and suitable manner, qualifications of applicants for employment in specific positions. (337)

Examination, Fitness-For-Duty—An agency directed examination given by a Federal medical officer or an employee-designated, agency-approved physician to determine the employee's physical, mental, or emotional ability to perform assigned duties safely and efficiently. (339, 831)

Examination, Unassembled—An examination in which applicants are rated on their education, experience, and other qualifications as shown in the formal application and any supportive evidence that may be required, without assembling for a written or performance test. (337)

Excepted Service—Positions in the Federal civil service not subject to the appointment requirements of the competitive service. Exceptions to the normal, competitive requirements are authorized by law, executive order, or regulation. (213, 302)

Exclusive Recognition—The status conferred on a labor organization which receives a majority of votes cast in a representation election, entitling it to act for and negotiate agreements covering all employees included in an appropriate bargaining unit. The labor organization enjoying this status is known as the exclusive representative, exclusive bargaining representative, bargaining agent, or exclusive bargaining agent. (711)

Executive Inventory—An OPM computerized file which contains background information on all members of the Senior Executive Service and persons in positions at GS-16 through GS-18 or the equivalent, and individuals at lower grades who have been certified as meeting the managerial criteria for SES. It is used as an aid to agencies in executive recruiting and as a planning and management tool. (920)

Executive Resources Board—Panel of top agency executives responsible under the law for conducting the merit staffing process for career appointment to Senior Executive Service (SES) positions in the agency. Most Boards are also responsible for setting policy on and overseeing such areas as SES position planning and executive development. (920)

F

Federal Labor Relations Authority (FLRA)—Administers the Federal service labor-management relations program. It resolves questions of union representation of employees; prosecutes and adjudicates allegations of unfair labor practices; decides questions of what is or is not negotiable; and on appeal, reviews decisions of arbitrators. (5 USC 7104)

Federal Personnel Manual (FPM)—The official publication containing Federal personnel regulations and guidance. Also contains the code of Federal civil service law, selected Executive orders pertaining to Federal employment, and civil service rules. (171)

Federal Service Impasses Panel (FSIP)—Administrative body created to resolve bargaining impasses in the Federal service. The Panel may recommend procedures, including arbitration, for settling impasses, or may settle the impasse itself. Considered the legal alternative to strike in the Federal sector. (711)

Federal Wage System (FWS)—A body of laws and regulations governing the administrative processes related to trades and laboring occupations in the Federal service. (532)

Full Field Investigation—Personal investigation of an applicant's background to determine whether he/she meets fitness standards for a critical-sensitive Federal position. (736)

Function—All, or a clearly identifiable segment, of an agency's mission, including all the parts of the mission (e.g. procurement), regardless of how performed. (351)

G

General Position—A position within the Senior Executive Service that may be filled by a career, noncareer, or limited appointment. (920)

General Schedule—(GS)The graded pay system as presented by Chapter 51 of Title 5, United States Code, for classifying positions. **(511)**

Grade—All classes of positions which, although different with respect to kind or subject matter of work, are sufficiently equivalent as to (1) level of difficulty and responsibility, and (2) level of qualification requirements of the work to warrant the inclusion of such classes of positions within one range of rates of basic compensation. (511, 532)

Grade Retention—The right of a General Schedule or prevailing rate employee, when demoted for certain reasons, to retain the higher grade for most purposes for two years. (536)

Grievance, (Negotiated Procedure)—Any complaint or expressed dissatisfaction by an employee against an action by management in connection with his job, pay or other aspects of employment. Whether such complaint or expressed dissatisfaction is formally recognized and handled as a "grievance" under a negotiated procedure depends on the scope of that procedure. (711)

Grievance (Under Agency Administrative Procedure)—A request by an employee or by a group of employees acting as individuals, for personal relief in a matter of concern or dissatisfaction to the employee, subject to the control of agency management.

Grievance Procedure—A procedure, either administrative or negotiated, by which employees may seek redress of any matter subject to the control of agency management. (711, 771)

H

Handbook X-118— The official qualification standard a manual for General Schedule Positions. (338)

Handbook X-118C—The official qualification standards manual for Wage System positions. (338)

Hearing—The opportunity for contending parties under a grievance, complaint, or other remedial process, to introduce testimony and evidence and to confront and examine or cross examine witnesses. (713, 771, 772)

I

Impasse Procedures—Procedures for resolving deadlocks between agencies and union in collective bargaining. (711)

Incentive Awards—An all-inclusive term covering awards granted under Part 451 or OPM regulations. Includes an award for a suggestion submitted by an employee and adopted by management; a special achievement award for performance exceeding job requirements, or an honorary award in the form of a certificate, emblem, pin or other item. (451)

Indefinite—Tenure of a nonpermanent employee hired for an unlimited time. (316)

Injury, Work Related—For compensation under the Federal Employees' Compensation Act, a personal injury sustained while in the performance of duty. The term "injury" includes diseases proximately caused by the employment. (810)

Injury, Traumatic—Under the Federal Employees' Compensation Act, for continuation of pay purposes, a wound or other condition of the body caused by external force, including stress or strain. The injury must be identifiable by time and place of occurrence and member or function of the body affected, and be caused by a specific event or incident or series of events or incidents within a single day or work shift. (810)

Intergovernmental Personnel Assignment—Assignments of personnel to and from the Executive Branch of the Federal Government, state and local government agencies, and institutions of higher education up to two years, although a two-year extension may be permitted. The purpose is to provide technical assistance or expertise where needed for short periods of time. (334)

Intermittent—Less than full-time employment requiring irregular work hours which cannot be prescheduled. (610)

J

Job Analysis—Technical review and evaluation of a position's duties, responsibilities, and level of work and of the skills, abilities, and knowledge needed to do the work. (511, 532)

Job Enrichment—Carefully planned work assignments and/or training to use and upgrade employee skills, abilities, and interests; and to provide opportunity for growth, and encourage self-improvement. (312)

Job Freeze—A restriction on hiring and/or promotion by administrative or legislative action. (330)

Job Title— The formal name of a position as determined by official classification standards. (511, 532)

Journeyman Level—(Full Performance Level)The lowest level of a career ladder position at which an employee has learned the full range of duties in a specific occupation. All jobs below full performance level are developmental levels, through which each employee in the occupation may progress to full performance. (511)

L

Labor-Management Relations—Relationships and dealings between employee unions and management. (711)

Labor Organization—An organization composed in whole or in part of employees, in which employees participate and pay dues, and which has as a purpose dealing with an agency concerning grievances and working conditions of employment. (711)

Lead Agency—Under the Federal Wage-System, the Federal agency with the largest number of Federal wage workers in a geographical area; consequently, it has the primary role for determining wage rates for all Federal employees who work in that area and are covered by the System. (532)

Leave, Annual—Time allowed to employees for vacation and other absences for personal reasons. (630)

Leave, Court—Time allowed to employees for jury and certain types of witness service. (630)

Leave, Military—Time allowed to employees for certain types of military service. (630)

Leave, Sick—Time allowed to employees for physical incapacity, to prevent the spread of contagious diseases, or to obtain medical, dental or eye examination or treatment. (630)

Leave Without Pay (LWOP)—A temporary nonpay status and absence from duty, requested by an employee. The permissive nature of "leave without pay" distinguishes it from "absence without leave." (630)

Level of Difficulty—A classification term used to indicate the relative ranking of duties and responsibilities. (511, 532)

M

Maintenance Review—A formal, periodic review (usually annual) of all positions in an organization, or portion of an organization, to insure that classifications are correct and position descriptions are current. (511)

Major Duty—Any duty or responsibility, or group of closely related tasks, of a position which (1) determines qualification requirements for the position, (2) occupies a significant amount of the employee's time, and (3) is a regular or recurring duty. (511)

Management Official—An individual employed by an agency in a position whose duties and responsibilities require or authorize the individual to formulate, determine or influence the policies of the agency. (711)

Management Rights—The right of management to make day-today personnel decisions and to direct the work force without mandatory negotiation with the exclusive representative. (See "Reserved Rights Doctrine.") Usually a specific list of management authorities not subject to the obligation to bargain. (117)

Mediation—Procedure using a third-party to facilitate the reaching of an agreement voluntarily. (711)

Merit Promotion Program—The system under which agencies consider an employee for internal personnel actions on the basis of personal merit. (335)

Merit Systems Protection Board (MSPB)—An independent agency which monitors the administration of the Federal civil service system, prosecutes and adjudicates allegations of merit principle abuses, and hears and decides other civil service appeals. (5 USC 1205)

N

National Agency Check and Inquiry (NACI)—The Investigation of applicants for nonsensitive Federal positions by means of a name check through national investigative files and voucher inquiries. (731)

National Consultation Rights—A relationship established between the headquarters of a Federal agency and the national office of a union under criteria of the Federal Labor Relations Authority. When a union holds national consultation rights, the agency must give the union notice of proposed new substantive personnel policies, and of proposed changes in personnel policies, and an opportunity to comment on such proposals. The union has a right to: (1) suggest changes in personnel policies and have those suggestions carefully considered; (2) consult at reasonable times with appropriate officials about personnel policy matters; and (3) submit its views in writing on personnel policy matters at any time. The agency must provide the union with a written statement (which need not be detailed) of reasons for taking its final action on a policy. (711)

Negotiability—A determination as to whether a matter is within the obligation to bargain. (711)

Negotiated Grievance Procedure—A procedure applicable to members of a bargaining unit for considering grievances. Coverage and scope are negotiated by the parties to the agreement, except that the procedures may not cover certain matters designated in Title VII of the CSRA as excluded from the scope of negotiated grievance procedures. (711)

Negotiations—The bargaining process used to reach a settlement between labor and management over conditions of employment. (711)

Nominating Officer—A subordinate officer of an agency to whom authority has been delegated by the head of the agency to nominate for appointment but not actually appoint employees. (311)

O

Objection—A written statement by an agency of the reasons why it believes an eligible whose name is on a certificate is not qualified for the position to which referred. If the Examining Office sustains the objection, the agency may eliminate the person from consideration. (332)

Occupational Group—Positions of differing kinds but within the same field of work. For example, the GS-500 Accounting and Budget Occupational Group includes: General Accounting Clerical and Administrative Series; Financial Management; Internal Revenue Agent Accounting Technician; Payroll; etc. (511, 532)

Office of Personnel Management (OPM)—Regulates, administers, and evaluates the civil service program according to merit principles. (5 USC 1103)

Office of Workers Compensation Programs (OWCP)—In the Department of Labor, administers statutes that allow compensation to employees and their survivors for work-related injuries and illnesses. Decides and pays claims. (810)

Official Personnel Folder (OPF)—The official repository of employment records and documents affecting personnel actions during an employee's Federal civilian service. (293)

Overtime Work—Under Title 5, U.S. Code, officially ordered or approved work performed in excess of eight hours in a day or 40 hours in a week. Under the Fair Labor Standards Act, work in excess of 40 hours in a week by a nonexempt employee. (550, 551)

P

Pass Over—Elimination from appointment consideration of a veteran preference eligible on a certificate (candidate list), to appoint a lower ranking nonveteran, when the agency submits reasons which OPM finds sufficient. (332)

Pay Retention—The right of a General Schedule or prevailing rate employee (following a grade retention period or at other specified times when the rate of basic pay would otherwise be reduced) to continue to receive the higher rate. Pay is retained indefinitely. (536)

Pay, Severance—Money paid to employees separated by reduction-in-force and not eligible for retirement. The following formula is used, but the amount cannot be more than one year's pay:
> *Basic Severance Pay— One* week's pay for each year of civilian service up to 10 years, and two weeks' pay for each year served over 10 years, plus
> *Age Adjustment Allowance* —10 percent of the basic severance pay for each year over age 40. (550)

Performance Appraisal—The comparison, under a performance appraisal system, of an employee's actual performance against the performance standards previously established for the position. (430)

Personal Action— The process necessary to appoint, separate, reinstate, or make other changes affecting an employee (e.g., change in position assignment, tenure, etc.). (296)

Personnel Management—Management of human resources to accomplish a mission and provide individual job satisfaction. It is the line responsibility of the operating supervisor and the staff responsibility of the personnel office. (250)

Position—A specific job consisting of all the current major duties and responsibilities assigned or delegated by management. (312)

Position Change—A promotion, demotion, or reassignment. (335)

Position Classification—Analyzing and categorizing jobs by occupational group, series, class, and grade according to like duties, responsibilities, and qualification requirements. (511, 532)

Position Classifier—A specialist in job analysis who determines the titles, occupational groups, series, and grades of positions. (312)

Position Description—An official written statement of the major duties, responsibilities and supervisory relationships of a position. (312)

Position Management—The process of designing positions to combine logical and consistent duties and responsibilities into an orderly, efficient, and productive organization to accomplish agency mission. (312)

Position Survey—Agency review of positions to determine whether the positions are still needed and, if so, whether the classification and position description are correct. (312)

Position, "PL 313 Type"—Positions established under Public Law 80-313 of August 1, 1947, or similar authorities. A small group of high level professional and scientific positions generally in the competitive service, but not filled through competitive examinations. Salaries are set between GS-12 and GS-18. (534)

Preference, Compensable Disability ("CP")—Ten-point preference awarded to a veteran separated under honorable conditions from active duty, who receives compensation of 10 percent or more for a service-connected disability. Eligible "CP" veterans are placed at the top of civil service lists of eligibles for positions at GS-9 or higher. (211)

Preference, 30 Percent or More, Disabled ("CPS")—A disabled veteran whose disability is rated at 30 percent or more, entitled to special preference in appointment and during reduction in force.

Preference, Disability ("XP")—Ten-point preference in hiring for a veteran separated under honorable conditions from active duty and who has a service-connected disability or receives compensation, pension, or disability retirement from the VA or a uniformed service. (211)

Preference, Mother ("XP")—Ten-point preference to which the mother of a deceased or disabled military veteran may be entitled. (211)

Preference, Spouse ("XP")—Ten-point preference to which a disabled military veteran's spouse may be entitled. (211)

Preference, Tentative ("TP")— Five-point veteran preference tentatively awarded an eligible who served on active duty during specified periods and was separated from military service under honorable conditions. It must be verified by the appointing officer. (211)

Preference, Veteran—The statutory right to special advantage in appointments or separations; based on a person's discharge under honorable conditions from the armed forces, for a service-connected disability. *Not* applicable to the Senior Executive Service. (211)

Preference, Widow or Widower ("XP")—Ten-point preference to which a military veteran's widow or widower may be entitled. (211)

Premium Pay—Additional pay for overtime, night, Sunday and holiday work. (550)

Prevailing Rate System—A subsystem of the Federal Wage System used to determine the employee's pay in a particular wage area. The determination requires, comparing. the_. rate of pay with the private sector for similar duties and responsibilities. (532)

Probationary Period—A trial period which is a condition of the initial competitive appointment. Provides the final indispensable test of ability, that of actual performance on the job. (315)

Promotion—A change of an employee to a higher grade when both the old and new positions are under the same job classification system and pay schedule, or to a position with higher pay in a different job classification system and pay schedule. (335)

Promotion, Career—Promotion of an employee without current competition when: (1) he/ she had earlier been competitively selected from a register or under competitive promotion procedures for an assignment intended as a matter of record to be preparation for the position being filled; or (2) the position is reconstituted at a higher grade because of additional duties and responsibilities. (335)

Promotion, Competitive—Selection of a current or former Federal civil service employee for a higher grade position, using procedures that compare the candidates on merit. (335)

Promotion Certificate—A list of best qualified candidates to be considered to fill a position under competitive promotion procedures. (335)

Q

Qualifications Review Board—A panel attached to OPM that determines whether a candidate for career appointment in the Senior Executive Service meets the managerial criteria established by law.

Qualification Requirements—Education, experience, and other prerequisites to employment or placement in a position. (338)

Quality Graduate—College graduate who was a superior student and can be hired at a higher grade than the one to which he/she would otherwise be entitled '(338)

Quality Increase—An additional within-grade increase granted to General Schedule employees for high quality performance above that ordinarily found in the type of position concerned (531).

R

Reassignment—The change of an employee, while serving continuously within the same agency, from one position to another, without promotion or demotion. (210)

Recognition—Employer acceptance of a labor organization as authorized to negotiate, usually for all members of a bargaining unit. (711) Also, used to refer to incentive awards granted under provisions of Parts 451 and 541 of OPM Regulations, and Quality Increases granted under Part 531.

Recruitment—Process of attracting a supply of qualified eligibles for employment consideration. (332)

Reduction-in-Force (RIF)—A personnel action that may be required due to lack of work or funds, changes resulting from reorganization, downward reclassification of a position, or the need to make room for an employee with reemployment or restoration rights. Involves separating an employee from his/her present position, but does not necessarily result in separation or downgrading. (351) (See also *Tenure Groups.*)

Reemployment Priority List—Career and career-conditional employees, separated by reduction-in-force, who are identified, in priority order, for reemployment to competitive positions in the agency in the commuting area where the separations occurred. (330)

Reemployment Rights—Right of an employee to return to an agency after detail, transfer, or appointment to: (1) another Executive agency during an emergency; (2) an international organization; or (3) other statutorily covered employment, e.g., the Peace Corps. (352)

Register—A list of eligible applicants compiled in the order of their relative standing for referral to Federal jobs, after competitive civil service examination. (332,210)

Reinstatement— Noncompetitive reemployment in the competitive service based on previous service under a career or career-conditional appointment. (315)

Removal—Separation of an employee for cause or because of continual unacceptable performance. (432, 752)

Representation—Actions and rights of the labor organization to consult and negotiate with management on behalf of the bargaining unit and represent employees in the unit. (711)

Representation Election—Election conducted to determine whether the employees in an appropriate unit (See *Bargaining Unit)* desire a labor organization to act as their exclusive representative. (711)

Reprimand—An official rebuke of an employee. Normally in writing and placed in the   temporary side of an employee's OPF-(751)

"Reserved Rights Doctrine"—Specific functions delegated to management by Title VII of CSRA that protect management's ability to perform its necessary functions and duties. (See Management Rights.) Delegates to management specific functions not subject to negotiation except as to procedures and impact. (711)

Resignation—A separation, prior to retirement, in response to an employee's request for the action. It is a voluntary expression of the employee's desire to leave the organization and must not be demanded as an alternative to some other action to be taken or withheld. (715)

Restoration Rights—Employees who enter military service or sustain a compensable job-related injury or disability are entitled to be restored to the same or higher employment status held prior to their absence. (353)

Retention Preference—The relative standing of employees competing in a reduction-inforce. Their standing is determined by veteran's preference, tenure group, length of service, and performance appraisal. (351)

Retention Register—A list of all employees, arranged by competitive level, describing their retention preference during reductions-in-force. (351)

Retirement—Payment of an annuity after separation from a position under the Civil Service Retirement System and based on meeting age and length of service requirements. The types of retirement are:

> *Deferred* - An employee with five years civilian service who separates or transfers to a position not under the Retirement Act, may receive an annuity, does not withdraw from the Retirement Fund. (.83:1)
>
> *Disability* - An immediate annuity paid to an employee under the retirement system who has completed five years of civilian service and has suffered a mental, emotional, or physical disability not the result of the employee's vicious habits, intemperance, or willful misconduct, (831)
>
> *Discontinued Service* - An immediate annuity paid to an employee who is involuntarily separated, through no personal fault of the employee, after age 50 and 20 years of service, or at any age with 25 years of service. This annuity is reduced by 1/6 of one percent for each full month under age 55 (two percent per year). (831)
>
> *Optional* - The minimum combinations of age and service for this kind of immediate annuity are: age 62 with five years of service; age 60 with 20 years of service; age 55 with 30 years of service. (831)

Review, Classification—An official written request for reclassification of a position. Previously called a classification appeal.

S

Schedules A, B, and C—Categories of positions excepted from the competitive service by regulation. (213)

> *Schedule A—Positions* other than confidential or policy determining, for which it is not practical to examine.
> *Schedule B*— Positions other than confidential or policy determining for which it is not practical to hold a competitive examination.
> *Schedule* C—Positions of a confidential or policy determining character.

Senior Executive Service—A separate personnel system for persons who set policy and administer programs at the top levels of the Government (equivalent to GS-16 through Executive Level IV). (920)

Service Computation Date-Leave—The date, either actual or adjusted, from which service credit is accumulated for determining the rate of leave accrual; it may be different from the service computation date, which determines relative standing in a subgroup for reduction-in-force, or service computation date for retirement. (296)

Service Record Card (Standard Form 7)—A brief of the employee's service history. It is kept on file in accordance with agency disposition instructions. (295)

Special Salary Rates—Salary rates higher than regular statutory schedule; established for occupations in which private enterprise pays substantially more than the regular Federal Schedule. (530)

Spoils System—The personnel system characterized by the political appointment and removal of employees without regard to merit. (212)

Staffing—Use of available and projected personnel through recruitment, appointment, reassignment, promotion, reduction-in-force, etc., to provide the work force required to fulfill the agency's mission. (250)

Standard Form—171 ("Personal Qualification Statement") Used in applying for a Federal position through a competitive examination. (295)

Standards of Conduct For Labor Organization—In the Federal sector, a code governing internal democratic practices and fiscal responsibility, and procedures to which a labor organization must adhere to be eligible to receive any recognition. (711)

Steward (Union Steward)—A local union's representative in a plant or department, appointed by the union to carry out union duties, adjust grievances, collect dues and solicit new members. Stewards are employees trained by the union to carry out their duties.

Strike—Temporary stoppage of work by a group of employees to express a grievance, enforce a demand for changes in conditions of employment, obtain recognition, or resolve a dispute with management. *Wildcat strike*- a strike not sanctioned by union and which may violate a collective agreement. *Quickie strike*- a spontaneous or unannounced strike of short duration. *Slowdown-a* deliberate reduction of output without an actual strike in order to force concessions from *an* employer. *Walkout* -same as strike. Strikes are illegal for Federal employees. (711)

Suitability—An applicant's or employee's fitness for Federal employment as indicated by character and conduct. (731)

Supervisor—An individual employed by an agency having authority, in the interest of the agency, to hire, direct, assign, promote, reward, transfer, furlough, lay off, recall, suspend, discipline-or remove employees, to adjust their grievances, or to effectively recommend such action-if the exercise of the authority is not merely routine or clerical in nature but requires the consistent exercise of independent judgment. With respect to any unit which includes firefighters or nurses, the term "supervisor" includes only those individuals who devote a preponderance of their employment time to exercising such authority. (711).

Survey, Classification—An intensive study of all positions in an organization or organizational segment to insure their correct classification.

Suspension—Placing an employee, for disciplinary reasons, in a temporary status without duties and pay. (751, 752)

T

Tenure—The time an employee may reasonably expect to serve under a current appointment. It is governed by the type of appointment, without regard to whether the employee has competitive status. (210)

Tenure Groups—Categories of employees ranked in priority order for retention during reduction in force . Within each group, veterans are ranked above nonveterans. For the competitive service, the tenure groups are, in descending order:
Group I—Employees under career appointments and not serving probation.
Group II—Employees serving probation, career-conditional employees, and career employees in obligated positions.
Group III—Employees with indefinite appointments, status quo employees under any other nonstatus, nontemporary appointment. (351)
For the *excepted service,* they are in descending order:
Group I—Permanent employees, not serving a trial period, whose appointments carry no restriction or condition, such as "indefinite" or "time-limited".
Group II—Employees serving trial periods, those whose tenure is indefinite because they occupy obligated positions, and those whose tenure is equivalent to career-conditional in the competitive service.
Group III—Employees whose tenure is indefinite, but not potentially permanent, and temporary employees who have completed one year of current continuous employment. (351)

Tenure Subgroups—The ranking of veterans above nonveterans in each tenure group, as follows:

Subgroup AD—Veterans with service-connected disability of 30% or more.
Subgroup A— All other veterans
Subgroup B—Nonveterans

Time-in-Grade Restriction—A requirement intended to prevent excessively rapid promotions in the General Schedule. Generally, an employee may not be promoted more than two grades within one year to positions up to GS-5. At GS-5 and above, an employee must serve a minimum of one year in grade, and cannot be promoted more than one grade, or two grades if that is the normal progression. (300)

Tour of Duty—The hours of a day (a daily tour of duty) and the day of an administrative workweek (weekly tour of duty) scheduled in advance and during which an employee is required to work regularly. (610)

Training—Formal instruction or controlled and planned exposure to learning. (410)

Transfer—A change of an employee, without a break in service of one full workday, from a position in one agency to a position in another agency. (315)

Transfer of Function—For reduction-in-force, the transfer of a continuing function from one agency or competitive area to another, or when the competitive area in which work is performed is moved to another commuting area. (315)

U

Unemployment Compensation—Income maintenance payments to former Federal employees who: (1) are unemployed; (2) file a claim at a local employment office for unemployment compensation; and (3) register for work assignment. The program is administered through state and D.C. employment service offices, which determine eligibility and make the payments. (850)

Unfair Labor Practices—Prohibited actions by agency management and labor organizations. (711)

Union—See *Labor Organization.*

Upward Mobility—Systematic career development requiring competitive selection in positions that provide experience and training leading to future assignments in other, more responsible positions.(410)

V

Veteran—A person entitled to preference under 5 USC 2108, including a spouse, widow, widower, or mother entitled to preference under the law. (211)

Voucher—In staffing terms, a formal inquiry to employers, references, professors, and others who presumably know a job applicant well enough to describe job qualifications and personal character. (337)

W

Wage Employees—Those employees-in trades, crafts, or labor occupations covered by the Federal Wage System, whose pay is fixed and adjusted periodically in accordance with prevailing rates. (532)

Within-Grade Increase—A salary increase provided in certain Government pay plans based upon time-in-grade and acceptable or satisfactory work performance. Also known as "periodic increase" or "step increase." (531)

NOTE:

    Numbers in parentheses after the definitions refer to the appropriate FEDERAL PERSONNEL MANUAL (FPM) Chapter indicated.